Palgrave Historical Studies in Witchcraft

Series Editors: **Jonathan Barry, Willem de**

Titles include:

Edward Bever
THE REALITIES OF WITCHCRAFT AND POPULAR
MODERN EUROPE
Culture, Cognition and Everyday Life

Alison Butler
VICTORIAN OCCULTISM AND THE MAKING OF MODERN MAGIC
Invoking Tradition

Julian Goodare (*editor*)
SCOTTISH WITCHES AND WITCH-HUNTERS

Julian Goodare, Lauren Martin and Joyce Miller (*editors*)
WITCHCRAFT AND BELIEF IN EARLY MODERN SCOTLAND

Jonathan Roper (*editor*)
CHARMS, CHARMERS AND CHARMING

Alison Rowlands (*editor*)
WITCHCRAFT AND MASCULINITIES IN EARLY MODERN EUROPE

Rolf Schulte
MAN AS WITCH
Male Witches in Central Europe

Laura Stokes
DEMONS OF URBAN REFORM
Early European Witch Trials and Criminal Justice, 1430–1530

Forthcoming:

Johannes Dillinger
MAGICAL TREASURE HUNTING IN EUROPE AND NORTH AMERICA
A History

Soili-Maria Olli
TALKING TO DEVILS AND ANGELS IN SCANDINAVIA, 1500–1800

Robert Ziegler
SATANISM, MAGIC AND MYSTICISM IN FIN-DE-SIÈCLE FRANCE

Palgrave Historical Studies in Witchcraft and Magic
Series Standing Order ISBN 978–1403–99566–7 Hardback 978–1403–99567–4 Paperback
(*outside North America only*)

You can receive future titles in this series as they are published by placing a standing order. Please contact your bookseller or, in case of difficulty, write to us at the address below with your name and address, the title of the series and the ISBN quoted above.

Customer Services Department, Macmillan Distribution Ltd, Houndmills, Basingstoke, Hampshire RG21 6XS, England

---

Also by Julian Goodare

SIXTEENTH-CENTURY SCOTLAND: Essays in Honour of Michael Lynch (*co-edited with Alasdair A. MacDonald*)

WITCHCRAFT AND BELIEF IN EARLY MODERN SCOTLAND (*co-edited with Lauren Martin and Joyce Miller*)

THE GOVERNMENT OF SCOTLAND, 1560–1625

THE SCOTTISH WITCH-HUNT IN CONTEXT (*editor*)

THE REIGN OF JAMES VI (*co-edited with Michael Lynch*)

STATE AND SOCIETY IN EARLY MODERN SCOTLAND

Scottish Witches and Witch-Hunters

Edited by

Julian Goodare
Reader in History, University of Edinburgh, UK

First published 2013 by
PALGRAVE MACMILLAN

Palgrave Macmillan in the UK is an imprint of Macmillan Publishers Limited,
registered in England, company number 785998, of Houndmills, Basingstoke,
Hampshire RG21 6XS.

Palgrave Macmillan in the US is a division of St Martin's Press LLC,
175 Fifth Avenue, New York, NY 10010.

Palgrave Macmillan is the global academic imprint of the above companies
and has companies and representatives throughout the world.

Palgrave® and Macmillan® are registered trademarks in the United States,
the United Kingdom, Europe and other countries.

ISBN 978–1–137–35593–5

This book is printed on paper suitable for recycling and made from fully
managed and sustained forest sources. Logging, pulping and manufacturing
processes are expected to conform to the environmental regulations of the
country of origin.

A catalogue record for this book is available from the British Library.

A catalog record for this book is available from the Library of Congress.

Contents

Maps, Figures and Tables

Maps

Figures

Tables

Preface and Acknowledgements

Scottish Witches and Witch-Hunters is a collection of essays that showcases some of the latest research on Scottish witchcraft. It has been planned to range over the whole topic: from beginning to end of the period of witch-hunting; from individual case studies to international connections; from the perspective of central government to the perspective of local communities. As well as fresh studies of the well-established topic of witch-hunting, the book also launches an exploration of some of the more esoteric aspects of magical belief and practice.

This book is to some extent a follow-up to two previous books: Julian Goodare (ed.), *The Scottish Witch-Hunt in Context* (Manchester: Manchester University Press, 2002) and Julian Goodare, Lauren Martin and Joyce Miller (eds.), *Witchcraft and Belief in Early Modern Scotland* (Basingstoke: Palgrave Macmillan, 2008). The latter book, indeed, was the first volume in the present series, Palgrave Historical Studies in Witchcraft and Magic. Three of the contributors to the present book also contributed to these earlier collections, though on very different subjects. For seven of the other contributors, their chapter will be their first publication.

I am particularly grateful to Professor Brian P. Levack for friendship, advice and encouragement. Dr Joyce Miller and Dr Louise Yeoman have provided regular inspiration. Karen Howie helped me with the map. The series editors, Professor Jonathan Barry, Dr Willem de Blécourt and Professor Owen Davies, have been consistently supportive, as have the publishers.

Julian Goodare
April 2013

Abbreviations

APS	*Acts of the Parliaments of Scotland*, 12 vols., eds. Thomas Thomson and Cosmo Innes (Edinburgh, 1814–1875)
BL	British Library, London
Chambers, *Domestic Annals*	Robert Chambers, *Domestic Annals of Scotland*, 3 vols. (2nd edn., Edinburgh, 1860–1861)
CSP Scot.	*Calendar of State Papers relating to Scotland and Mary, Queen of Scots, 1547–1603*, 13 vols., eds. Joseph Bain *et al.* (Edinburgh, 1898–1969)
FM	Finnmark District Magistrate
HCP	High Court Processes (NRS)
HMC	Historical Manuscripts Commission
HP	*Highland Papers*, 4 vols., ed. J. R. N. Macphail (SHS, 1914–1934)
Hunter (ed.), *Occult Laboratory*	Michael Hunter (ed.), *The Occult Laboratory: Magic, Science and Second Sight in Late Seventeenth-Century Scotland* (Woodbridge, 2001)
NAD	National Archives of Denmark, Copenhagen
NLS	National Library of Scotland, Edinburgh
Normand and Roberts (eds.), *Witchcraft*	Laurence Normand and Gareth Roberts (eds.), *Witchcraft in Early Modern Scotland: James VI's* Demonology *and the North Berwick Witches* (Exeter, 2000)
NRS	National Records of Scotland, Edinburgh
ODNB	*Oxford Dictionary of National Biography* (2004)
Pitcairn (ed.), *Trials*	*Criminal Trials in Scotland, 1488–1624*, 3 vols., ed. Robert Pitcairn (Edinburgh, 1833)
PSAS	*Proceedings of the Society of Antiquaries of Scotland*
RAT	Regional State Archives of Tromsø

RMS	*Registrum Magni Sigilli Regum Scotorum (Register of the Great Seal of Scotland)*, 11 vols., eds. J. M. Thomson *et al.* (Edinburgh, 1882–)
RPC	*Register of the Privy Council of Scotland*, 38 vols., eds. J. H. Burton *et al.* (Edinburgh, 1877–)
RPS	Records of the Parliaments of Scotland, ed. Keith M. Brown *et al.* (www.rps.ac.uk, 2007)
SHR	*Scottish Historical Review*
SHS	Scottish History Society
SJC	*Selected Justiciary Cases, 1624–1650*, 3 vols., eds. S. I. Gillon and J. I. Smith (Stair Society, 1954–1974)
Spalding Misc.	*Miscellany of the Spalding Club*, 5 vols. (1844–1852)
SSW	Julian Goodare, Lauren Martin, Joyce Miller and Louise Yeoman, 'The Survey of Scottish Witchcraft, 1563–1736' (www.shc.ed.ac.uk/Research/witches/, archived January 2003, updated November 2003)
STS	Scottish Text Society
TA	*Accounts of the (Lord High) Treasurer of Scotland*, 13 vols., eds. T. Dickson *et al.* (Edinburgh, 1877–)

Contributors

Victoria Carr is a postgraduate student at the University of Bristol, UK. She is a graduate of the Universities of Swansea and Edinburgh, UK. Her chapter in this volume arose from research towards her MSc by Research degree in Edinburgh.

Anna Cordey is a history teacher at Robert Gordon's College, Aberdeen. She is a graduate of the Universities of Oxford and Edinburgh, UK; her chapter in this volume arose from her MSc by Research thesis in Edinburgh.

Margaret Dudley is a community worker in Edinburgh. Her chapter in this volume arose from her honours dissertation at the University of Edinburgh, UK.

Julian Goodare is Reader in History, University of Edinburgh, UK. His books include *The Scottish Witch-Hunt in Context* (2002) (as editor) and *Witchcraft and Belief in Early Modern Scotland* (2008) (as co-editor with Lauren Martin and Joyce Miller). He was Director of the Survey of Scottish Witchcraft, which went online in 2003.

Alistair Henderson recently qualified as an archivist following postgraduate studies at the University of Dundee, UK. His chapter in this volume arose from his honours dissertation at the University of Edinburgh, UK.

Alexandra Hill is a solicitor at a London law firm. Her chapter in this volume arose from her honours dissertation at the University of Edinburgh, UK.

Paula Hughes recently completed her thesis 'The 1649–50 Scottish Witch-Hunt, with Particular Reference to the Synod of Lothian and Tweeddale' (University of Strathclyde PhD thesis, 2008).

Lauren Martin is Director of Research at the Urban Research Outreach-Engagement Center at the University of Minnesota, US. She is co-editor of *Witchcraft and Belief in Early Modern Scotland* (2008) (with Julian

Goodare and Joyce Miller). She was a researcher with the Survey of Scottish Witchcraft, which went online in 2003.

Laura Paterson is a postgraduate student at the University of Strathclyde, UK. Her chapter in this volume arose from her honours dissertation at the University of Edinburgh, UK.

Michael Wasser teaches at Dawson College in Montreal, Canada. He is the author of several articles on crime, witchcraft and the law in Scotland. He is currently working on a book provisionally titled *Violence on Trial: Elite Violence and State-Building in Early Modern Scotland, 1573–1638*.

Emma Wilby is an Honorary Fellow in History, University of Exeter, UK. She is author of *Cunning Folk and Familiar Spirits: Shamanistic Visionary Traditions in Early Modern British Witchcraft and Magic* (2005) and *The Visions of Isobel Gowdie: Magic, Witchcraft and Dark Shamanism in Seventeenth-Century Scotland* (2010).

Liv Helene Willumsen is Professor of History, Department of History and Religious Studies, University of Tromsø, Norway. She has published several books and articles on Scottish and Norwegian witchcraft. Her books include *Witchcraft Trials in Finnmark, Northern Norway* (2010) and *Witches of the North: Scotland and Finnmark* (2013).

Map of Scotland showing counties and principal towns

1	Edinburgh
2	Aberdeen
3	Glasgow
4	Dundee
5	St Andrews
6	Dumfries
7	Perth
8	Inverness
9	Montrose
10	Ayr
11	Stirling

Principal towns

50 miles

Source: This work is based on data provided through EDINA UKBORDERS with the support of the ESRC and JISC, based on boundary mapping created by Great Britain Historical GIS Project, copyright University of Portsmouth.

Introduction

Julian Goodare

Witch-hunting was on the mind of Christopher Lowther, an English visitor to Scotland, in November 1629. The third of Scotland's five great witchcraft panics, that of 1628–1631, was in full spate. As Lowther stood on Salisbury Crags near Edinburgh, he took in a splendid view of the city and its surroundings, as he recorded in his journal: 'The hemisphere's circumference from Edinburgh is mountains, as is Westmoreland from about Lowther, but something plainer, and their mountains not so high. In view from Edinburgh 4 miles southwards is Keeth, a borough where all the witches are burned.'[1]

'Keeth [...] where all the witches are burned' was in fact Dalkeith. Although no full study has been made of the panic of 1628–1631 as it took place there, its outline can readily be reconstructed with the aid of the online Survey of Scottish Witchcraft. This shows that in the presbytery of Dalkeith, a group of sixteen parishes to the south and east of Edinburgh, there were fourteen cases of witchcraft in 1628 and nineteen in 1629. This compares with a total of nine cases for *all* years before 1628. Lowther's remark is relevant to several points that I will return to shortly, including panics, execution methods, and the role of towns in witch-hunting. Later in this introduction I will also say more about the Witchcraft Survey.

I

This book's title phrase 'Witches and Witch-Hunters' is a starting point in indicating its contents. Witches and witch-hunters are inseparable. Witches would not have existed in early modern Scotland if people had not hated and feared them; witches were generally labelled by others rather than self-identified. Yet witch-hunters were unusual people.

1

Most people in early modern Scotland, most of the time, lived with those neighbours whom they thought to be witches without displaying a desire to prosecute them. Only occasionally were there outbursts of panic.

The panic in Dalkeith featured some notable local witch-hunters. They included two local lairds, Mr Patrick Hamilton of Little Preston and Robert Cass of Fordell. They were involved as commissioners of justiciary in thirty-one cases altogether; in sixteen of these they acted together, while Hamilton handled eight further cases, and Cass seven, without the other. Cass was also requested to help arrest a suspect. All this activity occurred between 1628 and 1630. Usually there were between four and eight commissioners appointed to hold a trial, and in the Witchcraft Survey one can see teams forming and combinations changing.

Men like Hamilton and Cass were not only important in their localities, but were also able to connect these localities to central government – a necessary requirement, since Scottish witch-hunting was supervised centrally. Commissions of justiciary, which enabled lairds like Hamilton and Cass to act as judges and to convene a court to try a witchcraft suspect, were granted by the privy council. With Dalkeith so close to Edinburgh, both Hamilton and Cass had good central connections. Cass was an advocate (a lawyer representing clients in the court of session, the central civil court), while Hamilton was the brother of the earl of Haddington, a leading government minister.[2] A systematic study of Scottish witch-hunters remains to be carried out, but several chapters of this book take the subject further.

The phrase 'Scottish witch-hunters' often brings King James VI to mind – the intellectual king who participated in the North Berwick witchcraft panic of 1590–1591 and in the subsequent panic of 1597, and whose book, *Daemonologie*, was published in 1597.[3] There is some discussion of James in this book, but there are also reasons for looking more broadly at the question of 'witch-hunters'.

One reason for looking beyond James comes in Michael Wasser's chapter on the panic of 1568–1569.[4] The idea that James *initiated* Scottish witch-hunting is surely mistaken. The Scottish Reformation occurred officially in 1560, the witchcraft act was passed in 1563, and the new church and secular authorities knew that witchcraft was one of the offences that they should punish. Yet, witchcraft prosecution was a complex business involving the co-operation of several different authorities. As Wasser shows, the Scottish authorities had not yet worked out how to carry out large-scale witch-hunting successfully.

During the North Berwick panic, James busily interrogated Agnes Sampson and stoked his suspicions of the earl of Bothwell. However, other witch-hunters had their own agendas. One such witch-hunter was William Douglas, ninth earl of Angus, whose predecessor as earl, his cousin Archibald Douglas, had died suddenly in 1588. Victoria Carr's chapter meticulously follows the clues that enable her to reconstruct how the ninth earl's suspicions fell on Jean Lyon, the eighth earl's widow.[5] We also learn that the ninth earl had a personal grudge against Lyon – which probably tells us, not that he pursued a witchcraft case against her cynically, but that he found it plausible that someone as bad as her could be a witch. I am not going to give away the plot here, but the drama of the earl and countess of Angus was surely, for a time, as intense as the drama of the king and the earl of Bothwell.

The panics of the 1590s are also relevant to another witch-hunter, discussed in Liv Helene Willumsen's chapter.[6] This was John Cunningham, the seafaring son of a Fife laird, who grew up in the 1590s during a period of intense witch-hunting in Fife. Cunningham's career took him to Denmark, to Greenland, and finally to a job as governor of Finnmark in northern Norway. There, beyond the Arctic Circle, he used some of the ideas that he had learned in Scotland to launch his own witch-hunt, distinctively different from what happened in the rest of Norway.

Much Scottish witch-hunting occurred in bursts of panic. Paula Hughes's chapter is the first published study of the panic of 1649–1650, one of the five biggest national panics.[7] Until recently it has been a little-known episode, with the other four big panics – those of 1590–1591, 1597, 1628–1631 and 1661–1662 – having received recent scholarly attention.[8] Hughes's study, like Wasser's, shows how administratively complicated it was to prosecute large numbers of witches. The revolutionary regime of the late 1640s, despite its many other commitments including warfare with England, made godliness and discipline high priorities, to deadly effect.

Hughes mentions a number of local commissioners, but does not single out any particular 'witch-hunter' or 'witch-hunters'. This may be because she surveys the panic from the top down, and the most single-mindedly zealous witch-hunters were more likely to be found at a local level. Even the notorious Matthew Hopkins in England was essentially a local figure; national politicians had so many other calls on their attention that they could rarely be seen to pursue witches single-mindedly. I have outlined a definition of 'witch-hunters' in this sense as 'men who did not merely carry out their duty in trials, but who went out of their way to orchestrate and promote them'.[9] Using the example of the English magistrate Robert Hunt, Jonathan Barry has recently pointed out that apparent local 'witch-hunters' might in fact be zealous prosecutors of crime in general, rather than singling out witches for special attention.[10] Further study of this is required. Hughes's chapter reminds us that witchcraft panics could occur in unusual political conditions, and future studies of local panics and local witch-hunters should pay close attention to the local political context.

Panics involved prosecutions of multiple witches, with one prosecution leading on to another in a chain reaction. The smallest example of a chain reaction is the linked prosecution of two witches. This is relevant to the decline of the Scottish witch-hunt because part of the story is the decline of panics. The last of the really big panics was from 1661 to 1662; after that there were several smaller panics. One of these, in the west of Scotland from 1699 to 1700, resulted in a spate of acquittals and has been argued to be the last of its kind.[11] Which may be so – but Alexandra Hill's chapter shows that the period from 1701 to 1727 (when the last execution occurred) contained numerous instances of linked, chain-reaction prosecutions.[12]

II

Early modern Scotland was largely a peasant society, as Christina Larner, the influential pioneer of Scottish witchcraft studies, recognised.[13] Yet she also drew attention to its status as a 'middle-range' society, neither fully primitive nor fully technological, and thus distinctively different from the tribal societies studied by anthropologists who had carried out some of the most influential witchcraft studies of the time when she was working. A 'middle-range' society required towns as well as peasants, but Larner regarded towns as unimportant for witch-hunting.[14] Could there be more to be said about towns?

Robin Briggs, who has written influentially about peasants in a European context, has also dismissed the idea of urban witch-hunting:

> For reasons which remain obscure, the urban milieu does not seem to have generated many witchcraft cases in most parts of Europe. The obvious exceptions are the pandemics which afflicted some German towns and the more routine persecution found in parts of the southern Netherlands, the latter an exceptionally urbanized region suffering from severe economic dislocation. It may be that elsewhere even these relatively small urban populations were just sufficiently mobile and anonymous to discourage the long build-up

of hostility characteristic of witchcraft accusations in tight-knit rural societies.[15]

Briggs's 'long build-up of hostility' is a familiar and indeed essential idea in witchcraft studies. I will come back to this, but I first want to use Briggs's remarks about the 'urban milieu' to introduce Alistair Henderson's chapter on that subject.[16] Henderson employs a statistical analysis of the data in the Witchcraft Survey to reconstruct the varying intensity of witchcraft prosecution in Scottish towns of different sizes. The results show a fascinating and complex pattern, but one simple point can be made: Scottish towns were certainly not immune from witch-hunting, and small towns even seem to have hunted witches with particular intensity. Which is what Christopher Lowther seems to have been told when he looked out from Salisbury Crags. Witch-hunting was associated with small towns like Dalkeith, not large towns like Edinburgh.

The 'long build-up of hostility' is well exemplified by Lauren Martin's chapter reconstructing the career of one witch, Isobel Young, in detail.[17] Young's trial for witchcraft took place in 1629, but Martin traces the development of her reputation back to the late sixteenth century, with a series of quarrels connected with landholding and money-lending, and reports of unauthorised ritual healing. Young had a long-running dispute with a neighbouring family, and quarrels with her own husband led him to testify against her at her trial.

On the other hand, Anna Cordey's chapter on the presbytery of Dalkeith shows that the 'long build-up of hostility' was not the only pattern.[18] She looks at two panics in the area, those of 1649–1650 and 1661–1662, and asks how many of the witches prosecuted in the area actually had reputations in their communities. Proving a negative is always difficult, but she finds strong indications that many witches were not identified as such in their communities before their arrest. She also contributes to the discussion of 'witch-hunters' by showing that William Scott, bailie of Dalkeith, seems to have gone out of his way to frame Janet Cock in 1661. The Witchcraft Survey shows that Scott took various roles in twelve witchcraft cases.

These chapters draw on a wide range of documents, such as property records and minutes of kirk sessions and presbyteries. This gives us a more holistic view of Scottish witch-hunting than we would have had by relying wholly on trial documents, as some Continental studies do. Trial records, the usual sources for witch-hunting, are indispensable – but, as Cordey and Martin both point out, they can be coloured by hindsight.

The 'long build-up of hostility' was recorded after the event. In Martin's and Cordey's chapters, we can see some future witches in action before they become witches. Martin shows that Isobel Young was alleged in 1619 to have a Devil's mark; this was not pursued at the time, but it came up again at her trial in 1629. This testimony from 1619 was given and recorded at the time, giving it a different quality from trial testimonies about events 'ten years ago'.

This shows that we have much work still to do on the nature of people's recollections, and we should beware of assuming that recollections were accurate. Cordey's concept of 'instant reputation' outlines an important way in which testimony could be unwittingly reshaped to make it appear as if a reputation stretched back a long way. People reinterpreted earlier events to make it look as if there had been a 'long build-up of hostility' – but perhaps, at the time, nobody thought that the events had anything to do with witchcraft.

Another chapter using unusual sources is Laura Paterson's chapter on the process of execution.[19] Information about this is often found in burgh accounts, since both rural and urban witches were often executed in towns, and it was towns that bore the cost of the arrangements. When Christopher Lowther mentioned witches being 'burned', he may have been struck by Scotland's difference from England, where witches were hanged like ordinary felons. Burning, as Paterson shows, had dramatic significance as a public spectacle. Condemned witches were usually strangled before the pyre was lit, but burning was still a particularly degrading way to die.

III

Recent research has begun to show that early modern Scotland was a stranger and more uncanny place than once thought. Some chapters of this book pursue themes related to popular belief and practice in the areas of visionary experience, magical healing and flying. Such phenomena were once the province of 'folklore', but historians have recently begun to investigate them as aspects of lived experience. Nobody is suggesting that early modern witches really flew through the air, or really visited the fairies; but we are beginning to take seriously the reports in which they said that they had done these things. Some strange confessions followed a demonological formula and can be assumed or suspected to have been shaped by leading questions, but close examination of confessions and other evidence has shown that there is also a layer of genuine folk belief and practice to be investigated.

It may seem unlikely that the modern experience of abduction by aliens could have anything to do with early modern witchcraft. However, the two are in fact linked by the condition of sleep paralysis, as argued in the chapter by Margaret Dudley and myself.[20] Diagnosing medical conditions at a distance of centuries is usually difficult, but here the evidence seems clear enough. Dudley and I build on a brilliant pioneering study by Owen Davies, who argued that sleep paralysis lay behind many reports by witches' victims complaining that the witch had assaulted them in their bed.[21] However, we go beyond Davies in showing that sleep paralysis can also be used to explain some reports by witches themselves – confessions in which they were led to interpret an episode of sleep paralysis as a visitation by the Devil. This is literally nightmarish territory.

One of the most famous of all Scottish witches has always been Isobel Gowdie from Auldearn in 1662. Emma Wilby, who recently published a remarkable book analysing Gowdie's extraordinary confessions in detail, here draws on anthropological studies of tribal societies to elucidate one of the strangest aspects of the confessions: dark shamanism.[22] Shamanism has provided a useful, if sometimes controversial, set of concepts for scholars to analyse visionary magical practices. European visionaries did not engage in the public ritual performances of the tribal shaman in Siberia or elsewhere, so European 'shamanism' lacked some important attributes; nevertheless, visionaries like Gowdie did experience flight, trances and visits to spirits in other worlds. They also used these experiences in some similar ways to tribal shamans, bringing information from their spirit contacts to aid them in magical healing and divination. Even conventional shamanism of this kind was remarkable enough, but 'dark shamanism' takes us into a world of predatory flights and almost random destruction. The dark shaman, Wilby argues, was nevertheless not simply a killer, but a messenger of fate.

The recent discovery of a shamanistic cult in Scotland, the 'seely wights', provides some kind of context for Gowdie's strange and gloomy world-view. Seely wights (the phrase roughly meant 'magical beings') were nature spirits similar to fairies, and human members of the cult flew out in trances to meet them.[23] Fairies were the most important nature spirits in early modern Scotland, but there was a wider world of 'spirits' that is only now being opened up.[24] Isobel Gowdie may or may not have been part of a 'cult', but her visionary activities were some of the most remarkable on record.

The broader topic of popular belief in witches' flight is the subject of my own chapter.[25] By arguing that witches were usually assumed to be able to fly, this underlines how remarkable witchcraft was. The chapter draws some of its concepts from neuroscience journals like *Cognitive Neuropsychiatry* and *Cortex*, where topics like 'out-of-body experiences' and 'hallucinations' are studied scientifically. Neuroscience is very different, incidentally, from psychoanalysis, the discipline that has more often been used by witchcraft historians who have drawn on 'psychology'.[26] Ultimately, though, my chapter argues for a cultural interpretation of witches' flight, as a set of motifs that could be deployed to make sense of witchcraft and to tell stories about it.

IV

Most of the chapters of this book make use of the online Witchcraft Survey, a database of Scottish witchcraft cases.[27] It may help to say a few words here about the Survey, its varied sources, and the varied uses to which it can be put. It can be used to trace statistical patterns and trends, or to identify individual cases with particular characteristics. This introduction, for instance, began with an outline of the panic of 1628–1629 in the presbytery of Dalkeith. The information in this outline was gathered by using the online user interface via the 'Search the database/Search for accused witches by name, place' options. Entering 'Dalkeith' in the 'Place of residence' query box, selecting 'Presbytery', and entering a pair of dates in the 'Case dates between' boxes, brings up a list of names of witches which can be counted or examined individually. The user interface allows straightforward searches of this kind to be undertaken online. Users wanting to approach the data in more sophisticated or unusual ways can also download the entire data set – the information that lies behind the website's user interface. They can then run their own queries on it using Microsoft Access.

Any discussion of the Witchcraft Survey is indebted to the detailed analysis of it published by its two full-time researchers, Lauren Martin and Joyce Miller.[28] This analysis provides answers to a number of important queries, with detailed information about the chronology of Scottish witch-hunting and the social profiles of accused witches. My purpose here is simpler: to comment on the ways in which the Survey can best be used, using some of the chapters of the present book to illustrate its strengths and weaknesses. Some of the weaknesses derive from the limitations of the sources, a few from limitations of its own design; avoiding these limitations will enable other users to get the most out of this resource.

There are three levels in the database: the 'person', the 'case' and the 'trial'. In the online user interface, these are displayed with three different colours. Usually there is one 'case' for each 'person', but a few people were investigated more than once. And not everybody had a 'trial', or was known with certainty to have a 'trial'. The most typical 'case' was based on a commission of justiciary – a document ordering a trial to be held. The Survey provides 3,212 names of people accused of witchcraft (a few of whom had more than one 'case'), and has a further 625 records for unnamed people or groups of unnamed people, making a total of 3,837 cases (including some groups of unknown size). For statistical purposes, we counted all the groups as groups of 3 although many groups were probably larger.[29] The Survey gathered detailed information on each case, with 634 data fields that could be filled. Even this number does not guarantee comprehensiveness; we neglected to include a field (or group of fields) for 'flight', an omission perhaps atoned for in my chapter below on that subject. My chapter does in fact indicate some fields from which relevant information can be drawn in the Survey.

One good thing about the sources for Scottish witchcraft is that they provide wide coverage, at least after 1608. The earlier coverage is less consistent, since it is only after that date that a central register of commissions survives.[30] But once we have that register, we can gather the names of most accused witches. This contrasts with England, where most assize court records have disappeared, and where some of the most detailed sources are pamphlets that are more or less literary or even fictionalised.[31] Studies of English witch-hunting have very few statistics with which to work. In Scotland, we can produce graphs and charts, and carry out studies of incidence and distribution, like those by Hughes, Cordey and Henderson below. Another good thing is that some very detailed material survives. We have depth as well as breadth, and can reconstruct quite a few cases – like those of Isobel Young or Isobel Gowdie – in detail.

However, most cases survive only in outline, with record survival being not only patchy but also skewed towards certain types of case – particularly those witches who, like Young, were tried in the central justiciary court. The records of the justiciary court survive better than those of evanescent local courts, but cases sent to that court may not have been typical of the others. Because the detailed cases are only a minority, one question must always be kept in mind: Is this case typical? One of the best-known Scottish witches is Alison Balfour from Orkney in 1594. She not only suffered severe physical tortures, but her husband, son and seven-year-old daughter were tortured in front of her until she confessed.[32] There is quite a lot about Balfour on the internet, often seeming to assume that this was typical. In fact, as far as we know, it was unique.

Loss of most local trial records means that, for nine-tenths of our witchcraft cases, we have no direct record of whether the person was executed or not. We suspect they were in most cases, for various reasons. One reason is that it is fairly common to come across remarks like Christopher Lowther's mention of 'Keeth, a borough where all the witches are burned'. The Witchcraft Survey has only partial information on the fate of Dalkeith's thirty-three witchcraft suspects from 1628 and 1629. For only eleven of them do we have any trial records, and for only two, Janet Bishop and Margaret Cuthbertson, do we have sentences (although these were both sentences of death by burning). Lowther's remark indicates that many of the others were also burned.

Shortage of information about executions means that scholars studying statistical patterns of Scottish witch-hunting usually study 'cases' of witchcraft – people who were formally accused, whether or not we know what their fate was. There are three main categories of 'cases' of witchcraft with unknown outcomes. First, there are those for whom we have pre-trial documents showing them to have been formally investigated for witchcraft. Second, there are those for whom we know that a commission of justiciary – an order empowering commissioners to hold a trial – was issued. For these two categories we may not have any actual trial records. Third, there are those who are named as accomplices in another witch's trial record. We know that many such people were subsequently investigated and tried, so we take this formal accusation as a significant first step towards such action. Looking beyond those who were executed can be an advantage, as Michael Wasser's chapter shows. We may call these people 'witches' as a kind of shorthand, but if we do, we must bear in mind that it is shorthand for 'someone who was formally accused of witchcraft' rather than 'someone who was executed for witchcraft'.

We also excluded people who were accused of other magical practices that were not called 'witchcraft' or anything like it. The church courts often prosecuted 'charmers' (magical practitioners) for 'superstitious' practices, usually making them do penance. This was hardly ever considered to be 'witchcraft' unless there was a suggestion of harm done or open demonic involvement. We also excluded people who merely had a popular reputation for witchcraft. In one of my early publications I mentioned as a witch Major Thomas Weir, executed in 1670 mainly for incest.[33] He was said to have a magic staff, various strange occurrences were described around him, and his sister Jean Weir was formally charged with witchcraft. But my colleagues in the Witchcraft Survey persuaded me to omit Thomas on the grounds that he was never officially charged with witchcraft. He had a popular reputation, but if we included everyone with a reputation, then what about the reformer John Knox? – his Catholic critics sometimes accused him of necromancy.[34] Better to stick to official accusations. Gaps in the evidence can be interpreted in different ways. Wolfgang Behringer, quoting Larner's remark that there was 'no witch-hunting' in the Highlands, 'or none that reached the records', interprets it thus: 'In other words: nobody knows what happened up there.'[35] Behringer seems to be willing to allow his readers to gain the impression that there may have been extensive witch-hunting in the Highlands, perhaps even more extensive for having been unregulated by the authorities. Recent studies of the Highlands have not taken this view, however, and have regarded witch-hunting there as having indeed been small scale.[36]

The Witchcraft Survey was fortunate to be able to draw on the researches of previous projects, notably the 1977 *Source-Book of Scottish Witchcraft* that resulted from a project directed by Christina Larner.[37] The Survey used the *Source-Book* as a source for about 263 cases taken from out-of-the-way printed sources. Its 'Case details' for these cases typically include the phrase: 'The project did not check Larner's reference to this printed secondary source as part of the research.' This is hoped to be rectified in a future update to the Survey (it is not being updated regularly at the moment, but I am gathering material and hope in due course to obtain funds for an update). In the meantime, scholars wanting to go from the Survey to the primary sources for these cases have to go via the *Source-Book*. Here it might be added that most of these cases were derived by the *Source-Book* from printed sources previously identified by G. F. Black or John Gilmore.[38] Black and Gilmore hardly looked at any manuscripts, but they gathered many references to witches from out-of-the-way printed works – editions of primary sources, or local histories quoting extensively from primary sources. Their works are still worth consulting, with Black in particular having a convenient chronological arrangement and a paragraph or two of text summarising each case. His *Calendar* allows an introductory flavour to be gained of significant cases at any given date.

However, Black and Gilmore did not always use the same standards as the Witchcraft Survey. As a result, several cases have crept into the

Survey that ought not to be there because they are not, by the Survey's standards, cases of 'witchcraft'. This is particularly so for the last few decades of Scottish witch-hunting, the period studied below by Alexandra Hill. The central register of commissions was discontinued when the privy council was abolished in 1708. References to later cases, though plentiful, are scattered through sources of varying nature, which provide no single guiding standard for what constitutes a case of 'witchcraft'.

Hill has thus scrutinised and sifted the original sources more carefully than previous scholars. The need for this can be illustrated from a related pair of cases (originally identified by Gilmore) – cases that Hill wisely omits. In the parish of Minnigaff in 1702, Janet McGuffock, the young Lady Tonderghie, and her Irish servant Molly Redmond, were accused by the kirk session of 'that piece of devilrie commonly called turning the riddle' – a familiar divinatory ritual in which a sieve (riddle) was balanced and made to turn, and the turning was interpreted as answers to questions. Redmond was banished while McGuffock was made to subscribe a declaration, read out in church, 'abhorring and renouncing all spelles and charmes usual to wizards'.[39] Despite the use of the words 'devilrie' and 'wizards', neither McGuffock nor Redmond seem to have been suspected of actual witchcraft. The pair were punished simply as magical practitioners – quite mildly in the case of McGuffock, a member of the propertied elite.

As well as these avoidable shortcomings, the Witchcraft Survey also has unavoidable limitations which must be understood if it is to be used to best effect. It can easily generate misleading statistics for those unfamiliar with the source material on which it is based. For instance, a simple search for all cases mentioning any aspect of 'Demonic pact' retrieves 355 cases.[40] Recalling the overall total of 3,837 cases, can we conclude from a quick calculation that only 9 per cent of Scottish witches made a demonic pact? Such a conclusion would be highly unwise, since for most of the remaining 91 per cent the documentation is insufficient for us to be able to tell, one way or the other. The role of the Devil in Scottish witch-hunting has generated some interest, so this is an important question.[41] However, the question should be pursued primarily through qualitative study of the more detailed cases, rather than through statistics.

Another example of dodgy statistics concerns marital status. Here one can generate the precise-seeming statistic that 77 per cent of female witches (499 out of 650 with known marital status) were married, with the remainder being either single (1.5 per cent) or widowed (21.5 per cent). Yet, the total of individual female witches is 2,702, meaning that the marital status of 2,052 is 'Not known'. Were the 650 women with known status typical of the total of 2,702? Almost certainly not. Marital status was not recorded systematically, but mentioned only when it seemed relevant to the narrative of the witch's activities. There were various reasons to mention a living husband in the records: he had an interest in his wife's case and might intervene actively in it (as with Isobel Young), or he might simply be mentioned as having been present (or absent) when witchcraft-related activities took place. By contrast, there were few reasons to mention the marital status of a woman without a living husband. This can be underlined by glancing at the Survey's figures for male witches: 78 married, 5 single, 385 'Not known'. Not a single man was recorded as being widowed – surely not because there were no widowed men, but because no reason to record such a man's marital status presented itself.[42] The marital status of Scottish witches is an interesting question, but the Survey's statistics in themselves cannot answer it. Here, as with the demonic pact, what the Survey can do is to guide the user towards the cases with more recorded information, which can then be analysed in their own right and assessed for their typicality.

V

Like all good databases, the Witchcraft Survey aims to stimulate and facilitate further research. The contributors to this book have used it in various ways. For some, like Hughes, Cordey, Henderson and Hill, it has provided a framework for their investigations. For others, like Paterson and myself, it has been a quarry for materials. The way it has been used goes beyond the specific reference notes citing the 'SSW', since it has often guided contributors towards sources that they could investigate in their own right. On the other hand, some contributors, like Carr, Willumsen, Martin and Wilby, have found it unnecessary to make much use of the Survey in their concentrated studies of individual episodes. In the future, the most important project that the Survey could facilitate would be a study of witch-hunters using a combination of qualitative and quantitative methods. In the meantime, here are twelve chapters that investigate Scottish witches and witch-hunters through a variety of methods.

Notes

1. [Christopher Lowther,] *Our Journall Into Scotland, Anno Domini 1629, 5th of November, From Lowther*, ed. W[illiam] D[ouglas] (Edinburgh, 1894), 22. Christopher Lowther (1611–1644) was the second son of Sir John Lowther of Lowther Hall, Westmorland.

2. *RMS*, viii, 331, 698.
3. See Brian P. Levack, 'King James VI and witchcraft', in his *Witch-Hunting in Scotland: Law, Politics and Religion* (London, 2008), 34–54.
4. Michael Wasser, 'Scotland's first witch-hunt: the eastern witch-hunt of 1568–1569', Chapter 1 in this volume.
5. Victoria Carr, 'The countess of Angus's escape from the North Berwick witch-hunt', Chapter 2 in this volume.
6. Liv Helene Willumsen, 'Exporting the Devil across the North Sea: John Cunningham and the Finnmark witch-hunt', Chapter 3 in this volume.
7. Paula Hughes, 'Witch-hunting in Scotland, 1649–1650', Chapter 5 in this volume.
8. For studies of the other major panics, see in particular: Normand and Roberts (eds.), *Witchcraft*; Jenny Wormald, 'The witches, the Devil and the king', in Terry Brotherstone and David Ditchburn (eds.), *Freedom and Authority: Scotland, c.1050–c.1650* (East Linton, 2000), 165–80; Julian Goodare, 'The Scottish witchcraft panic of 1597', in Julian Goodare (ed.), *The Scottish Witch-Hunt in Context* (Manchester, 2002), 51–72; Julian Goodare, 'The Aberdeenshire witchcraft panic of 1597', *Northern Scotland*, 21 (2001), 1–21; Elizabeth Robertson, 'Panic and Persecution: Witch-Hunting in East Lothian, 1628–1631' (University of Edinburgh MSc by Research thesis, 2009); Brian P. Levack, 'The great Scottish witch-hunt of 1661–2', in his *Witch-Hunting in Scotland*, 81–97.
9. Julian Goodare, 'Men and the witch-hunt in Scotland', in Alison Rowlands (ed.), *Witchcraft and Masculinities in Early Modern Europe* (Basingstoke, 2009), 148–70, at p. 152. A thought-provoking study of such men is Louise Yeoman, 'Hunting the rich witch in Scotland: high-status witchcraft suspects and their persecutors, 1590–1650', in Goodare (ed.), *The Scottish Witch-Hunt in Context*, 106–21.
10. Jonathan Barry, *Witchcraft and Demonology in South-West England, 1640–1789* (Basingstoke, 2011), 26–51.
11. Michael Wasser, 'The western witch-hunt of 1697–1700: the last major witch-hunt in Scotland', in Goodare (ed.), *The Scottish Witch-Hunt in Context*, 146–65.
12. Alexandra Hill, 'Decline and survival in Scottish witch-hunting, 1701–1727', Chapter 12 in this volume.
13. Her Gifford lectures of 1982 were originally published as Christina Larner, *The Thinking Peasant: Popular and Educated Belief in Pre-Industrial Culture* (Glasgow, 1982). For a revised edition, see Christina Larner, *Witchcraft and Religion: The Politics of Popular Belief* (Oxford, 1984), 95–165.
14. Larner, *Witchcraft and Religion*, 159; Christina Larner, *Enemies of God: The Witch-Hunt in Scotland* (London, 1981), 47–8.
15. Robin Briggs, *Witches and Neighbours: The Social and Cultural Context of European Witchcraft* (2nd edn., Oxford, 2002), 265.
16. Alistair Henderson, 'The urban geography of witch-hunting in Scotland', Chapter 10 in this volume.
17. Lauren Martin, 'The witch, the household and the community: Isobel Young in East Barns, 1580–1629', Chapter 4 in this volume.
18. Anna Cordey, 'Reputation and witch-hunting in seventeenth-century Dalkeith', Chapter 6 in this volume.

19. Laura Paterson, 'Executing Scottish witches', Chapter 11 in this volume.
20. Margaret Dudley and Julian Goodare, 'Outside in or inside out: sleep paralysis and Scottish witchcraft', Chapter 7 in this volume.
21. Owen Davies, 'The nightmare experience, sleep paralysis, and witchcraft accusations', *Folklore*, 114 (2003), 181–203.
22. Emma Wilby, ' "We mey shoot them dead at our pleasur": Isobel Gowdie, elf arrows and dark shamanism', Chapter 8 in this volume. For the book, see Emma Wilby, *The Visions of Isobel Gowdie: Magic, Witchcraft and Dark Shamanism in Seventeenth-Century Scotland* (Brighton, 2010).
23. Julian Goodare, 'The cult of the seely wights in Scotland', *Folklore*, 123 (2012), 198–219. This paper also reviews the debate on shamanism in more detail than can be undertaken here.
24. Julian Goodare, 'Boundaries of the fairy realm in Scotland', in Karin E. Olsen and Jan R. Veenstra (eds.), *Airy Nothings: Imagining the Otherworld of Faerie from the Middle Ages to the Age of Reason* (Leiden, 2013, forthcoming), 147–78.
25. Julian Goodare, 'Flying witches in Scotland', Chapter 9 in this volume.
26. A much-cited example is Lyndal Roper, *Oedipus and the Devil: Witchcraft, Sexuality and Religion in Early Modern Europe* (London, 1994). See also Katharine Hodgkin, 'Gender, mind and body: feminism and psychoanalysis', in Jonathan Barry and Owen Davies (eds.), *Palgrave Advances in Witchcraft Historiography* (Basingstoke, 2007), 182–202.
27. Julian Goodare, Lauren Martin, Joyce Miller and Louise Yeoman, 'The Survey of Scottish Witchcraft, 1563–1736' (www.shc.ed.ac.uk/Research/witches/, archived January 2003, updated November 2003).
28. Lauren Martin and Joyce Miller, 'Some findings from the Survey of Scottish Witchcraft', in Julian Goodare, Lauren Martin and Joyce Miller (eds.), *Witchcraft and Belief in Early Modern Scotland* (Basingstoke, 2008), 51–70.
29. See Hughes, 'Witch-hunting in Scotland, 1649–1650', for more on the issue of counting witches in groups.
30. For the interpretation of earlier sources, see Julian Goodare, 'The framework for Scottish witch-hunting in the 1590s', *SHR*, 81 (2002), 240–50.
31. James Sharpe, *Instruments of Darkness: Witchcraft in England, 1550–1750* (London, 1996), 105–8. For a study of pamphlets, see Marion Gibson, *Reading Witchcraft: Stories of Early English Witches* (London, 1999).
32. Peter D. Anderson, *Black Patie: The Life and Times of Patrick Stewart, Earl of Orkney, Lord of Shetland* (Edinburgh, 1992), 49–52, 156–7.
33. Julian Goodare, 'Women and the witch-hunt in Scotland', *Social History*, 23 (1998), 288–308, at p. 305.
34. Julian Goodare, 'John Knox on demonology and witchcraft', *Archiv für Reformationsgeschichte*, 96 (2005), 221–45, at pp. 235–7.
35. Wolfgang Behringer, *Witches and Witch-Hunts: A Global History* (Cambridge, 2004), 124, quoting Larner, *Enemies of God*, 80.
36. Lizanne Henderson, 'Witch hunting and witch belief in the *Gàidhealtachd*', in Goodare, Martin and Miller (eds.), *Witchcraft and Belief*, 95–118; Ronald Hutton, 'Witch-hunting in Celtic societies', *Past and Present*, 212 (August 2011), 43–71.
37. Christina Larner, Christopher H. Lee and Hugh V. McLachlan, *A Source-Book of Scottish Witchcraft* (Glasgow, 1977). For the strengths and weaknesses of

this work today, see my review of it when it was reprinted in 2005: *SHR*, 86 (2007), 338–40.

38. G. F. Black, *A Calendar of Cases of Witchcraft in Scotland, 1510–1727* (New York, 1938); John Gilmore, 'Witchcraft and the Church in Scotland subsequent to the Reformation' (University of Glasgow PhD thesis, 1948).

39. P. H. McKerlie, *History of the Lands and their Owners in Galloway*, 5 vols. (Edinburgh, 1870–1879), i, 487–8.

40. A slightly different search, for cases mentioning 'Non-natural beings', reveals 392 mentions of such beings by 226 different people: Joyce Miller, 'Men in black: appearances of the Devil in early modern Scottish witchcraft discourse', in Goodare, Martin and Miller (eds.), *Witchcraft and Belief*, 144–65, at p. 160.

41. Stuart Macdonald, 'In search of the Devil in Fife witchcraft cases, 1560–1705', and Lauren Martin, 'The Devil and the domestic: witchcraft, quarrels and women's work in Scotland', both in Goodare (ed.), *The Scottish Witch-Hunt in Context*, 33–50, 73–89.

42. Cf. Martin and Miller, 'Some findings', 60–1; Goodare, 'Women and the witch-hunt', 290. These figures do not add up to the headline figure of 3,837 because the latter incorporates groups of which the gender breakdown is unknown.

1
Scotland's First Witch-Hunt: The Eastern Witch-Hunt of 1568–1569

Michael Wasser

The pioneering modern scholar of Scottish witch-hunting, Christina Larner, clarified the pattern of Scottish witch-hunting and showed that much of it occurred in brief bursts.[1] Larner listed five major peak periods which she called national witch-hunts: 1590–1591, 1597, 1628–1630, 1649 and 1661–1662.[2] The recent Survey of Scottish Witchcraft confirms this pattern, even as it increases the numbers based on further research.

However, the 1590–1591 witch-hunt was not the first of its kind. A previously unnoticed Scottish witch-hunt occurred in the years 1568–1569 in the eastern sheriffdoms of Scotland, from Fife to Elgin. Its size corresponds to Larner's second category of witch-hunts, a large-scale local hunt, existing just below the scale of a national hunt.[3] How was it possible for such a large witch-hunt to be previously undetected? Large witch-hunts were usually spectacular occurrences, accompanied by a moral panic and such wide publicity that it could not be hidden.

The explanation lies in the failure of the hunt. As I will argue below, two important characteristics of a witch-hunt were present. There was a determination on the part of the legal and political authorities to pursue witches as a public menace and there were large-scale accusations against suspected witches. However, the element of moral panic was not exclusive to witches, but was diffused among other offenders against God's law such as adulterers. This was part of a campaign of godly reform under the regime of the 'good regent', the earl of Moray. Also, the witch-hunters did not systematically organise the trials and evidence in advance, so they were often unable to secure convictions. Finally, Moray's regime was unstable and ended with his assassination. The instability detracted from a campaign of law and order; the assassination brought it to an end. The result was a failed witch-hunt: many

17

people were accused as witches, efforts were made to bring them to justice, but few were actually executed. The witch-hunt was lost from sight among these wider issues.

I

The evidence for a witch-hunt in the years 1568–1569 consists of a number of distinct sets of records. At the December 1567 parliament, a commission drafting legislative proposals discussed 'how witchecraft salbe puneist and Inquisitioun takin thairof'.[4] There was probably no formal response, but it was followed in the next two years by a succession of prosecutions or attempted prosecutions of witches. In April 1568, there was a commission to try many people in Forfarshire, and at least one other person was subsequently investigated in May.[5] On 2 August 1568 Sir William Stewart, the Lord Lyon, was arrested on charges of treason and using witchcraft against Regent Moray. He was later tried and executed.[6] In the late spring of 1569, Moray conducted a justice ayre (a travelling criminal court) up the east coast of Scotland, during which large numbers of witches were accused, and ten were executed.[7] Finally, there was another isolated case on 12 August 1569.[8] The political context for these events was Moray's regency, which lasted from August 1567 until his assassination in January 1570.

The two main incidents of witch-hunting were the commission of 1568 and the justice ayre of 1569. The April 1568 commission was issued to try thirty-eight individual witches in Angus. It was to last for six months and allowed for the investigation and trial of any other suspected witches as well.[9] The commission is an example of how research expands our knowledge. It lay in the archives of the earls of Airlie until it was discovered by Arthur Williamson and mentioned in his book, *Scottish National Consciousness in the Age of James VI*, published in 1979. This late discovery meant that Larner was not aware of it. Since Williamson was not primarily interested in witchcraft, the commission occupied only part of a paragraph in his book and was not explored further.[10] The discovery slowly percolated into the wider scholarly community. It formed a major part of the 1998 conference paper on which this chapter is based and was addressed in Peter Maxwell-Stuart's 2001 book, *Satan's Conspiracy*.

A little over a year after the commission was issued, in May and June of 1569, Moray personally conducted a justice ayre up the east coast of Scotland, from Fife to Elgin, putting down political opposition and prosecuting criminals. This circuit included the Forfarshire territory where the 1568 commission had been based. According to Robert Lindsay of Pitscottie, Moray executed two witches in St Andrews, two in Dundee and various others in other places – ten witches in total.[11] The names of four witches who were accused but whose fate is unknown appear in the treasurer's accounts via payments made to messengers to summon an assize.[12] One witch, named 'Niknevin', is known from a number of sources and is the only one of the ten executed witches whose name we know.[13] In a letter written to the General Assembly after the justice ayre, Moray complained that he had been unable to convict most of the accused witches presented to him for lack of evidence.[14] This means that the ten executed witches were drawn from a much larger number of accused witches, of which we have no record. I have therefore added an estimate of thirty witches, accused but not executed, to accompany the ten witches mentioned by Pitscottie, a three to one ratio. This extrapolation is based on other examples of the imperfections of Scottish record-keeping. For example, in 1607 and 1628, approximately 75 per cent of the original bills for trials before the privy council did not appear in the subsequent trial records – also a three to one ratio.[15]

When we add these numbers together, we have a total of eighty-one accused witches, of whom eleven (including Sir William Stewart) are known to have been executed. This estimate for the accused witches should be seen as conservative; the actual number might have been considerably higher. For example, the justice ayre of 1569 passed through five sheriffdoms: Fife, Forfar, Aberdeen, Banff and Elgin. In one of those sheriffdoms, Forfar, there had been thirty-eight witches judicially accused the year before. Regent Moray complained that what he had during the ayre was merely 'a generall delation of names'[16] – which is what had also been provided in the 1568 commission. What if this 'generall delation of names' in 1569 had *averaged* thirty-eight witches for each sheriffdom? This would give us a total of 190 accused witches! Consider also that our knowledge of the 1568 commission is due solely to its accidental survival. Were there others? We cannot know. Moreover, Moray conducted six other justice ayres during his regency.[17] There are no mentions of witchcraft prosecutions concerning any of them, but perhaps there were attempts on a smaller scale. Finally, the 1568 witchcraft commission was issued by the earl of Argyll, who was justice general of Scotland, while he was holding a justice ayre in the west of Scotland. If he issued a commission to try witches in the east, might he have been holding his own trials in the west? There are no surviving records to tell us.[18] Yet if he was doing so, this would have been a national witch-hunt, not a regional one. The purpose of this speculation is not to encourage an expansion of the numbers beyond the conservative estimate of eighty-one accused witches, but to demonstrate that this figure is indeed conservative and that 1568–1569 constituted a period of large-scale witch-hunting. On the available evidence, it is just short of one of Christina Larner's 'national hunts'. Her examples of the category just below the national hunt were the Inverkeithing hunt of 1623 when twenty-two people were accused and the Paiston, East Lothian hunt in 1678 when eighteen people were accused.[19] Both the 1568 commission and the 1569 justice ayre were larger than these witch-hunts. In fact, the figure of eighty-one accused witches approaches that of 1590–1591 when the Witchcraft Survey lists 119 entries for accused witches.[20]

II

The existence of a large but relatively invisible witch-hunt in the years 1568–1569 raises a number of questions. Why was the effort made to prosecute large numbers of witches? Is it justified to treat the 1568 commission and the 1569 justice ayre as part of a single concerted effort to hunt witches? And why did the witch-hunt fail?

The answer to the first two questions begins with two of the men responsible for the prosecutions. Regent Moray personally led the 1569 justice ayre. John Erskine of Dun was one of the seven commissioners in 1568, and one of the two who had to be of the quorum.[21] Both men were prominent and powerful supporters of the Protestant kirk and of its agenda, which included a rigorous enforcement of the law. The argument is that Moray's regency saw a new spirit of co-operation between the royal government and the kirk, and that one specific instance of this co-operation was the attempt by two 'godly magistrates', Moray and Erskine of Dun, to prosecute witches.[22] This is why there was a witch-hunt in 1568–1569, and why the two distinct episodes in 1568 and 1569 deserve to be treated together.

In the eyes of the reformers, crimes were sins and sins were crimes.[23] Men like Moray, Erskine of Dun, and John Knox were oriented in the direction of the Old Testament and wanted to see its judicial laws enforced in society. In the kirk's fourth general assembly, on 29 June 1562, the second item of the assembly's supplication to the queen and her council called for 'punishment of horrible vices' which 'for laike of punishment, doe even now so abound, that sinne is reputed to be no sinne'. It continued:

If anie object that punishment cannot be commanded to be executed without a parliament, we answere, that the Eternall God, in his parliament, hath pronounced death to be the punishment of adulterie and of blasphemie; whose acts, if yee putt not in execution, (seing that kings are but his lieutenants, having no power to give life where he commandeth death,) as that he will repute you and all others who foster vice patrons of impietie, so will he not faile to punishe you for neglecting of his judgements.[24]

Three things need to be stressed concerning this pronouncement. The first is the presence of the death penalty. The kirk was not concerned only with questions of worship and belief, which were held to be exclusive to itself, nor was it concerned only with moral offences that could be handled exclusively through the godly discipline of church courts. If the kirk wanted the death penalty enforced, then it needed the active co-operation of the civil magistrates who wielded the sword.[25] The second is the clear link that is made between the execution of sinners and the good of the kingdom and its rulers – God will punish those who fail to enforce his judgments. The third is that witchcraft is nowhere mentioned.

This neglect of witchcraft may have been no more than an oversight; it was no doubt implicitly included under the rubric of 'horrible vices'. At any rate, this relative neglect of witchcraft was about to end. Beginning at the next general assembly in December 1562 and culminating in the parliament of May and June 1563, witchcraft rose to a position of importance among the moral offences that the kirk wanted punished by death. Julian Goodare has shown that the witchcraft act of 1563 was probably a fragment of a wider programme of legislation prepared initially by the December 1562 general assembly and introduced to the parliament in May. Most of this programme was not enacted, especially those aspects dealing with 'a full Protestant legislative settlement' in which the acts of the 1560 Reformation Parliament would finally have been confirmed.[26] However, the witchcraft act was passed, witchcraft did become a statutory capital crime, and the way was now clear for the prosecution of witches in the secular courts of the realm.

Or was it? To pass a law is one thing, to see it enforced is another. Law enforcement was not a strong point of early modern Scottish administration, and there were particular problems in enforcing a kirk-supported agenda during the reign of Mary Queen of Scots. For one thing, it was difficult for a Protestant church to co-operate with a Catholic queen. The kirk's dissatisfaction with Mary's enforcement of the law can be seen on 25 June 1565, when the tenth general assembly made the following appeal to Mary:

> That suche horrible crimes as now abound in this realme without correctioun, to the great contempt of God and his holie word, as idolatrie, blaspheming of God's name, manifest breache of the Sabboth-day, witchecraft, sorcerie, and inchantment, adulterie, incest, whooredom, maintenance of brothells, murther, slaughter, reafe, spoilzie, with manie other detestable crimes, may be severlie punished; and judges appointed in everie province or diocie, with power to execute, and that by Act of Parliament.[27]

Witchcraft had now made it into the list by name. Complaints about serious crimes were repeated later in 1565 and again in 1566.[28] On 24 July 1567 Queen Mary abdicated following her defeat at the battle of Carberry, and on 22 August the earl of Moray was appointed regent for the infant James VI.

Moray's regency, like his sister's reign, was marked by political difficulties, rebellions and threatened rebellions. These finally resulted in his assassination in January 1570 and the outbreak of a more widespread civil war. But so long as he was in power, Moray vigorously pursued the material and moral interests of the kirk. The contrast with what came before and what came after, together with the glow of martyrdom that assassination brings, resulted in his reputation as 'the good regent' in Protestant hagiography.[29] On the issue of justice, one anonymous poet wrote that 'Baith murtheraris, theifis, and Witches he did dant'.[30]

Moray did actively pursue criminals. In October 1567 he made a raid in the West March. In March 1568 he held a justice ayre in Glasgow, in July an expedition was made to Fife, in September there was another border raid, and yet another in April 1569. In May and June 1569, there was the justice ayre from Fife to Elgin that this essay addresses and in September 1569 there was another border expedition.[31] Many of these endeavours were linked to establishing his authority as regent. Both the 1568 witchcraft commission and the witch-hunting of the May–June 1569 justice ayre occurred during peak periods of Moray's authority. A parliament in December 1567 began a process of acceptance of Moray's rule and the April 1568 commission came at the height of this process. Queen Mary's escape on 2 May interrupted it and, despite her defeat and flight to England, it was not until the spring of 1569 that he re-established his authority in much of Scotland. The primary purpose of the May–June justice ayre in 1569 was to receive the submission of nobles who had continued to support Mary.[32] There is a strong correlation, therefore, between Moray's political authority and the 1568–1569 witch-hunt.

This is not to say that Moray was a paragon of consistency in all he did. As a politician, he knew when to compromise, which infuriated his less realistic colleagues such as John Knox.[33] Nonetheless, his enforcement of criminal justice during his regency was indubitable. One minor theme noticed by Amy Blakeway is that justice was more strongly affected by Moray's death than was religion. On his tomb, the figure of Justice was visibly more upset than the figure of Religion.[34]

But however important Moray was, no single man can ever be wholly responsible for implementing a policy of law enforcement. Other people are needed to provide help and aid. It is thus significant that Moray was not directly involved in the 1568 commission in Forfarshire. Instead, it was handled by people who were his allies and who shared his views. As seen above, the earl of Argyll issued the commission. Argyll had been a colleague of Moray in the Lords of the Congregation, and his brother-in-law and political supporter after this. Moray and Argyll did have a personal falling out in the summer of 1567 over Mary's deposition and Moray's opposition to Argyll's desire to divorce his wife. Nonetheless they were still formally co-operating in April 1568, prior to Mary's escape from Lochleven, as seen by Argyll conducting a justice ayre under Moray's regime.[35] Although Campbell power was greatest in the southwestern highlands, Argyll also played a local role in Forfarshire, both through direct landholding, and ties to kinsmen who were resident there.[36]

The commission was granted to seven men, including James, Lord Ogilvy, John Erskine of Dun and Sir John Ogilvy of Inverquharity.[37] All seven were committed Protestants,[38] but Peter Maxwell-Stuart and I have independently concluded that John Erskine of Dun was probably the man most responsible for the commission.[39] Erskine was a leading reformer, uniquely combining a theological and ministerial role with that of a secular baron.[40] Erskine's lands and power base were in the Mearns in northern Forfarshire. He was also superintendent of Angus and the Mearns, exercising spiritual jurisdiction over all of Forfarshire. Maxwell-Stuart concludes that the commission might have been due to 'Erskine's wish to exert a renewed discipline and control over certain areas within his jurisdiction'.[41]

Additional arguments can be found in Erskine's secular role as a magistrate accustomed to meting out justice. In 1556, he acted as a justice depute for the fourth earl of Argyll, father of the man who granted the

1568 commission. Beginning on 16 August, he held a justice ayre in the north of Scotland, starting in Elgin and ending two months later on 19 October in Aberdeen. It heard well over a hundred cases (none involving witchcraft).[42] In 1579 and 1581, he was employed to raise an army and enforce the king's law against people laying siege to Redcastle in Forfarshire.[43] Erskine's judicial role, when tied to his position as superintendent of Angus and the Mearns, and his close relationship with the earl of Moray, suggests that he was the key man in the commission.

He did not, however, act alone. In order for courts to be held, a quorum of three men was necessary, and both Erskine and Lord Ogilvy had to be of the quorum. As Maxwell-Stuart has noted, the courts were to be held in Arbroath in the southern part of Angus, and as he has shown, most of the accused witches came from southern Angus, but Erskine's power base was further north in the Mearns. The point is the same as has been made concerning Moray: no one man can be wholly responsible for a large-scale operation like a witch-hunt, but you do need a small number of men to take the lead and provide the motive force which others can then follow. This seems to have been the role of Moray in particular, but also of Erskine of Dun.

Moray's regency, therefore, can be seen as a period of fruitful co-operation between the secular authorities and the kirk in pursuit of the godly commonwealth. Moray himself, with his personal piety, commitment to Protestantism and vigorous enforcement of the laws, set the tone. Other magistrates such as Erskine of Dun, who shared his qualities and goals, followed suit. The policies pursued included the suppression of crime, and the new conflation of sin and crime insisted upon by the kirk meant that some moral offences, such as adultery and witchcraft, had been redefined as capital crimes and were to be as vigorously pursued as theft and murder. Thus, we have parliament's concern over witchcraft, the granting of a commission to try dozens of witches in Forfarshire, Moray's pursuit of witches during at least one of his justice ayres, and at least two scattered witchcraft trials, one of a high-ranking official, the other of an ordinary woman in Dunkeld. But it must be stressed that the pursuit of witches was merely one part of a greater whole.[44] It was not emphasised and could easily be lost sight of among all the other demands of state at the time. This returns us to the final question: Why did the witch-hunt fail?

III

One characteristic of the European witch-hunt was the way in which witchcraft was often viewed as a *crimen exceptum*, that is 'a category of criminal offenses that were so serious and often so difficult to prove that they justify both irregular legal procedure – often summary – and also deserve neither Christian charity nor imperial *clementia* (clemency) in the matter of sentencing'.[45] These two elements – a serious crime that was difficult to prove – could certainly apply to witchcraft. The witches' dealings were in secret, and the supposed harm that they caused was by invisible magic working at a distance, much harder to prove than a theft or a murder, which proceeds by physical means and can be seen by witnesses. Rules of evidence and procedure were loosened in several ways. Torture was used in a more extreme and otherwise illegal manner. Circumstantial evidence was given more credence than usual. Witnesses whose testimony would not normally be allowed, such as criminal accomplices (other accused witches), women and children were admitted. This allowed the conviction and execution of hundreds and thousands of women and men who otherwise would have gone free.[46] In the eyes of zealous believers, this was a good and godly thing.

Eventually this attitude towards witchcraft was adopted in Scotland. Brian Levack has shown how the use of torture to extract confessions and other evidence in Scottish witch trials was technically illegal but nonetheless tolerated and accepted.[47] At times the *crimen exceptum* model was rejected. This is what occurred between 1597 and 1628 in a reaction against the excesses of the 1597 witch-hunt.[48] This temporary rejection of witchcraft as a *crimen exceptum* can be seen in detail in the case of Geillis Johnstone in 1614, when a panel of high-ranking judges led by the earl of Dunfermline systematically barred the jury from hearing evidence that they considered to be tainted. Johnstone was consequently acquitted.[49] In 1568–1569, however, witchcraft had not yet come to be seen as a *crimen exceptum*. This can be seen from a letter written by Regent Moray to the general assembly in July 1569 outlining his difficulties in achieving convictions during his recent justice ayre:

Before our coming from Fife, and sensyne, we have been verie willing to do justice on all persons suspected of witchecraft; as also upon adulterers, incestuous persons, and abusers of the sacraments; wherin we could not have suche expedition as we would have wished, because we had no other probabilitie to trie and convict them, but a generall delation of names, the persons suspected not being for the most part tried and convicted by order of the kirk of before. This hindered manie things that otherwise might have beene done. And, therefore, we pray you appoint and prescrive how the judgement of the kirk may proceed and be executed against all suche trespassers, before complaint be made to us, that when we come to the countrie we may caus execute the law, and be releeved of the triell and inquisitioun heeranant.[50]

Witchcraft, although it was mentioned first, was not the sole focus of Moray's concern. He also mentioned adultery, incest and abuse of the sacraments as crimes that concerned the kirk. This is consistent with previous pronouncements of the general assembly, as we have seen. However, a witch-hunt, to be successful, needed to focus on witches. This is what happened in the national witch-hunts and even the regional witch-hunts beginning in 1590–1591. It did not happen in the 1569 justice ayre.

Even more important than a lack of focus was a lack of evidence. Moray was clear that he had been unable to 'have such expedition as we would have wished' because the lists of names which he received were unaccompanied by any evidence. He thus had to engage in a lengthy process of 'triell and inquisitioun' in order to achieve convictions. This was the case not just with accused witches, but with the perpetrators of the other three crimes as well. The lists of names of witches, adulterers, incestuous persons and abusers of the sacraments presented to Moray had probably been gathered by the individual congregations of the kirk; this had been proposed for adulterers and incestuous persons a year and a half earlier.[51]

The result so far as witches were concerned can be seen in a letter from Sir John Muir of Caldwell to the earl of Eglinton. It was written on 10 May 1569 from St Andrews, where Moray was holding the first stage of his justice ayre. Muir reported Moray's interrogation of a witch known as 'Niknevin', mentioning that both 'the Lord Regent' and 'the ministeris' were questioning her. We see here the reality of Moray's complaints: Niknevin had not been adequately interrogated before she reached the justice ayre. We also see the intimate co-operation between Moray and the ministers. Niknevin was resistant on two points. First, she refused to make a confession concerning any 'wytchcreftis nor gilt'. Second, she refused to name any other people as witches. This suggests that the lists of witches given to Moray did not contain names provided by other accused witches and reinforces the likelihood that they were given by members of congregations (or the minister, exhorter or reader). Muir reported that Niknevin was due to be tried 'this Tysday' and that public opinion was divided on whether she would be convicted and executed.[52] We know from another source that Niknevin was indeed executed.[53] Therefore, far from going to extraordinary lengths to gather evidence, the 1569 justice ayre suffered from a dearth of evidence due to a lack of effort by local authorities. This is the opposite of treating witchcraft as a *crimen exceptum*, and it is no wonder that there were not a larger number of executions.

A third issue that needs to be highlighted is Moray's vision of the proper role of the kirk in enforcing the law. He complained that the accused had not been '*tried and convicted by order of the kirk of before*' (emphasis mine). He then requested the general assembly to 'appoint and prescrive how the judgement of the kirk may proceed and be executed against all suche trespassers, before complaint be made to us'. Moray did not just want the kirk to gather evidence for him, he wanted it actually to try and convict the accused criminals before handing them over to the secular authorities.[54] This is a procedure akin to that of the Catholic Inquisition, and it is not what eventually pertained in Scotland. The kirk was eventually barred from trying people accused of capital crimes.[55]

While Moray's letter to the kirk shows that his witch-hunt was a relative failure, the same is not as obvious for the thirty-eight witches named in the 1568 witchcraft commission. Since the commissioners were directed to try witches only, there was no problem with a lack of focus. Moreover, the commission's call for further investigation of witches seems to have been heeded by the burgh authorities of Arbroath. In May 1568 they imprisoned Agnes Fergusson, who was not named in the commission, as a suspected witch.[56] However, circumstantial evidence suggests that very few if any of the accused were ever executed. First is the argument from silence. Chroniclers did mention the ten people executed by Moray; wouldn't they have done as much for a larger number from a small geographical area and associated with Erskine of Dun, one of the most respected of the reformers? There is also an analogy to be drawn from Moray's letter to the general assembly. If his lists were unaccompanied by the necessary evidence for a conviction, isn't it likely that the same was true for the commission, which was issued a year earlier? The strongest evidence, however, is derived from chronology. The commission was granted in April 1568 (the exact day was left out) and was to endure for six months, but on 2 May Queen Mary escaped from her imprisonment in Lochleven. She rallied her supporters and fought the regent's forces at Langside on 13 May. Although she was defeated and fled, the political crisis continued.[57] Forfarshire for the most part supported the queen until February of 1569. The members of the commission took different approaches. Lord Ogilvy was a leader of the queen's party while his kinsman John Ogilvy of Inverquharity supported the king. John Erskine of Dun remained neutral. Another commissioner, Sir David Graham of Fintry, also supported the queen. The difficulty of enforcing justice under these circumstances can be seen by what happened when Graham was to be tried for wrongful imprisonment on 27 July 1568: the court was attacked by an army under the leadership of the earl of Huntly.[58] Given this upheaval and the divisions among the commissioners, it is likely that the commission fell by the wayside, and in October 1568 it expired.

IV

It is instructive to compare the relative futility of the 1568–1569 witch-hunt with the success achieved by James VI at the North Berwick witch-trials in 1590–1591. James's bride, Princess Anne, had been prevented by storms from reaching him, so he sailed to Norway to reach her. After he returned to Scotland, he convinced himself that the storms that had threatened him and Anne had been raised by a conspiracy of witches in order to kill him.[59] Thus began the North Berwick witch trials, which resulted in the execution of dozens of people and which tried but failed to include the earl of Bothwell among them.[60] During the witch-hunt and in its wake, James addressed some of the problems that had hampered the earlier witch-hunt. In particular, he altered the law by pressing the court of session to issue an opinion saying that in cases of *lèse-majesté* and heresy 'infamous persons, weomen, bairns, et conscii criminis' could be admitted as witnesses against the accused. This ruling was applied to witches as well.[61] It was a direct application of the *crimem exceptum* theory. As has been argued above, without treating witchcraft as a *crimen exceptum*, it would have been impossible to achieve large numbers of convictions and executions. Certainly the testimony of women and 'conscii criminis' (criminal associates, or other witches) was important in furthering the witch-hunt. James also used and authorised the use of torture at this time, although the legal use of torture did not continue.[62]

The contrast with Regent Moray's efforts is striking. Whereas Moray had grouped witchcraft with other crimes, preventing an exclusive focus on it, James singled out witchcraft as *the* great crime to be fought, and gave it his undivided attention. Moray had also allowed witches to go free for lack of evidence, while James made sure that evidence was forthcoming, one way or another. Intertwined with what was probably a genuine belief went a political purpose. James set himself up as the great enemy of the witches in part to establish himself as a 'godly magistrate', God's instrument against Satan.[63] Moray had been known as the 'good regent'; James wanted this type of moral authority for himself and combating witches provided him with one means of achieving it. The kirk's programme of eradicating sin by prosecuting crime was continuing, but now witchcraft had been elevated to the status of the great *crimen exceptum*.

One witchcraft case, in between the two hunts of 1568–1569 and 1590–1591, can further illustrate these points and shed light on both witch-hunts. On 24 October 1577, Violet Mar was tried and convicted for using witchcraft to try to kill Regent Morton.[64] The record of the trial is sketchy, but a letter discussing the planning of the trial throws light on how the conviction was obtained. The letter was from Annabell, countess of Mar, to her sister's husband, Robert Murray of Abercairny, and is dated a month and a half before the trial. Annabell told Murray that the regent was delayed by dealings with England, and that therefore he was to keep Violet Mar with him for the time being. She then went on to tell him what to do with her while he was waiting:

> Praying you in the meintyme to caus try [*sic*] put the personis that suld accuse hir quhom scho hes abusit, as I wrett to you afoir, to be in reddiness to cum hier with thair accusatiounes in write agane the tyme ye appointit, as alsua to caus hir renew the speiking scho deponit afoir, befoir the ministeris was present of befoir, and that tua notaris be present to pen thir depositioune under ther forme of instrument, as my sister and I ressonit with you at being hier. Gif James my brother be thair, ye will mak him participant heirof, as alsua to mak my hartlie commendatiounes to him.[65]

Here was the beginning of a solution to Regent Moray's problem. It did not involve trial and conviction by the kirk, but it did involve participation by ministers. Annabell wanted to make sure that the case against Violet was secure. The witnesses were to be primed in their testimony, Violet's own testimony was to be repeated, the ministers who had been present at her original testimony were to be present again, and the whole was to be recorded in writing by two notaries. Convicting a witch was hard work, but unfortunately it was work that many Scots were happy to do throughout the period of the witch-hunts.

Annabell was the widow of Regent Mar and the foster mother of King James VI. At the time that she was co-ordinating the case against Violet Mar, James was a ten-year-old boy in her care. Is it possible that she gave James his early attitudes towards witches, which then provided a foundation for his later beliefs and actions? Certainly his actions in the North Berwick witch-hunt were in line with (but on a much larger scale than) what his foster mother had helped arrange thirteen years earlier.

V

The discovery of a witch-hunt prior to the North Berwick episode in 1590–1591 adds depth to our understanding of the witch-hunt as a whole but also emphasises the continuing lacunae in our knowledge. The lack of success in 1568–1569 points to the importance of hard work, co-operation between church and state, and viewing witchcraft as a *crimen exceptum* in order to achieve convictions in the courts. There are two periods, the 1590s and 1640s, which were periods of extensive witch-hunting for which the records are particularly incomplete.[66] Perhaps there were more accusations, prosecutions and executions in these two periods than our current extrapolations suggest. Estimated numbers of executed witches have fallen over the years as scholars gained more of a mastery of the sources. However, perhaps this process has gone too far. I would suggest that the next series of estimates for Europe as a whole might increase, as they have done for Scotland.[67]

Notes

1. An earlier version of this chapter was presented at the Scottish Studies Fall Colloquium, 'Witchcraft, Punishment and Popular Culture in Scotland', at the University of Guelph in 1998. I would like to thank the organisers and the participants, including Peter Maxwell-Stuart and Stuart Macdonald.
2. Christina Larner, *Enemies of God: The Witch-Hunt in Scotland* (London, 1981), 60–2.
3. Ibid., 61.
4. *APS*, ii, 44 (RPS, 1567/12/97).
5. NRS, Airlie Muniments, GD16/25/4; Arbroath burgh court book, 1563–1575 (Arbroath Library), fo. 40r. I would like to thank Julian Goodare for the Arbroath reference.
6. Sir James Balfour, *Historical Works*, 4 vols., ed. J. Haig (Edinburgh, 1824–5), i, 345; Pitcairn (ed.), *Trials*, i, 510*, n. 2; P. G. Maxwell-Stuart, *Satan's Conspiracy: Magic and Witchcraft in Sixteenth-Century Scotland* (East Linton, 2001), 57–60.
7. Robert Lindesay of Pitscottie, *The Historie and Cronicles of Scotland*, 3 vols., ed. Æ. J. G. Mackay (STS, 1899), ii, 217–18.
8. *TA*, xii, 167.
9. NRS, GD16/25/4. In a few instances part of the name is left out or is supplied by a description rather than a name.
10. Arthur H. Williamson, *Scottish National Consciousness in the Age of James VI* (Edinburgh, 1979), 56.
11. Lindesay, *Historie*, ii, 217–18.
12. *TA*, xii, 161, 163.
13. Sir John Muir of Caldwell to Hugh, third earl of Eglinton, 10 May 1569, HMC, *Reports on the Manuscripts of the Earl of Eglinton* (London, 1885), 42–3; Chambers, *Domestic Annals*, i, 60. She would have been one of the two

witches whom Robert Lindsay of Pitscottie says were executed at St Andrews: Lindesay, *Historie*, ii, 217–18. For more on the name as a witches' soubriquet, see Alison Hanham, ' "The Scottish Hecate": a wild witch chase', *Scottish Studies*, 13 (1969), 59–65, and Julian Goodare, 'Nicneven', in Elizabeth Ewan *et al.* (eds.), *The Biographical Dictionary of Scottish Women* (Edinburgh, 2006), 284.

14. David Calderwood, *The History of the Kirk of Scotland*, 8 vols., ed. Thomas Thomson (Wodrow Society, 1842–1849), ii, 501–2.

15. Michael Wasser, 'Violence and the Central Criminal Courts in Scotland, 1603–1638' (Columbia University PhD dissertation, 1995), 223.

16. Calderwood, *History*, ii, 501–2.

17. Chambers, *Domestic Annals*, i, 45, 52–3, 60.

18. The commission was issued from Glasgow in April 1568. From 8 March to 1 May 1568 the earl of Argyll was engaged in the justice ayre mentioned above. See Jane E. A. Dawson, *The Politics of Religion in the Age of Mary, Queen of Scots: The Earl of Argyll and the Struggle for Britain and Ireland* (Cambridge, 2002), 58, n. 54. Her source was the *Treasurer's Accounts*. While these accounts record payments made to people who helped to run the justice ayre, they contain no information on the crimes that were prosecuted. *TA*, xii, 113, 118, 121–2.

19. Larner, *Enemies of God*, 61.

20. SSW. This figure includes people from before the North Berwick witch-hunt began in November 1590.

21. The other, Lord Ogilvy, will be discussed below.

22. Cf. Keith Brown, 'In search of the godly magistrate in Reformation Scotland', *Journal of Ecclesiastical History*, 40 (1989), 553–81. Brown acknowledges Moray as the archetypal godly magistrate and also mentions Erskine of Dun: pp. 556, 559.

23. For the wider programme of 'godly discipline' in the church courts, see Michael R. Graham, *The Uses of Reform: 'Godly Discipline' and Popular Behavior in Scotland and Beyond, 1560–1610* (Leiden, 1996), and Margo Todd, *The Culture of Protestantism in Early Modern Scotland* (New Haven, Conn., 2002). Moray's policy of enforcing the law in a spirit of co-operation with the kirk has never been systematically studied, but has been frequently commented on: e.g. Maurice Lee, *James Stewart, Earl of Moray: A Political Study of the Reformation in Scotland* (New York, 1953), 219.

24. Calderwood, *History*, ii, 189.

25. Graham, *Uses of Reform*, 46–8. See also James Kirk, 'Minister and magistrate', in *Patterns of Reform: Continuity and Change in the Reformation Kirk* (Edinburgh, 1989), 232–79, especially pp. 270–9, for a discussion of ecclesiastical and civil jurisdictions.

26. Julian Goodare, 'The Scottish witchcraft act', *Church History*, 74 (2005), 39–67, at p. 42.

27. Calderwood, *History*, ii, 289.

28. Ibid., 301–2, 330.

29. Lee, *James Stewart*, is still the only full biography of Moray, but he features in most of the works dealing with the 1560s. Amy Blakeway, 'The response to the Regent Moray's assassination', *SHR*, 88 (2009), 9–33, shows how he was perceived as forwarding the interests of the kirk, which included a vigorous enforcement of the law.

30. 'Ane Tragedie in forme of ane Diallog betwix honour, Gude fame, and the Authour heirof in a Trance', in James Cranstoun (ed.), *Satirical Poems of the Time of the Reformation*, 2 vols. (STS, 1891–1893), i, 93.
31. Chambers, *Domestic Annals*, i, 45, 52–3, 60.
32. Gordon Donaldson, *Scotland: James V – James VII* (Edinburgh, 1965), 158–61.
33. Both Julian Goodare and Amy Blakeway remind us of the conflicts between Moray and Knox, which were most contentious over Moray's acquiescence to Mary's wishes in the 1563 parliament. Goodare, 'Scottish witchcraft act', 43; Blakeway, 'Regent Moray's assassination', 23–4.
34. Blakeway, 'Regent Moray's assassination', 26.
35. Dawson, *Politics of Religion*, 36, 87–96, 112–26, 153–4.
36. Frank D. Bardgett, *Scotland Reformed: The Reformation in Angus and the Mearns* (Edinburgh, 1989), 53, 72–3, 77, 119, 122, 124, 126, 131. See also Edward J. Cowan, 'The Angus Campbells and the origin of the Campbell-Ogilvie feud', *Scottish Studies*, 25 (1981), 25–38.
37. NRS, GD16/25/4.
38. Lord Ogilvy, Erskine of Dun and Ogilvy of Inverquharity are all listed as members of the 'Party of Revolution, 1559–1560' in Gordon Donaldson, *All the Queen's Men: Power and Politics in Mary Stewart's Scotland* (London, 1983), 161.
39. For Maxwell-Stuart's analysis, see *Satan's Conspiracy*, 52–7.
40. There is no modern biography of Erskine, but see D. F. Wright, 'John Erskine of Dun', in H. C. G. Matthew and Brian Harrison (eds.), ODNB, 60 vols. (Oxford, 2004), xviii, 540–2, and Frank D. Bardgett, 'John Erskine of Dun: a theological reassessment', *Scottish Journal of Theology*, 43 (1990), 59–85. Erskine also features prominently in Bardgett, *Scotland Reformed*.
41. Maxwell-Stuart, *Satan's Conspiracy*, 57.
42. NLS, Adv. MS 34.2.16, fos. 112r.–28v.
43. HMC, *Appendix to the Fifth Report* (London, 1877), 636, 641.
44. The way in which witchcraft was subsumed within a larger agenda before 1590 is also explored by Williamson, *Scottish National Consciousness*, 53–62.
45. Edward Peters, 'Crimen exceptum', in Richard M. Golden (ed.), *The Encyclopedia of Witchcraft: The Western Tradition*, 4 vols. (Santa Barbara, Calif., 2006), i, 232. See also Christina Larner, '*Crimen exceptum*? The crime of witchcraft in Europe', in *Witchcraft and Religion: The Politics of Popular Belief* (Oxford, 1984), 34–67.
46. Peters, 'Crimen exceptum', 233; Brian P. Levack, *The Witch-hunt in Early Modern Europe* (3rd edn., Harlow, 2006), 80–8.
47. Brian P. Levack, *Witch-Hunting in Scotland: Law, Politics and Religion* (London, 2008), 21–4.
48. Michael Wasser, 'The privy council and the witches: the curtailment of witchcraft prosecutions in Scotland, 1597–1628', *SHR*, 82 (2003), 20–46.
49. Michael Wasser and Louise A. Yeoman (eds.), 'The trial of Geillis Johnstone for witchcraft, 1614', *SHS Miscellany*, xiii (2004), 83–145.
50. Calderwood, *History*, ii, 501–2.
51. John Row, *The History of the Kirk of Scotland, 1558–1637*, ed. David Laing (Edinburgh: Wodrow Society, 1842), 35.
52. Sir John Muir of Caldwell to Hugh, third earl of Eglinton, 10 May 1569, HMC, *Reports on the Manuscripts*, 42–3.

53. Chambers, *Domestic Annals*, i, 60.
54. The bailies of the Canongate, when criticised by the superintendent for not punishing whores and harlots, responded that it was the responsibility of the kirk session to first call these people before it and convict them, then hand them over to the secular authorities for punishment: Kirk, 'Minister and magistrate', 274.
55. Julian Goodare, *State and Society in Early Modern Scotland* (Oxford, 1999), 186–92. It should not be thought, however, that Moray was insisting on prior church conviction as necessary for a secular trial. After all, he did execute ten witches in 1569 and the point of making witchcraft a statutory crime was to allow the state to proceed without the need for prior church conviction.
56. NRS, GD16/25/4. For Fergusson, see Arbroath burgh court book, 1563–1575 (Arbroath Library), fo. 40r.
57. Lee, *James Stewart*, 222–34; Donaldson, *James V – James VII*, 159–60.
58. Bardgett, *Scotland Reformed*, 127–33.
59. Jenny Wormald has shown that there was more to the 1590–1591 witch-hunt than North Berwick and King James's participation in it, but James's involvement is nonetheless what gave the hunt its publicity and its success. Jenny Wormald, 'The witches, the Devil and the king', in Terry Brotherstone and David Ditchburn (eds.), *Freedom and Authority: Scotland, c.1050–c.1650* (East Linton, 2000), 165–180.
60. For a recent study concerning the North Berwick trials, see Victoria Carr, 'The countess of Angus's escape from the North Berwick witch-hunt', Chapter 2 in this volume.
61. Sir Thomas Hope, *Major Practicks, 1608–1633*, 2 vols., ed. J. A. Clyde (Stair Society, 1938), ii, 268; *CSP Scot.*, x, 522. This issue deserves further study from a legal history point of view.
62. Julian Goodare, 'The framework for Scottish witch-hunting in the 1590s', *SHR*, 81 (2002), 240–50.
63. Stuart Clark, 'King James's *Daemonologie*: witchcraft and kingship', in Sydney Anglo (ed.), *The Damned Art: Essays in the Literature of Witchcraft* (London, 1977), 156–81; Williamson, *Scottish National Consciousness*, 53–62.
64. Pitcairn (ed.), *Trials*, i, 76–7.
65. Annabell, Countess of Mar to Robert Murray of Abercairny, HMC, *Appendix to the Third Report* (London, 1872), 419. It is interesting to see how two women, Annabell and her sister, were responsible for the trial of another as a witch. There is no mistaking the tone of command that Annabell adopts towards her brother-in-law. This is the type of action that official records and chronicles would never show, since all formal power was in the hands of men. 'James my brother' was James Murray of Pardewis, younger brother of Sir William Murray of Tullibardine.
66. For the later 1640s, see Paula Hughes, 'Witch-hunting in Scotland, 1649–1650', Chapter 5 in this volume.
67. Cf. Wolfgang Behringer, *Witches and Witch-Hunts: A Global History* (London, 2004), 157.

2
The Countess of Angus's Escape from the North Berwick Witch-Hunt

Victoria Carr

The North Berwick witch-hunt began in the autumn of 1590 when the bailie of Tranent, David Seton, was suspicious about the late night excursions of his servant, Geillis Duncan. Questioned under torture, she revealed to him the existence of a large group of witches who met throughout East Lothian. Although Seton was particularly interested in witches plotting attacks on himself, he also uncovered hints of plans to cause a storm to coincide with Anne of Denmark's voyage to Scotland to marry James VI. As a result the king became convinced that a conspiracy, plotted in North Berwick church during Halloween of 1590, had been directed at him personally.

Although the plot against the king became the main matter of the hunt, there were several sub-plots in the drama. Other people, some of them more influential than the bailie of Tranent, developed their own ideas about where the hunt should go. This chapter discusses one of these sub-plots: an attempt by relatives of the eighth earl of Angus, who had died in 1588, to blame his death on witches. Drawn into the hunt as a result of the eighth earl's death was his widow, Dame Jean Lyon.

I

Archibald Douglas, eighth earl of Angus, was a prominent and controversial political figure, head of the powerful Douglas family and a champion of the radical Protestant cause.[1] He had died after a long illness on 5 August 1588, aged only 33, and his biographer David Hume of Godscroft, among others, later reported that witchcraft had been suspected.[2] There is no evidence to suggest that any action was taken on this matter before the North Berwick hunt began, but it was only a few months into the hunt that the names of the earl and his countess began to be brought in.

Numerous people from all levels of society were accused of being involved in these alleged attacks, and so the brief involvement of the countess was not wholly unique. Not only was a poor cunning-woman, Agnes Sampson, heavily involved, but so were Barbara Napier and Euphame MacCalzean, both from the higher levels of Edinburgh society. It is through some of the witches from more noble backgrounds that a connection was made with Jean Lyon. Barbara Napier and Janet Stratton, another accused witch, both had connections with the eighth earl of Angus through Jean. Euphame was connected with the couple through her husband.[3] Janet Stratton's background is uncertain, but she definitely knew the countess somehow. Another witch, Richard Graham, had his own connections not only with Francis Stewart, earl of Bothwell, who was to become the most prominent target of the hunt, but also with Bothwell's enemy, the chancellor, John Maitland of Thirlestane.[4]

II

Jean Lyon was the daughter of John Lyon, eighth Lord Glamis (*c.*1544–1578), and his wife Janet Keith, sister of the fourth Earl Marischal. She was probably born in the early 1560s, her parents having married in 1561. She herself was married three times, with each of her marriages having some connection to the North Berwick hunt. Her first marriage, in 1583, was to Robert Douglas, eldest son of William Douglas of Lochleven. William Douglas became the sixth earl of Morton in 1588 after the death of Jean Lyon's second husband, the eighth earl of Angus (who had also held that earldom). William Douglas, as earl of Morton, was also present during some of the examinations of the North Berwick hunt, which will be discussed later. Robert Douglas, however, was lost at sea in 1585, and there is no evidence that witchcraft was suspected by contemporaries. Jean's marriage to Robert Douglas produced a son, who eventually became the seventh earl of Morton, and also meant that she had a powerful father-in-law in the sixth earl.[5]

Two years after the death of Robert Douglas, Jean married Archibald Douglas, eighth earl of Angus. The eighth earl himself had previously been married twice. His first wife, Mary Erskine, had died in 1575, and his second marriage to Margaret Leslie ended in divorce due to her alleged infidelity.[6] Jean Lyon was only married to the eighth earl for one year prior to his death, and at the time of his death she was pregnant with his only child. This second marriage of Jean's was also her second and final marriage into the Douglas family. The importance of this shall be considered later. In May 1590 she was married again, this time to Alexander Lindsay, shortly to become Lord Spynie. Spynie was, by 1590, briefly a favourite of James VI; he had accompanied the king on his voyage to Denmark in 1589–1590. Lindsay's friendship with James was to be important for Jean.

The approach taken below will be similar to that taken by Louise Yeoman in her exploration of the importance of David Seton to the North Berwick hunt. As a result of Yeoman's work, we now know that there was a connection between David Seton and the accused witch Euphame MacCalzean, who were related through a mutual father-in-law. Both people were involved in a family feud, which included a substantial inheritance.[7] What Yeoman has done here has not only increased our knowledge of the people in the hunt but has also provided an interesting insight into the hunt itself. Yeoman's approach has inspired the work below, for considering Jean Lyon in the light of the hunt has led to a further appreciation of what was going on in the background during the examinations and trials.

Jean Lyon has been briefly discussed by historians in the light of her connection with the North Berwick witch-hunt. P. G. Maxwell-Stuart deals with the eighth earl of Angus's death, Jean's relationship with Barbara Napier and her habit of consulting witches, but he does not ask why this was not taken further, although he is aware of Jean being accused of involvement in the eighth earl's death.[8] Charles Kirkpatrick Sharpe also briefly noticed Jean's presence in the hunt and even expressed surprise that she was able to escape prosecution.[9] Even in Sir William Fraser's *Douglas Book*, Jean's association with witches was not ignored, although Fraser did not connect it with the earl's death.[10] These are worthwhile insights into Jean Lyon's presence in the hunt, and it is time to take them further.

The argument that will be considered here is that Jean's presence in the hunt was the result of an adversary taking advantage of a situation that could have led to a grave outcome for her. Jean and the eighth earl's presence in the documents will be discussed in the light of this possible attack. However, even the most repeated idea about her – that she consulted witches – did not cause her to be arrested or examined, and this too must be explored to better understand her presence. Ultimately, the most important question will be: Who would have had the inclination and ability to bring Jean Lyon's name into the examinations?

As we shall see, the king is unlikely to have instigated the campaign against Jean. James's letters to both Alexander Lindsay and Jean Lyon reveal his feelings towards the two. In one letter to Jean, concerning a proposed marriage with Alexander Lindsay, he wrote to her that 'I haue oft promeisit unto you, I sall euer remaine best freinde to you baith, be your patrone in all your adoes, and reuenger of all tortis [i.e. wrongs] that any darr offer to ather of you'. While James showed some affection towards Jean, and declared his wish to defend her, his letter remained quite formal. By comparison, his letter to Lindsay was informal, showing his closeness to his favourite, 'Sandie'.[11] James's declared willingness to defend Jean could have been important later, when her name was suddenly dropped from the hunt. As for Spynie, Caroline Bingham argues that he was not a typical favourite for James, as the king was less emotionally involved with him.[12] James also warned Spynie to 'mynd Jean Lyon, for her auld tout will mack yow a new horne' – a proverbial expression, but one that could also have been a joke about the horns of the cuckold.[13]

This may show that Jean had a dubious reputation, although James generally treated her marriage to his favourite as positive for him. We have little information on the state of her previous two marriages. James also made a similar comment to Jean, saying that he had nothing to add to his previous support of Lindsay except 'a new tout in an aulde horne'.[14] This also suggests that James had spoken directly to Jean on the subject, and that his support of their marriage was more than just a series of letters to the two.[15]

Lindsay was considered 'ane great courtiour' in 1588, and as he was created Lord Spynie in November 1590, he was evidently still in favour then.[16] Royal favour might help explain why the entire theme of his wife was dropped from the hunt. Yet during the North Berwick witch-hunt Lindsay's own position in court began to change.[17] In 1591, he was trusted enough to apprehend the master of Glamis (Jean's uncle) for the king, so at least Spynie was still agreeable to some extent to the king.[18] By 1592, Lindsay had lost James's favour, but this was after the danger to Jean had passed, as will be discussed below.

III

Jean's relationship with the house of Douglas was crucial to her involvement in the hunt. The Douglas family, with their two earldoms, could be either a powerful ally or a dangerous enemy. Part of the predicament that Jean Lyon was in by 1591 can be explained by the position of Scottish women within marriage: women were considered to have closer ties to their natal kin than to the family they acquired through marriage. The Douglases were therefore not inclined to express any loyalty to one who had twice been married into their family but had since married out.[19] As for her own kin, the head of the Lyon family was her uncle, Thomas Lyon, master of Glamis. There is little to suggest that Jean had a strong relationship with him, and he tended to pursue his own agenda; he was also connected with the Douglas family and so might not have wanted to defend Jean against them.[20] He was at least friendly with Jean's husband, Spynie, at the time of the latter's ennoblement in November 1590.[21]

Central to Jean Lyon's presence in the hunt was the matter of her second husband, the eighth earl of Angus. It is difficult to have a clear understanding of their relationship; it is almost impossible to understand a relationship four centuries ago, and the marriage only lasted a year.[22] When Jean Lyon entered the marriage she already had a child by her previous husband, while the eighth earl had been married twice before with neither marriage having produced children. Whether this caused conflict is difficult to know, but Janet Stratton's deposition mentioned an 'eindling', or jealousy, between Jean Lyon and the eighth earl.[23] What this concerned is unknown, but it could have related to Jean's child and the eighth earl's lack of an heir. There is also the slight possibility that it could have been related to the possible allusion to the cuckold's horns discussed above. Nevertheless, before Archibald Douglas died he was almost certainly aware that his countess was pregnant, as it was mentioned in his testament.[24] Early modern widows were 'custodians of property and wealth'.[25] This role of the widow is useful in trying to understand Jean Lyon's position in life. Her widowhood left her with a portion of her husband's land and wealth, which would have been returned to the heir to the earldom only upon her own death.

The death of the eighth earl was sometimes attributed to witchcraft, even after the hunt. The eighth earl's biographer wrote that 'his death was ascribed to witchcraft: and one Barbary Nepair in Edinburgh ... was apprehended on suspition, but I know not whether shee was convicted of it or not: onely it was reported that she was found guiltie, and that execution was deferred'. He went on to describe how 'Anna Simson, a famous witch, is reported to have confessed at her death, that a picture of waxe was brought to her, having *A. D.* written on it, which (as they said to her) did signifie *Archibald Davidson*', which was later revealed to be Archibald Douglas, the eighth earl of Angus.[26] David Calderwood, too, briefly described how

Archibald Erle of Angus departed this life taikin away, as was vehementlie suspected, by witchecraft... He gave a prooffe of his religioun and pietie at his last and greatest extremitie; for howbeit he was assured that he was bewitched, yitt refused he all helpe by witches, but referred the event to God. It was constantlie reported that his bodie pynned and melted away with sweates, and, in the meane tyme, the witches were turning his picture in waxe before a fire.[27]

Spottiswoode's description of the same events was similar, although it adds that the earl rejected the assistance of Richard Graham, who was later executed as one of the North Berwick witches.[28] Although Godscroft, Spottiswoode and Calderwood all wrote long after the events, they were alive during the hunt, so their versions of the events may either reveal what they knew to be true, or at least what they had heard and so what others believed to be true.

Another description of the eighth earl's death was given by the earl of Bothwell during his trial in 1593. Bothwell's version of events included the use of witchcraft: 'thErle of Angishe being sick, his lady sent for me to requyre me to send for Richard Greyme to her husband... And a long tyme after, thErle of Anguishe falling sick againe, his lady requyred me to send, as I did before'.[29] The importance of Bothwell's statement lies in the similarities between his own accusation and the accusation he was laying before Jean Lyon. Although the charge against him was witchcraft rather than consulting with witches, Bothwell was not accused of casting spells himself but of commissioning other witches to do so on his behalf. Jean Lyon, likewise, was clearly believed by some to have had frequent contact with witches such as Agnes Sampson and maybe even Richard Graham.

All these descriptions of the earl's death can be brought together to describe how the earl's sickness led Jean to seek help from Richard Graham – help that the earl refused. As Godscroft was closest to the earl, his opinion may be the most important, but he did not discuss Richard Graham as Bothwell, Spottiswoode and Calderwood did. Bothwell certainly knew the earl well – he was married to his sister. Godscroft's omission of Jean Lyon's involvement may at least show that the idea of her being involved in the earl's death did not necessarily persist. At any rate, it may not have taken much effort to drop her name into the hunt if she was already associated both with the eighth earl's recent death and with consulting witches during that period. We are left with the likelihood that if there were people pushing for her name to be mentioned in the examinations, it was at least partly because they were aware of her real past.

IV

Who could have brought Jean's name into the hunt? There are not many candidates with the ability, the contacts or the inclination to do this, but there was at least one: the heir to the earldom of Angus. William Douglas, ninth earl of Angus, reappeared again and again in connection with Jean and had obvious reasons to be opposed to her. He was older than the eighth earl and only distantly related to him, being a great-grandson of the fifth earl who had died in 1513, but he was a diligent upholder of the Douglas family interest. He did not gain the earldom immediately, for the king raised a legal challenge against his inheritance. James was himself descended from the sixth earl of Angus, but his claim was rejected by the court of session on the grounds that the sixth earl had entailed the earldom in the male line. James's claim derived from the sixth earl's daughter, his own grandmother, Margaret Douglas, countess of Lennox. Had the earldom not been entailed, indeed, it would presumably have been inherited in 1588 by another Margaret Douglas, the eighth earl's posthumous daughter by Jean.

Jean, together with her future third husband, Alexander Lindsay, incurred the ninth earl's wrath by supporting the king's rival claim to the earldom. The ninth earl and Lindsay had a further dispute in June 1590, just after Lindsay married Jean.[30] The ninth earl would have been extremely angry with Jean and her new husband by the time of the North Berwick hunt. As a result of the couple's actions he had to wait until 7 March 1589 to obtain his earldom.[31] Upon defeat, James demanded 40,000 merks from the new earl.[32] That William Douglas's brief tenure of the earldom was not included in Godscroft's *History of the Houses of Douglas* may indicate that Godscroft did not become a part of the ninth earl's circle, and thus may not have wished to promote any of the earl's grudges. This might explain why he did not mention Jean in relation to the eighth earl's death.

There was more to the ninth earl's animosity towards Jean and Spynie than the struggle for his earldom. James Lumsden of Airdrie, who seems to have known Jean Lyon through her marriage to the eighth earl, had his own problems with them, which he brought to the attention of the ninth earl. A bond of maintenance and assistance between Lumsden and the ninth earl was concluded on 24 July 1590. The bond related that Lumsden had 'incurrit the indignation off Dame Jeane Lyone, relict off wmquhill Archibald Erle of Anguis, our predecessour, and Mr. Allexander Lindsay, now hir spous'. Lumsden's immediate motive was financial, for Jean owed him substantial debts. Among these were 'nyne thousand twa hundreth and aucht pundis', 'the sowme off aucht thousand merkis', 'ane zeirlie pensione for the space of twelff zeiris' and 'dewties off hir coiunct fie and lyfrent landes of Kinros, the Thomeccane, Lathrow and wtheris'.[33] Lumsden's pursuit of Jean became an issue for the ninth earl of Angus, whose influence could have caused his allies to take advantage of the brief mentions of Jean when they were brought up. Examples of this shall be discussed later.

It was not without precedent for such a bond to hold malicious intent.[34] Lumsden's own issues with Jean can well be seen as a motive for plots or for simply encouraging trouble for the countess. Beyond the items listed in the bond, the lands of Lochleven had been promised to Lumsden on 15 January 1589, five months after the eighth earl's death. It may be important that in the document Jean refers to her 'gud friend James Lumsden of Ardrie'.[35] The previous month Lumsden was given the feudal right of the marriage of Jean's infant daughter 'gotten betwix the ssaid umqhille erle my spous and me'.[36] Jean also referred to Lumsden as 'my vaillielint frieind James Lumsden of Ardraie'.[37] These two documents show Jean referring to Lumsden fondly, and yet clearly she failed to keep her promises to him, thus leading to the bond of maintenance as discussed above. Debts seem to have been something that Jean was expert at collecting and not repaying.

In the second half of 1590, soon after the bond of maintenance had been given, James Lumsden was ordered before the privy council regarding a ring that was said to belong to the king, and so Lumsden, and his servants were 'to be denounced rebels'.[38] A few months later, in October, he was brought before the privy council again regarding the same ring, where it was revealed that he 'ressavit a jewell fra Dame Jeane Lyoun, Countesse of Angus, quhilk, at hir desire, he laid in pledge of a soume of money to Jacob Barroun, burges of Edinburgh, unknawne to the said James that it appertenit to his Majestie'.[39] As this event occurred after the bond of maintenance had been written, it is likely that Lumsden's anger towards Jean was even greater than what is evident from the bond. Once she had caused him to be accused of almost stealing from the king, it is arguable that he would have had a grudge against her that would not disappear easily. His connection with the ninth earl is clearly important, as the ninth earl was in a perfect position to use his power and influence in the North Berwick witch-hunt.

James Lumsden's place in these events becomes all the more important when considering his role in Spynie's downfall in 1592. It was reported at the time that 'some suit is made for Ardrye's life, who pleads that he came to Leith to talk with Colonel Stewart, having warrant to confer with all men for the furtherance of his proof against Spynie'.[40] The incident harmed Spynie's standing in court and the king's attitude towards him. That Lumsden was involved in providing evidence against Spynie for Colonel William Stewart to use shows that Lumsden took the issues he had with Spynie seriously. Lumsden took these actions at great personal risk to himself, for he was obviously not meant to be there with Stewart. The result was that the alleged alliance between Spynie and Bothwell was brought to the king's attention by Colonel Stewart, who accused Spynie of being involved in some of Bothwell's conspiracies.[41]

The ninth earl's connection to the hunt can be drawn closer still. James VI himself had requested Angus to be present in some manner during the hunt. A letter from Angus to Morton shows a connection between the two earls at a time when Morton had already attended at least one examination of witches. Written on 8 April 1591, when Jean's name was still being brought up, the letter shows how the king had wished for the ninth earl's presence:

> to haue sen justice vsit aganis sic personnes as hes ettellit [i.e. planned] mischewous pratekceis aganis his majesties awin estait and persoune, as also aganis myne and youris Lordshipis wmquhill last predicessoure that died of guid memorie... Seing his majesties intentione tendis bayth to the weillfaire of the countery, and speciallie to the veillfair and standing of our house.[42]

Angus thus thought that the witches who had killed the eighth earl were also guilty of involvement in the subsequent conspiracy against the king.

The letter clearly shows that the eighth earl's death was being taken seriously as a case of witchcraft and that it was a major family issue for the Douglases. If this attitude persisted throughout the house of Douglas, then it is possible that Jean may have had more enemies than just the ninth earl, as her alleged habit of consulting with witches during her marriage to the eighth earl may have been a cause for wider concern. Morton himself had also received a letter from the king regarding the hunt, in which James described how 'Sathan and his ministeris' plotted against not only himself, but also 'our richt traist cousing and counsellour the umquhile erll of Angus'.[43] James had also demanded Morton's presence on 11 April to assist him in the matter.[44] If James put all the pieces of the jigsaw in place at this point, then he will have realised that the chief suspect in the death of the 'umquhile erll of Angus' was his widow, Jean Lyon.

Morton's presence in the hunt also extended to the escheat of Barbara Napier. Winifred Coutts's work shows that James VI gifted the escheat to Mr Robert Leirmont, who then gave it to the earl of Morton, who then 'maid and constitute the complener and hir airs [Janet Douglas, Napier's daughter] thair undoutit cessionar, assignay and procurator in *rem suam*'.[45] The interesting route that the escheat took – via Morton – brings up yet again his involvement in the hunt. Morton may have been trying to protect Napier's family because of their connection with the house of Douglas. Morton was also the grandfather of Jean Lyon's son, William Douglas, who was to become the seventh earl of Morton. Not much is known about the future seventh earl's early life and so it is necessary here to consider what little information there is.[46] He may have been in the care of the ninth earl of Angus throughout the time of the hunt, giving Angus power over the future earl of Morton. In 1597, William Douglas was residing with the tenth earl of Angus and, according to a licence by James VI, he was to be removed and placed into the care of Jean Lyon.[47] From this we know that he had somehow been placed into the care of the earl of Angus instead of Morton. Once again we see the problem Jean faced by marrying outside the Douglas family. It also adds an interesting dynamic to the relationship between the ninth earl and Jean Lyon.

V

Thus Jean Lyon, in 1591, had lost the kinship ties between herself and the Douglases, and she was in debt to many people. Her presence in the hunt and the dates she was mentioned, along with how she was mentioned, are better understood if placed into this context. The first examination that brought Jean Lyon close to the hunt was when the eighth earl's death was first mentioned, on 15 January 1591. At this date, the death was not ascribed to witchcraft, but merely used to illustrate when another event happened.[48]

In Agnes Sampson's examination of January 1591, perhaps later in the month, the subject of the countess was brought into the questioning again, this time more directly. That the accusation concerned Sampson enchanting a ring for Barbara Napier that would cause her to gain 'Jean Lyon's favour and love' is less important than the end of the examination, which says that Napier had 'sic other ends which are to be revealed in their own time'.[49] It may be suggested that this short passage reveals there was an intent to pursue the idea of Jean's involvement with witchcraft. Such an ominous ending to the examination does set up the idea that at least one of the people present was intent on pursuing the issue further, but unfortunately the document does not say who was present.

Later in January, Janet Stratton made a potentially damaging statement against Jean Lyon. Janet described an incident in 1588 where Agnes Sampson, Barbara Napier and Euphame MacCalzean met because they 'had something ado concerning a lord'.[50] After a possibly leading question, it was revealed that the meeting occurred because 'the earl of Angus' last wife called Lyon sent Barbara to Agnes Sampson for the effect because of an eindling betwixt her goodman and her'.[51] The indication that they had an unhappy marriage would have had to have contained some degree of truth if anyone who had known the couple was present. Morton had been present at the examination of Janet Stratton the day before, when Jean Lyon was mentioned in reference to being threatened by Euphame MacCalzean, on behalf of Barbara Napier.[52] It is therefore probable that Morton was present the following day when Janet Stratton revealed Jean to have consulted for the eighth earl's death. If Morton was involved in pursuing the subject of Jean, it is likely that there was a general sense of Douglas discontent towards her.

The letter of 8 April from the ninth earl to Morton, discussed above, shows that the king entertained the idea of Jean's guilt for a few months.[53] The idea of the eighth earl being killed by witchcraft was revisited in June during Janet Kennedy's deposition. Kennedy told how 'Agnes Sampson, who a summer night betwixt the Midsummer and Lammas had a long small picture of wax in her hand, black hued, which was devised for the earl of Angus' destruction and put in a ... basin full of water and made to grow weak and so to melt away'.[54]

That this version of events was still being told just before the whole subject of the eighth earl's death suddenly disappeared from the hunt indicates the possibility of a third party being involved in causing this idea to disappear. It is not always possible to know who was encouraging which lines of questioning and who was even present during some of the examinations and depositions. Apart from the one reference to Morton, it is generally a mystery as to who could have been present at these various examinations. Morton's name, however, does lend credibility to the argument that it was an attack led by some of the Douglases, which would have no doubt involved the ninth earl of Angus and possibly was even led by him. A connection between the countess and Barbara Napier continued to appear in the examinations throughout this stage of the hunt. In Napier's trial, from 8 to 10 May 1591, Napier was accused of having been an intermediary between Jean Lyon and Agnes Sampson, of having consulted with Sampson to win Jean's favour and of having worked towards the destruction of the eighth earl.[55] If it was believed that Napier was involved in the earl's death, why was the reference to Jean's involvement in his death not taken further as well? With Napier a constant feature in the references to the countess's presence in the hunt, it is also interesting that references to Jean Lyon and the death of the eighth earl of Angus disappeared from the hunt at the same time that Barbara Napier's assizers were tried for wilful error on 7 June. Only when Bothwell brought the subject up himself during his own trial in August 1593 was the issue ever revisited.[56]

VI

That this trial of Napier's assizers was arguably one of the most important of the hunt can only make the lack of subsequent references to the eighth earl even more intriguing. It could be that James was actually terrified of witches plotting his own death and thus that the prospect of one of these attackers being freed took all his attention.[57] James's opinion, given in *Daemonologie*, was that consulting witches was just as punishable as practising witchcraft, so we cannot assume that he would protect those whom he believed to have consulted a witch, especially for the death of their own husband.[58] In England, husband-murder was known as petty treason, and in Scotland too it was considered a terrible crime for a woman to commit.[59] As far as the king is concerned, we are left with two possibilities: either James was protecting Jean as he had promised or he had become so focused on the prospect of his own destruction that everything else became unimportant. A third possibility is that the motive force behind pursuing the countess's involvement disappeared for some reason unconnected with the king. It should be borne in mind that the impetus for *all* the prosecutions declined markedly after the execution of Euphame MacCalzean on 25 June 1591. The ninth earl of Angus died on 1 July 1591, round about the time when Jean's name was being dropped – which yet again points to his possible involvement in the attack on the countess. He was succeeded as tenth earl by his son, also William Douglas, but the tenth earl was a Catholic who had his own agenda – one that the rest of his family did not support. After the ninth earl's death, as we have seen, James Lumsden again attacked Jean and Spynie in 1592, outside the North Berwick witch-hunt. Morton's involvement hints at a larger discontent among the Douglases concerning Jean. Yet it seems likely that the ninth earl of Angus was the one pushing for an attack on Jean. As has been discussed, an understanding of a Scottish woman's position within the family of her husband is crucial in explaining how Jean Lyon could have so quickly fallen from favour among the Douglases.

VII

There are thus several reasons why there may have been a move to prosecute Jean Lyon for witchcraft: her marriage to the controversial Spynie, her large debts and people's perception of her as a consulter of witches around the time that her husband was believed to be murdered by witchcraft. There must be a reason as to why her name was brought into the hunt, then connected with the eighth earl's death and then suddenly disappeared. It has been argued here that it was a combination of all three of these issues. Related questions are who promoted the attack and whether they had motives other than belief in witchcraft for doing so. Here we can point to her debts owing to James Lumsden and to the fact that her manoeuvres in 1588–1589 incurred the wrath of the ninth earl of Angus. There could well have been more to Jean Lyon's presence than has thus far been discussed.

Even with the horrific execution of Euphame MacCalzean, and with it a clear signal that status would not be a barrier to witch-hunting, Jean Lyon was still able to escape from the tales that surrounded her during the North Berwick witch-hunt. She died much later, some time between 1607 and 1610, thus managing to outlive many of those caught up in the hunt.

Notes

1. K. M. Brown, 'In search of the godly magistrate in Reformation Scotland', *Journal of Ecclesiastical History*, 40 (1989), 553–81, at pp. 558, 577–80.
2. David Hume of Godscroft, *A General History of Scotland Together with a Particular History of the Houses of Douglas and Angus* (Edinburgh, 1648), 432.
3. *RMS*, v, 1483.
4. *Calendar of Border Papers*, 2 vols., ed. Joseph Bain (Edinburgh, 1896), ii, 487.
5. J. R. M. Sizer, 'Douglas, William, seventh Earl of Morton (1582–1648)', *ODNB*.
6. George R. Hewitt, 'Douglas, Archibald, eighth Earl of Angus and fifth Earl of Morton (c.1555–1588)', *ODNB*.

7. Louise Yeoman, 'Hunting the rich witch in Scotland: high-status witchcraft suspects and their persecutors, 1590–1650', in Julian Goodare (ed.), *The Scottish Witch-Hunt in Context* (Manchester, 2002), 106–21, at p. 107.

8. P. G. Maxwell-Stuart, *Satan's Conspiracy: Magic and Witchcraft in Sixteenth-Century Scotland* (East Linton, 2001), 159–60.

9. Charles K. Sharpe, *A Historical Account of the Belief in Witchcraft in Scotland* (Edinburgh, 1884), 74–5.

10. Sir William Fraser (ed.), *The Douglas Book*, 4 vols. (Edinburgh, 1885), ii, 366.

11. [Alexander,] Lord Lindsay, *Lives of the Lindsays*, 3 vols. (London, 1858), i, 322–3.

12. Caroline Bingham, *James VI of Scotland* (London, 1979), 115.

13. Sharpe, *Historical Account*, 75. In its usual form, 'a new tout [i.e. toot] in an aulde horne', the proverb meant 'an old idea expressed as something new'.

14. Fraser, *Douglas Book*, iv, 34.

15. Ibid.

16. David Moysie, *Memoirs of the Affairs of Scotland, 1577–1603*, ed. James Dennistoun (Bannatyne Club, 1830), 71, 85.

17. Rob Macpherson, 'Lindsay, Alexander, first Lord Spynie (c.1563–1607)', *ODNB*.

18. Moysie, *Memoirs*, 86–7.

19. Christine Peters, *Women in Early Modern Britain, 1450–1640* (Basingstoke, 2004), 7.

20. Michael J. Lyon, 'Family and Politics in Scotland, 1578–1596, with Particular Reference to the Master of Glamis' (University of Stirling PhD thesis, 2005), 204.

21. Robert Bowes to Lord Burghley, 7 November 1590, *CSP Scot.*, x, 416.

22. Keith M. Brown, *Noble Society in Scotland: Wealth, Family and Culture from Reformation to Revolution* (Edinburgh, 2000), 155; Robin Macpherson, 'Francis Stewart, 5th Earl Bothwell, c.1562–1612: Lordship and Politics in Jacobean Scotland' (University of Edinburgh PhD thesis, 1998), 136.

23. Normand and Roberts (eds.), *Witchcraft*, 169.

24. NRS, Edinburgh Commissary Court, testament of Archibald Douglas, eighth earl of Angus, CC8/8/20.

25. J. S. W. Helt, 'Memento mori: death, widowhood and remembering in early modern England', in Allison M. Levy (ed.), *Widowhood and Visual Culture in Early Modern Europe* (Aldershot, 2003), 39.

26. Hume, *General History*, 432.

27. David Calderwood, *History of the Kirk of Scotland*, 8 vols., ed. Thomas Thomson (Wodrow Society, 1842–1849), iv, 680.

28. John Spottiswoode, *History of the Church of Scotland*, 3 vols., eds. Michael Russell and Mark Napier (Spottiswoode Society, 1847–1851), ii, 389–90.

29. *Calendar of Border Papers*, i, 487.

30. Bowes to Burghley, 20 June 1590, *CSP Scot.*, x, 368.

31. *APS*, iii, 588, c. 92 (RPS, 1592/4/114).

32. *RPC*, iv, 360n.

33. Fraser, *Douglas Book*, iii, 296–7.

34. Jenny Wormald, *Lords and Men in Scotland: Bonds of Manrent, 1442–1603* (Edinburgh, 1985), 116.

35. NRS, Dame Jean Lyon to James Lumsden of Airdrie, 18 January 1589, GD150/1956.
36. This would have enabled Lumsden, once the daughter reached the marriageable age of 12, to offer her a suitable marriage partner and to collect a penalty in the event of a refusal. Lumsden and Jean seem thus to have expected at this point to remain friends for some considerable time.
37. NRS, Jean Lyon to Lumsden, December 1588, GD150/482.
38. *RPC*, iv, 51.
39. Ibid., 537.
40. *CSP Scot.*, x, 771.
41. Sir James Balfour Paul (ed.), *The Scots Peerage*, 9 vols. (Edinburgh, 1904–1914), viii, 100.
42. Fraser, *Douglas Book*, iv, 187.
43. *Registrum Honoris De Morton*, 2 vols., ed. Thomas Thomson, Alexander Macdonald and Cosmo Innes (Bannatyne Club, 1853), i, 170.
44. Ibid.
45. Winifred Coutts, *The Business of the College of Justice in 1600* (Stair Society, 2003), 183–4.
46. Sizer, 'Douglas, William, seventh Earl of Morton (1582–1648)', *ODNB*.
47. Fraser, *Douglas Book*, iv, 40–1.
48. Normand and Roberts (eds.), *Witchcraft*, 152.
49. Ibid., 157.
50. Ibid., 168.
51. Ibid., 169.
52. Ibid., 166–7.
53. Fraser, *Douglas Book*, iv, 187.
54. Ibid., 185.
55. Ibid., 249–51.
56. *Calendar of Border Papers*, i, 487.
57. Brian P. Levack, *Witch-Hunting in Scotland: Law, Politics and Religion* (New York, 2008), 34.
58. Normand and Roberts (eds.), *Witchcraft*, 378.
59. For a case of husband-murder in 1600, see Keith M. Brown, 'The laird, his daughter, her husband and the minister: unravelling a popular ballad', in Roger Mason and Norman Macdougall (eds.), *People and Power in Scotland* (Edinburgh, 1992), 104–25. The wife's crime in this case was murder, but, as was being envisaged with Jean Lyon, she had not carried out the killing herself but had instigated a servant to do it.

3
Exporting the Devil across the North Sea: John Cunningham and the Finnmark Witch-Hunt

Liv Helene Willumsen

European witchcraft trials were unevenly distributed from one district to a neighbouring one. The question why this happened still has to be answered, but there is consensus among witchcraft scholars that a complex of several factors together caused the trials, including top-down as well as bottom-up explanation models. This chapter will concentrate on the personal factor: how governmental representatives influenced the upsurge of witchcraft trials in their areas. One person, the Scotsman John Cunningham, and his influence on the seventeenth-century witch-hunt in Finnmark, the northernmost district of Norway, of which he was governor, will be highlighted.

In this chapter, it will be argued that John Cunningham's appointment in 1619 announced a new era for the Finnmark witch-hunt – a witch-hunt that had started in 1601 and would continue till 1692. This remote region experienced one of the most intense witch-hunts in Europe, relative to its population. Whereas the first two decades of the Finnmark witchcraft trials were focused on traditional sorcery carried out on an individual basis, Cunningham added new ideas. These ideas centred about the learned doctrine of demonology and referred to witchcraft performed on a collective basis, with the Devil's pact as its core.[1] When these thoughts were introduced into the witch-hunt, they changed judicial practice as well as the contents of the accused persons' confessions. Demonological ideas appeared in the court records. A specific Scottish connection can be argued on linguistic grounds; there are strong indications that expressions found in the accused persons' confessions during the Scottish witchcraft trials are also found in similar contexts in Finnmark.

I

John Cunningham entered the service of the Danish–Norwegian King Christian IV on 7 June 1603, employed as a naval captain under the name of Hanns Køningham.[2] The employment had effect from 20 January 1603. Cunningham was installed as district governor of Vardøhus and Finnmark on 26 March 1619.[3] He was based at Vardøhus Castle, near the Russian border. He kept his position as district governor until 1651, the year that he died.[4]

Cunningham's life was a varied one, even before he moved to the extreme north of Europe in 1619. He was an illegitimate son of John Cunningham of Barns, who had a son, John, who was legitimated on 16 April 1596.[5] He was probably born in *c*.1575. Barns was in the parish of Crail in Fife. Our John Cunningham's grandfather was William Cunningham of West Barns, from whom a continuous line of ancestors may be traced.[6] William Cunningham was the head of a large family, whose members can be traced in archival sources buying and selling property to each other related to marriage and death.[7] They were well-to-do people, burgesses of Crail with influence in local society. John Cunningham's contemporary relative Alexander Cunningham has a memorial inside the kirk of Crail, a carved oak panel with the initials A. C. on either side of the family coat of arms, a shake-fork with a star in chief.[8] John Cunningham's own coat of arms survives in Norway; this also has a shake-fork with a star in chief, with the name Hans Koninck, and in addition a unicorn. It is carved on the pulpit of the old Vardø church, today preserved in Trondheim.[9]

Unlike several of his cousins, John Cunningham did not study at the nearby University of St Andrews.[10] He was a man of the sea, and probably had more in common with his relative Alan Cunningham, who in 1600 paid money to get an English merchant ship released from the *Dunkirker*, a Spanish warship.[11] In several contexts John Cunningham is said 'to have travelled much and far, before he settled in Denmark',[12] to have been a 'widely travelled' man[13] and to have looked widely around in the world.[14] It has also been suggested that Cunningham was employed in the Danish navy due to his knowledge of 'Arctic waters'.[15] A contemporary source says that in his younger years Cunningham had sailed to 'Frisland' and other land towards the western side of the Atlantic.[16] When John Cunningham entered the service of King Christian IV, it was on King James's 'request and recommendation'.[17] Cunningham was allegedly sent to the Danish king in a costly ship at King James's coronation, thus giving rise to the name Køning Hans.[18]

John Cunningham married in Copenhagen in 1607, with King Christian IV present.[19]

There was a friendly relationship between King James and King Christian at the time Cunningham was employed, with frequent exchange of letters during the summer of 1603. James was invited to Denmark for the baptism of Christian's newborn son, though he declined to cross the North Sea again.[20] Cunningham must have been favoured by James in the years before he left for Denmark, and this favour continued after 1603. As a result of an apparent controversy between Cunningham and King Christian in 1605, Cunningham contacted King James, who wrote to his brother-in-law that

> the noble man, John Cunningham, descended from Scotland, who wished to devote his work to Your Serene Highness, we owe and give you our great thanks; and we thank you even more because he acknowledges and professes that he was received very kindly. What therefore, is there that we are requesting of Your Serene Highness on his behalf? Certainly that he may always be deemed worthy of the same kind and generous will, because that fact might seem doubtful to him. But since we favour him and wish him well, it will be very pleasing to us if he feels that your kindness has been strengthened and increased more and more at our request. And this will be reckoned by us as among the very many other proofs and indications of your good will toward us.[21]

The letter shows that King James knew Cunningham well and wanted him to be treated with respect. Christian IV seems to have taken the request seriously, because shortly afterwards Cunningham was entrusted with a difficult and important task. He was appointed captain of the ship *Trost* (*Thrush*), one of three ships which left Denmark in May 1605 on an expedition to Greenland.[22] The principal pilot of the *Trost*, James Hall, portrayed his captain in his diary as an eminent seaman and strong leader – loyal to the king, uncompromising, persevering and decisive.[23] When the ship encountered great icebergs near Greenland, the men were determined to return home, but 'the Captaine as an honest and resolute Gentleman stood by mee, protesting to stand by me so long as his blood was warme, for the good of the Kings Majestie, who had set us forth, and also to the performing of the Voyage'.[24] During this expedition several places in Greenland were put on the map, among them Mount Cunningham, Queen Anne's Cape and 'King Christianus Foord [*fiord*]'.[25]

However, Cunningham's unsavoury qualities should not be over-looked. He was characterised by people who met him as a strange and peculiar man, especially when drunk.[26] During the 1605 expedition, two men from the crew, 'both being Malefactors', were set ashore in Greenland, with some provisions to keep them alive.[27] The ship brought back to Denmark four natives from Greenland and, because they were troublesome on board, Cunningham shot one of them to make an example of him. The other three were taken to Denmark, and reportedly behaved well and attracted public interest.[28]

The following year, 1606, King Christian sent an expedition of five ships to Greenland.[29] John Cunningham was this time captain of the ship *Den røde Løve* (*The red lion*).[30] During this expedition he made a landing on the Labrador coast of modern Canada. It has been pointed out that 'by laying claim to Greenland on behalf of Christian IV he iron-ically placed his two benefactors at loggerheads'.[31] After the expeditions to Greenland, Cunningham was for several years a sea captain in the North Sea.[32] He took part in the Calmar War between Denmark–Norway and Sweden (1611–1613), initially as captain of the *Leopard*.[33] In 1612, Cunningham was captain of the *David*, another royal ship.[34] In time of peace he was often sent out 'to control the monarchy's territorial waters', especially the passage through Øresund.[35]

The new district governor of Finnmark, therefore, was a good seafarer, a man who could take quick decisions and deal with unexpected prob-lems, and a loyal servant. In addition, he was a person who was trusted to deal with the witches of the north – a problem of which the king had become aware during his visit to the northernmost parts of his kingdom, Finnmark and Kola, in 1599.[36] The ethnic conditions in the very north of King Christian's kingdom were distinctive, with Norwegian and Sami populations living side by side. Sami males had a reputation for sor-cery all over Europe at the time, being particularly well versed in selling wind to seafarers.[37] The new century made the king even more con-cerned about the danger of sorcery. The sudden death in 1601 of the governor of Finnmark, Hans Olsen Kofoed, was blamed on Sami sorcery, and the result was the first two witchcraft trials in Finnmark of Christen the Tailor and the Sami Morten Olsen.[38] No wonder that Christian IV in 1609 wrote to the next district governor, Claus Gagge, warning him to beware of witchcraft, especially Sami sorcery, and to show no mercy in such cases.[39] One of the main reasons for Cunningham's appoint-ment was allegedly the king's expectation that he would prosecute Sami sorcerers with a strong hand.[40]

II

Cleansing Finnmark of witches was only one of several demanding tasks Cunningham had to undertake as district governor. The king needed a strong man in several respects watching the northern borders of his kingdom. The fortress of Vardøhus had to guard the borders and the king's seas. The fortress had to be expanded. Churches had to be repaired.[41] Taxes had to be collected even in the most remote areas, among them the border areas towards Russia and Sweden. In some of these areas, for instance Kola, Russia also collected taxes. Cunningham applied in 1621 to cancel the taxation journey to Kola in order to save expenses, but the king ordered that he should continue.[42] The same point was repeated related to the Swedes.[43]

Finnmark had approximately 3,000 inhabitants in 1600, mainly peasants and fishermen.[44] The Bergen trade was important to the economy: fishermen from the north of Norway sailed with small cargo boats called 'jekter' to Bergen to sell stockfish in exchange for flour and other types of food.[45] The Bergen merchants, with roots going back to the Hanseatic League, had a monopoly of the Finnmark trade. However, in the period 1500–1650, the economy had shifted from expansion to stagnation.[46] People struggled to pay their taxes, and Cunningham applied successfully in 1628 to the king to get tax relief for the common people due to poor fisheries over many years.[47]

III

The Finnmark witchcraft trials changed character after Cunningham's arrival in 1619. The number of trials increased enormously from 1620 onwards, as the first panic started that year. Whereas before 1620 the focus was on traditional sorcery, there was now a shift towards demonological ideas, as seen through questions posed during interrogation as well as through the accused persons' confessions. While prosecutions of men and Sami sorcery often occurred during the first two decades of the witch-hunt in Finnmark, prosecutions of women and demonological witchcraft came to the fore after 1620. Traditional Sami sorcery was seen as an individual skill, displaying inherent magical power. Contrary to this was witchcraft learned from a pact with the Devil. Collective performance of witchcraft took over, highlighting witches' meetings and collective witchcraft operations.[48] The district of Finnmark was administratively divided into East Finnmark and West

Finnmark. East Finnmark bordered to Russia and included the fishing villages Vardø and Vadsø, with Vardøhus Castle as the most important place. West Finnmark covered the western part of the district, including the fishing villages Hammerfest and Honningsvåg. Whereas witchcraft trials in Finnmark before 1620 were scattered in East as well as West Finnmark, after 1620 the witchcraft trials were centred round Vardøhus Castle. So we see changes around 1620 related to the scale, the content and the location of the trials.

During the whole period of the Finnmark witchcraft trials, 135 persons were accused of witchcraft.[49] Of these, ninety-one persons were executed, an execution rate of 67 per cent. Among the accused persons, 82 per cent were females and 18 per cent males. This is similar to the percentage we find in most European countries, wherein women were clearly in the majority.[50] However, in a few countries and areas, for instance Iceland, Estonia, Russia and Normandy, fewer than half of those who were accused of witchcraft were women.[51] The male dominance was particularly clear in Iceland, where accusations were based on *maleficium*, not demonology. Only ten out of one hundred and twenty witchcraft trials concerned women, and only one woman was burned out of twenty-two in total.[52] In Finnmark, among the accused males, the Sami men were in a majority, as two-thirds of the males were Samis.[53]

During the first two decades of the seventeenth century, nine persons were accused of witchcraft, all executed. Demonological ideas were not mentioned during these trials, neither was the figure of the Devil. The collective element implied in witches' meetings and collective sorcery operations was absent. In 1617, a decree was issued for Denmark–Norway, stating that the 'real witches' were those who had sworn themselves to the Devil. With this decree, demonological elements had found their way into the laws of Denmark–Norway. For Finnmark, more than other regions in Norway with other ethnic conditions, this decree had the effect that demonological witchcraft and learned witchcraft ideas were adopted. In this way, the ground was prepared for a type of witch-hunting based on learned ideological grounds. The intensity of witchcraft persecution was particularly high in the district of Finnmark compared to the rest of Norway. With only 0.8 per cent of Norway's population at the time, Finnmark had 16 per cent of all Norwegian witchcraft trials and 31 per cent of all death sentences in witchcraft trials.[54] This points to the personal factor as important in promoting the prosecution of witches. The appointment of a new district governor is the most likely explanation for the new direction the Finnmark witch-hunt took after 1620.

IV

What kind of ideas about witchcraft did Cunningham bring with him to Finnmark? To answer this question we have to turn to the situation in Scotland and the early witchcraft trials there. Among the episodes that stand out as periods of high-level accusation and prosecution of witches there are two early ones, the 1590–1591 and 1597 panics.

During the North Berwick panic of 1590–1591, several persons from East Lothian and Edinburgh were accused of witchcraft.[55] The initial accusations were related to the raising of a storm against the ship of King James VI's future bride, Princess Anne from Denmark, sister of Christian IV, who was on her way to Scotland to meet her husband-to-be.[56] The North Berwick witches, in alliance with Danish witches, were believed to have raised a storm so that the princess's ship had to turn back to Norway. The 1590–1591 panic shows clear demonological ideas, including witches' meetings and digging up corpses near the church.[57]

John Cunningham had witnessed this panic as a young man, as the alleged evildoings had taken place near his birthplace, Barns in Fife, from where he could look across the firth to North Berwick. In an oral society, as the seventeenth century was, the stories emerging from the trials must have been hot news for people living nearby. In addition to the North Berwick cases, Cunningham must have known about early witchcraft trials in his home district of Fife.[58]

The other Scottish witchcraft panic that Cunningham probably knew thoroughly was the panic of 1597. This panic took place mainly in Aberdeenshire, Fife, Perthshire, Glasgow and Stirlingshire, and has been suggested to have involved about 400 cases, half of them resulting in executions.[59] Stuart Macdonald documents twenty-six cases in Fife in 1597, and there were certainly numerous further cases.[60] The 1597 hunt particularly affected the presbyteries of Kirkcaldy and St Andrews (including Crail).[61] King James was present during several witchcraft trials there in July. The 1597 panic was also noteworthy because many suspected persons were subjected to the water ordeal, which was unusual in Scotland. The water ordeal would be used extensively in Finnmark, as we shall see. Demonological notions were present during the 1597 panic, with the Devil's pact as well as the witches' sabbath as part of the confessions.[62] Like the 1590–1591 panic, this had a combination of witchcraft and treason at its centre. It certainly would have attracted public interest. Cunningham would surely have known about the trials, not least because some witches were prosecuted near Crail.

Cunningham's early years thus brought him into contact with two monarchs both concerned with hunting witches and with a strong anxiety for the evil deeds witches could perform. King James's active role during the early Scottish panics shows his strong conviction about what the witches could do. He was the only monarch in Europe to publish a treatise on demonology, *Daemonologie*, written between the 1590–1591 and the 1597 panics, and published in 1597.[63] King Christian IV was also a strong believer in the evildoings of witches, with a particular fear of the witches in the north of his kingdom. The influence on Cunningham in this respect must have gone only in one direction.

V

The echo of European demonological ideas was clearly heard during the first Finnmark panic, in 1620–1621. Thirteen women were implicated, twelve of whom were executed. The main accusation concerned a shipwreck in 1617, when ten boats with forty men from Kiberg and Vardø went down on Christmas Eve. The trial of a Sami woman, Karen Edisdatter, who was brought before the court on 13 May 1620, was the first.[64] The district governor, Cunningham, was present as well as the appeal court judge.[65] Central demonological elements, like the pact with the Devil, were now heard in the courtrooms in Finnmark for the first time.[66] Karen Edisdatter was accused of casting spells on persons, causing sickness and death. She was tried by the water ordeal and confessed afterwards as follows:

> The first time she was involved with the Devil was when she was but a lass and was tending herds in the fields. A heaviness came over her near a hill, and presently a big headless man came to her asking her whether she was asleep. She said, I am neither asleep nor awake. In his hand, he was holding a large ring of keys which he offered her, saying, If you accept these keys, all you wish to undertake in this world will come to pass. She noticed he had a beautiful ribbon and she said, Give me that ribbon, I do not know how to use the keys. She got her ribbon, and when she reached home, she became demented, and since then, she confessed, the Devil has always been with her, unless the minister was present and now, in the presence of the Reverend Master Mogens, while he prepared her spiritually, she confessed that she was to blame for the death of the said Abraham Nielsen and for the said Johannis's sake [*sic*], as has been touched upon.[67]

Karen Edisdatter denounced two other women, thus introducing the collective aspect of demonological trials:

> She confessed she was to blame for all of their deaths, for as soon as her anger flared and she said, may the Evil One take you, or if she hoped evil might strike them, the Evil One would be there at once. At the height of her distress, she screamed that Rasmus Joensen's Lisebet in Omgangh and Morten Nielsen's Anne in Langefiørd were both just as guilty as she in the handling of witchcraft. On the aforementioned grounds, and in accordance with her own confession, the court finds that she is to be punished in fire at the stake.[68]

We next see the same elements in the confession of Kirsten Sørensdatter, originally from Helsingør in Denmark, now living in the small fishing village of Kiberg in Finnmark. She was denounced by seven other women. On 26 April 1621, she was brought before the court at a session held at Vardøhus Castle, with the bailiff, the magistrate, the jurors and 'the illustrious Hans Køning' (Cunningham) present.[69] Kirsten Sørensdatter first denied knowing witchcraft:

> His Royal Majesty's bailiff, Søffren Nielsen, asked her why so many witches have denounced her for being familiar with witchcraft and sorcery, adding that if this was the case, and if she were willing to confess of her own accord, she would not be tortured. She fiercely denied she had any such skills; they had slandered her cruelly. Since seven witches have denounced her for being familiar with the craft, as she herself has heard from their testimonies about her, and since, according to their sentences that have been recited to her, she was their master and admiral and also learned a bit from them, the court found that she should be tried by the water ordeal.[70]

After this she confessed:

> When she heard she was to be tried by the water ordeal, she said she would confess what she knew of her own accord. First, that when she was sixteen years old, she went to Helsingør, to an old woman whose name she could not recall. One day, as she was on her way into the fields to fetch some geese for the old woman, Satan came to her in the likeness of a dog, saying, If you agree to learn witchcraft, all you undertake in this world will succeed. However, she had to forswear God and her baptismal pact with God; and he followed her into the

house to the old woman, who then read to her and taught her and tested her abilities with a ball of yarn on water. It rolled around on the water, and that amused her.[71]

The formulation about forswearing God and the baptismal pact is well known from witchcraft trials in other places, including Scotland; so is the image of Satan appearing in the shape of a dog.[72] Kirsten Sørensdatter, like many others in the seventeenth century, went north to Finnmark and settled there.

In addition to confessing to the Devil's pact, witches' meetings and collective witchcraft operations, fantastic elements were brought into the confessions – particularly the long distances witches managed to fly to attend meetings. The witches could fly from Vardø in Finnmark to the Lyder Horn, a well-known witches' mountain near Bergen, in a short time:

> She confessed she went carousing with the others, just as they have confessed about her, except that she was not here on Balduolden[73] last Christmas Eve; nor has she been on Lyder Horn since that summer when she sailed south, and there had been a whole bevy of them and she did not recognise nearly everyone. When asked if she was the cause of Hendrich Meyer's death, she confessed that they had a quarrel about a drying rack, and for that reason she had cursed him and wished him the worst, because when you are angry with someone you are not that person's well-wisher.[74]

Shape-shifting was another fantastic aspect of these witchcraft trials, and it was not always necessary to be shaped as birds to fly quickly:

> Moreover, she confessed that last Christmas night, Marrite Oelsdaatter, in the likeness of a dog, fetched her from Bergen and put her down here in Vardøen on Balduolden. As for herself, she was in the likeness of a bitch. Several others had been there, two of them in the shapes of wolves, one of which was thin and long and black around the head; that was Bertell Hendrichsen who did the writing for them. The other was fat with a white chest; that was Eluffue Oelsen. And they drank and danced and played, and Else Knudtzdaatter waited on them. She also confessed that Else's daughter Mette was with them, too, in the likeness of a grey cat. She generally confirmed everything the others had testified about her except that she was their admiral. She would gladly stake her

life upon the truth of what she had said, and accept the final rites.[75]

Shape-shifting and flying are similarly found in the early Scottish panics, for instance at the convention in Atholl in 1597 where 2,300 witches allegedly participated, 'and the Devill amongst them'.[76]

During Cunningham's period in office fifty-two persons were accused of witchcraft, of whom forty-one were executed. About half of the death sentences were passed at Vardøhus. Torture was frequently used, sometimes applied after sentence was passed in order to extort names of accomplices. Of those who received death sentences, twenty were tried by the water ordeal. Demonological elements recurred frequently.

VI

The most specific evidence of Scottish influence on the Finnmark witchcraft trials is linguistic. When particular words and linguistic images are found on both sides of the North Sea, but not in European witchcraft documents elsewhere, this cannot be accidental. In the following I will draw attention to two such linguistic images found both in Scottish and in Finnmark witchcraft trial documents.

The first of the expressions has to do with witches' meetings and the wording is that one person is 'admiral and master' for other witches during a witches' meeting. In the Scottish material this expression is first found in Euphemia MacCalzean's case in 1591. Several points concerning persons she had harmed, witches' meetings and witchcraft operations lead up to this one:

> Item i[n]dytit and accusit for ane conventioun haldin be yow and utheris notorious wiches youre associatis att the BrouneHoillis quhair ye and thay tuik the sea Ro[ber]t Greirsoun bei[n]g youre *admerall and m[aiste]r* man past owre the sea in ridillis to ane schip q[uhai]r ye enterit w[i]th the devill yo[u]r m[aiste]r th[air]in q[uhai]r eftir ye had eittin and drinkkin ye caist owr ane blak dog that skippit under the schip and th[air]by ye leving the devill yo[u]r m[aiste]r th[air]in quha drownit the schip be tumbling q[uhair]by the quene wes putt bak be storme.[77]
>
> (*my italics*)

The expression 'admiral and master' is an interesting one. The 'admiral' in Scotland was an officer of the crown; his job was to organise and command ships for the king, and to act as a judge in the admiral's court. At the time of the North Berwick panic, the admiral of Scotland was Francis Stewart, earl of Bothwell, the king's enemy on whose behalf the witches were accused of acting. The title was used by Bothwell himself, but he could appoint one or more deputes to do the actual work.[78] In England, too, it could be used in maritime connections, through the phrase 'admiral of the sea'.[79]

We also find the same expression, one person being an admiral for other persons at a witches' meeting, in the case of Kirsten Sørensdatter mentioned above: 'she was their master and admiral and also learned a bit from them'. Later in the same case a parallel wording is used: 'She generally confirmed everything the others had testified about her except that she was their admiral.' The idea of a military ranking system among the witches is found in Bohuslän in Sweden, where a woman led a 'Compagnie'.[80] But the crucial expression of being an 'admiral' does not occur. The meaning of the word 'admiral' in Danish and Norwegian would in a general sense be 'a naval officer'. In the setting of the court, it could additionally have referred to Cunningham himself, as he was known to have been a naval captain. This similarity is a strong argument that the image of a woman being the admiral for other witches is taken from Scotland and brought to Finnmark orally – presumably by the district governor himself. The expression could then have been spread among the common people as a result of interrogation at the court.

The other expression found in Scottish as well as in Finnmark witchcraft cases is the word 'Ball-Ley'. In the case of Barbara Bowndie (Orkney, 1644), she was repeatedly asked what she knew about Marjorie Paplay, who had been denounced for witchcraft earlier: 'Quarto, being posed in particular, concerning the Devill his apparitions in diverse shapes *upon the Ball-Ley*, and his having carnall copulation with Marjorie Paplay at that tyme, as a man hes adoe with a woman'.[81] (*my italics*) A 'ley' was a tract of grassland, meadow or pasture; it is also found as a second element in Scottish place-names.[82] With the addition of the element 'ball', today we would call this a playing field or a sports field, somewhere where ball games are played. Locations where games were held may be traced in place-names in Orkney back to the fourteenth century, like 'Leik-kvi' or 'Leikakvi'.[83] The word 'Ball-greene' or 'Balgrene' is used about a green on which ball games are played. The words 'Ba'Fields' and 'Ba'greens' are used with the same meaning at the time.[84] The word 'Ball-grene' is mentioned in Scottish court records in 1611.[85]

Several words similar to 'Ball-Ley' are used in Scottish witchcraft documents in the same context as 'Ball-Ley', namely a playing field used as a meeting place for witches and the Devil. In the case of Margaret Duchill, tried before Stirling Court 1659, the word 'croft' is used.[86] Margaret Duchill confessed that Elisabeth Blak came to her and took her to the 'crofts of Alloway', where the Devil came to them.[87] A 'croft' is a piece of enclosed land, or small field, used for tillage or pasture. A witches' meeting at the 'cuning yaird' (rabbit warren) is also mentioned in connection with Duchill.[88]

In Norwegian court records the parallel term is 'Balduolden'. The word is mentioned in the confession of Kirsten Sørensdatter, given on 26 April 1621 at Vardøhus: 'She confessed she went carousing with the others, just as they have confessed about her, except that she was not here *on Balduolden* last Christmas Eve.'[89] (*my italics*) The word next occurs during the interrogation of Mette Thorgiersdatter: 'Bastian Hess asked her whether she, too, was *on Balduolden* in Vardøen last winter, as Kirsten said in her denunciation.'[90] (*my italics*) The word reappears three years later, during the trial of Gundell Olsdatter, which started on 22 April 1624 at Vardøhus:

> On April 25, after she had been sentenced and the sentence had been explained, she confessed, however, without torture, that Oluff Mogensen's wife Ingeborgh from Haffningbergh was with them *on Balduolden* on Christmas night, together with the others, holding a piece of cloth in her hand, with a knot on it. She recognised nobody else, for the others were in the shapes of cats and dogs whereas she ran ahead of them and was shaped as a human, above her belt, but she was not thus shaped below. Now she was tortured and she confessed, in Ingeborgh's presence, that she [*Ingeborgh*] had a tall companion with her, someone in the likeness of a man, but she did not know him.[91]
>
> (*my italics*)

This last example also shows that the interrogator's main intention was to make the accused person confess not only participation at a witches' meeting, but also the Devil's presence there. It seems that the notion of witches' meetings on 'Balduolden' in Vardø was a consistent one, lasting for several years. However, the word does not occur in witchcraft trial records after 1624.

The word 'Balduolden' is a descriptive noun, the first part denoting a ball, the latter part denoting a piece of grassland or turf. Kirsten Sørensdatter uses the word about a place in Vardø where witches' meetings were held, probably a playing field. There is no place today called 'Balduolden' or 'Ballvollen' in Vardø. A somewhat shorter, but similar word, which also is a descriptive noun, is used in the trial of Lisebet Nilsdatter. In her confession she mentions 'Wolden' in the village Omgang, a word identical with the second element in 'Balduolden'.

When we find exactly the same image of witches' meeting at a 'Ball-Ley' in the Scottish material and 'Balduolden' in the Finnmark material, thus forming a Scottish connection, this is remarkable. When these words with identical meaning and used in the same semantic context are documented on both sides of the North Sea, this cannot be accidental. A link is shown on linguistic grounds.

VII

John Cunningham's influence on the Finnmark witchcraft trials may thus be traced in two ways. In general terms, his arrival at Vardøhus Castle coincided with, and may well have prompted, a shift in the contents and ideas of the trials. In special terms, he is a necessary link with regard to specific words and expressions found in the accused persons' confessions both in Scotland and in Finnmark.

In my view the particular expressions 'admiral' and 'Ball-Ley', used in similar contexts in witchcraft cases in Scotland and Norway, indicate a connection between these two areas as far as the contents of witchcraft trials are concerned. Both expressions are used to express demonological ideas. 'Admiral' refers to the ranking system among the witches. It also denotes the collective aspect of demonological witchcraft, in the sense that an accused person's confession gives information about many persons participating in a witches' meeting, thus making it possible for the witch-hunters to prosecute a group. 'Ball-Ley' denotes a place for a witches' meeting, and, in the examples above, the Devil was present at the meetings. When these expressions are known in Scottish witchcraft documents and found in Finnmark in court records after John Cunningham arrived there, there is reason to believe that the expressions are orally transmitted from one area to the other. Both linguistic images are distinct and easy to remember. In local societies, all news and traditions had to be transmitted orally. There had to be a person to transmit new ideas, including ideas related to witchcraft. John Cunningham's arrival in Finnmark was an opportunity for demonological notions from Scotland to acquire a foothold in Europe's northernmost land.

Notes

1. Liv Helene Willumsen, 'Seventeenth-Century Witchcraft Trials in Scotland and Northern Norway' (University of Edinburgh PhD thesis, 2008), 8–11.

2. In Danish his title was 'Skibshöffuidzmannd', meaning the leader of a crew; captain or mate. NAD, Danske Kancelli 232, Sjællandske Registre 1572–1660, Arkivnr. B 54D, protokoll 1596–1604, fos. 405v.–406r.
3. Otto Gr. Lundh and Johan Ernst Sars (eds.), *Norske Rigs-Registranter* (Christiania, 1861–1891), v, 12–14.
4. Buried 9 December 1651 Eggeslevmagle church: NAD, Church records Eggeslevmagle parish 1651.
5. *RMS*, vi, 430. This corresponds with information in Rune Hagen, 'At the edge of civilisation: John Cunningham, lensmann of Finnmark, 1619–51', in Andrew Mackillop and Steve Murdoch (eds.), *Military Governors and Imperial Frontiers, c.1600–1800* (Leiden, 2003). However, in *The Oxford Dictionary of National Biography*, Hagen has Alexander Cunningham as John Cunningham's father and Christiane Wood as his mother. This cannot be correct, as this couple had lived apart for two years in 1561 and were divorced in 1563: *St Andrews Kirk Session Register, 1559–1600*, 2 vols., ed. D. Hay Fleming (SHS, 1889–1890), i, 133–5; St Andrews University Library, Dept. of Special Collections, CH2/316/1/1; NRS, Register of Deeds, RD1/6, fo. 133. Research at NRS by Diane Baptie. See Liv Helene Willumsen and Diane Baptie, 'John Cunningham – karriere og bakgrunn', *Norsk slektshistorisk tidsskrift*, 1 (2013), 159–76, at p. 176.
6. Ole Kjølseth, '"Kong Hans" og hans dramatiske løpebane', *Slekt og data*, 4 (1996), 6–9, at p. 6; Willumsen and Baptie, 'Cunningham'; Liv Helene Willumsen and Diane Baptie, 'From Fife to Finnmark – John Cunningham's way to the North', *The Genealogist* (2013, forthcoming).
7. NRS, Register of Deeds, RD1/6, fo. 133; RD1/7, fo. 187; RD1/16, fo. 205.
8. The initials are on either side, with the motto 'Salus per Christum' above: *The Kirk of Crail* (folder published by Crail parish), p. 10. A shake-fork is a figure in the shape of a letter Y, three arms with the ends cut off in a straight line (couped). It is almost entirely confined to Scottish families, and chiefly to those of Cunningham, who bear it in a variety of ways: James Parker, *A Glossary of Terms used in Heraldry* (Oxford, 1894), s.v. Shake-fork.
9. Hans A. K. T. Cappelen, 'Det norske Cunningham-våpnet – en heraldisk identifisering –', *Heraldisk tidsskrift*, no. 26 (1972), 249–61, at pp. 249–50.
10. St Andrews University Library, Dept. of Special Collections, Acta Rectorum 1590–1620, UY305/3.
11. *CSP Scot.*, xiii, II, 659, 664.
12. C. C. A. Gosch (ed.), *The Danish Arctic Expeditions, 1605 to 1620* (Hakluyt Society, 1897), i, pp. xxviii–xxix.
13. C. Pingel, 'Om de vigtigste reiser, som i nyere tider ere foretagne fra Danmark og Norge, for igjen at opsöge det tabte Grönland og at undersöge det gjenfundne' in *Grønlandsk historiske mindesmærker* III (Copenhagen, 1845), 625–794, at p. 671.
14. *Dansk Biografisk Lexikon*, iv (Copenhagen, 1890).
15. *Dansk Biografisk Leksikon*, iii (3rd edn., Copenhagen, 1979).
16. Claus C. Lyschander, *Den Grønlandske Chronica* (2nd edn., Copenhagen, 1726; orig. publ. 1607), 96. Frisland was an imaginary island, a Venetian fabrication in the North Atlantic. An account of an alleged fourteenth-century voyage, with a map, was published by Nicolo Zeno the Younger in 1558. In 1569, Gerhard Mercator copied the Zeno map into his world map and

in 1595 included Frisland in a separate inset on his map of the North Pole. Thus Frisland came to be known as 'fact' and was copied by other cartographers.

17. NAD, Tyske Kancelli, Udenrigske Afdeling 1223–1770, Topografisk henlagte sager, England Breweksling mellom Kongehusene 1602–1625, 63:2, England AI 85. Letters from King James VI and I to Christian IV dated 18 February 1605.

18. After John Cunningham came to Scandinavia, he is mentioned as Hans Køning, Hans Kønning, Hans Kønigh and Hans Cunninghiemb in documents; even Hans Keymand is used, according to Lyschander, *Grønlandske*, 120. *Jon Olafsons oplevelser som bøsseskytte under Christian IV, nedskrevne af ham selv*, in the series Julius Clausen and P. Fr. Rist (eds.), *Memoirer og Breve* (Copenhagen 1905), 130–1. The surname Køning relates to the German term for king, *König*.

19. H. D. Lind, *Kong Kristian den fjerde og hans mænd paa Bremerholm* (2nd edn., Copenhagen, 1974), 166. The name of Cunningham's first wife is not known.

20. NAD, Tyske Kancelli, Udenrigske Afdeling 1223–1770, Topografisk henlagte sager, England Breweksling mellom Kongehusene 1602–1625, 63:2, England AI 85. Letters from King James VI and I to Christian IV dated 4 June 1603 and 4 July 1603. Translated from Latin into English by Frank Bigwood.

21. R. M. Meldrum (ed.), *Letters from James I to Christian IV, 1603–1625* (Washington, 1977), 40–1.

22. Pingel, 'Om de vigtigste', 671–2.

23. Samuel Purchas (ed.), 'James Hall his voyage forth of Denmarke for the discovery of Greeneland, in the yeare 1605', in *Purchas his Pilgrimes* (London, 1625), 318–53.

24. Purchas, 'James Hall his Voyage', 324.

25. Ibid., 326.

26. *Jon Olafsons*, 131.

27. Purchas, 'James Hall his Voyage', 335.

28. Pingel, 'Om de vigtigste', 686–7.

29. *Dansk Biografisk Leksikon*, iii (1979).

30. *Grønlandsk historiske*, iii, 690.

31. Steve Murdoch, 'Scotsmen on the Danish-Norwegian frontiers, *c.*1580–1680', in Mackillop and Murdoch (eds.), *Military Governors and Imperial Frontiers*, 6.

32. *Jon Olafsons*, 130–1.

33. 'Mogens Ulfelds Tog udi Østersøen med Kongelig Majestets Skibs-Flode 1611', *Danske Magazin*, 1. Række, i, 114–18, at p. 115.

34. E. F. Bricka, 'Gabriel Kruses Beretning om den danske Flaades Virksomhed i Efteraaret 1612', *Danske Magazin*, 4. Række, v, 280–8, at p. 286.

35. NAD, Danske Kancelli 232, Sjællandske Registre 1605–1612, B54E, fos. 236r., 263v., 296v., 297r., 425r.; ibid., Sjællandske Registre 1613–1619, B54F, fos. 23r.–v., 177v., 354v.–355v.

36. Einar Niemi, 'Christian 4s Finnmarksreise i 1599', *Årbok for Foreningen til norske fortidsminnesmerkers bevaring* (Oslo, 1988), 34.

37. Liv Helene Willumsen, *Trollkvinne i nord* (Tromsø, 1994), 51–2; Olaus Magnus, *Historia om de nordiska folken* (Uppsala, 1909); Peder Claussøn

Friis, *Norriges Beskriffuelse* (Copenhagen, 1632); Johan Schefferus, *Lapponia* (Frankfurt am Main, 1673).

38. National Archives of Norway, District Accounts for Vardøhus, 1601–1602, bundle 1.
39. Willumsen, *Trollkvinne*, 57.
40. *Jon Olafsons*, 131–2.
41. Lundh and Sars, *Norske Rigs-Registranter*, vi, 463.
42. Ibid., v, 190.
43. Ibid., vi, 167–8.
44. Hans Eivind Næss, *Trolldomsprosessene i Norge på 1500–1600-tallet* (Oslo, 1982), 32.
45. Alf Kiil, *Når bøndene seilte* (Oslo, 1993).
46. Einar Niemi, *Vadsøs historie*, i (Vadsø, 1983), 69–217; Randi Balsvik, *Vardø. Grensepost og fiskevær 1850–1950* (Vardø, 1989), 20–33.
47. Lundh and Sars, *Norske Rigs-Registranter*, vi, 60.
48. Willumsen, 'Seventeenth-Century Witchcraft Trials', 101–4.
49. Ibid., 94.
50. Ibid., 36.
51. Brian P. Levack, *The Witch-Hunt in Early Modern Europe* (3rd edn., Harlow, 2006), 142.
52. Kirsten Hastrup, 'Iceland: sorcerers and paganism', in Bengt Ankarloo and Gustav Henningsen (eds.), *Early Modern European Witchcraft: Centres and Peripheries* (Oxford, 1993), 383–401, at p. 386.
53. Willumsen, 'Seventeenth-Century Witchcraft Trials', 108.
54. Næss, *Trolldomsprosessene i Norge*, 32.
55. Normand and Roberts (eds.), *Witchcraft*, 22.
56. For more on North Berwick, see Victoria Carr, 'The countess of Angus's escape from the North Berwick witch-hunt', Chapter 2 in this volume.
57. Normand and Roberts (eds.), *Witchcraft*, 135–274.
58. Stuart Macdonald, 'In search of the Devil in Fife witchcraft cases, 1560–1705', in Julian Goodare (ed.), *The Scottish Witch-Hunt in Context* (Manchester, 2002), 33–50.
59. Julian Goodare, 'The Scottish witchcraft panic of 1597', in Goodare (ed.), *The Scottish Witch-Hunt in Context*, 51–72.
60. Stuart Macdonald, *The Witches of Fife: Witch-Hunting in a Scottish Shire, 1560–1710* (East Linton, 2002), 38. For some additional cases, see Goodare, 'The Scottish witchcraft panic of 1597', 57–8.
61. Macdonald, *Witches of Fife*, 59, 61.
62. Goodare, 'The Scottish witchcraft panic of 1597', 61, 55.
63. Normand and Roberts (eds.), *Witchcraft*, 327–8.
64. RAT, FM no. 6, fos. 10v.–12v.
65. Hans H. Lilienskiold, 'Troldom oc anden ugudelighed', National Library of Denmark, Thott's collection, 950, 2°, fo. 40r.
66. Cf. Julian Goodare, 'The Finnmark witches in European context', in Reidun Laura Andreassen and Liv Helene Willumsen (eds.), *Steilneset Memorial: Art, Architecture, History* (Stamsund, 2013, forthcoming).
67. RAT, FM no. 6, fo. 12r.–v. Translation of Norwegian sources into English is made by Katjana Edwardsen.
68. RAT, FM no. 6, fo. 12v.

69. RAT, FM, Court Records 1620–7, fo. 27r.
70. Ibid.
71. Ibid.
72. Normand and Roberts (eds.), *Witchcraft*, 145.
73. 'Balduolden', a descriptive noun composed of two elements, 'ball' and 'volden' (meadow, grassland); probably a field outside Vardø where people gathered, possibly for games.
74. RAT, FM, Court Records 1620–7, fos. 27v., 28r.
75. Ibid., fos. 28v., 29r.
76. Goodare, 'The Scottish witchcraft panic of 1597', 58; Julian Goodare, 'Flying witches in Scotland', Chapter 9 in this volume.
77. NRS, JC2/2, fo. 224r. Transcription by Diane Baptie. For modernised text with some different readings, see Normand and Roberts (eds.), *Witchcraft*, 267–8.
78. Julian Goodare, *The Government of Scotland, 1560–1625* (Oxford, 2004), 165–8.
79. *Oxford English Dictionary*.
80. Lars Mannfred Svennungsson, *Rannsakingarna om Trolldomen i Bohuslän, 1669–1672* (Uddevalla, 1970), 56.
81. Orkney Library and Archive, Kirkwall, Orkney Presbytery Records, CH2/1082/1, p. 255.
82. *Dictionary of the Older Scottish Tongue*, s.v. ley (4, 5).
83. The word is found in Orkney in 1329: *Records of the Earldom of Orkney, 1299–1614*, ed. J. Storer Clouston (SHS, 1914), 12.
84. John D. M. Robertson, *The Kirkwall Ba': Between the Water and the Wall* (2nd edn., Edinburgh, 2005), 230.
85. Pitcairn (ed.), *Trials*, iii, I, 214, 'the Reidhous was vpone the Ball-grene, playing with him'.
86. BL, Egerton MS 2879. I would like to thank Julian Goodare for letting me read his transcription of this document.
87. Ibid.
88. Ibid.
89. RAT, FM, Court Records 1620–7, fos. 27v., 28r.
90. Ibid., fo. 41r.
91. Ibid., fo. 94r.

4
The Witch, the Household and the Community: Isobel Young in East Barns, 1580–1629

Lauren Martin

Isobel Young had land, wealth and power. Most of her life looks successful by early modern standards. In her prime from 1590 to 1622, Young wielded influence over many people in her community. She was a competent, perhaps skilled, household manager. Her husband, George Smith, was the proprietor (holding a feu, a heritable lease) of a productive piece of land in East Barns in the parish of Dunbar, a fertile area of Scotland. She had four sons who brought wives into the household; she may also have had daughters. As well as controlling the labour of at least twelve servants, she also held sway over tenants and households to whom she lent money and leased land. In 1622, her eldest son John combined Smith's holding with his own – doubling the family's holding at a time when other comparable East Barns families either stayed the same or declined.

Yet, in 1629 Isobel Young was executed for witchcraft. Forty-five of her neighbours and relatives, including her husband, testified against her, telling a story that unfolded over four decades. Witnesses alleged that Young engaged in a wide range of witch-like activities, including causing magical harm following quarrels, shape-shifting into animals and carrying out healing rituals for humans and cattle. Strange portents accompanied her words and actions. She was widely regarded as ill-tempered, power-hungry and vengeful.

Quarrelsome and difficult women were not uncommon in early modern Scotland and across Europe.[1] Young's case, while outstanding in the amount and quality of its documentation, resonates with the primary themes in Scottish witchcraft. Like most witchcraft cases in Scotland, the case against Young had two main components, 'malefice' (magical harm) and her relationship with the Devil. The second of these was the centrepiece of her trial. But twenty out of the twenty-four formal accusations against her stemmed from long-term neighbourhood quarrels. Young was accused of using threatening language or curses, punctuated by unusual and magical occurrences, to enact magical harm. We know, in general, that many witches were quarrelsome and unpopular with their neighbours. What more can be learned about this subject, then, by examining Young's case? How and why did the community of East Barns, including many members of her own household, decide that Isobel Young was a witch?

I

Young's case illustrates some of the broader cultural formations, practices and power struggles at work in witchcraft belief, practice and accusation. Specifically, I believe that Young's case reveals links between witchcraft accusation and the domestic formations that shaped everyday forms of social organisation and practice of early modern communities.

The wide range of trial documents from 1628 and 1629, combined with witness statements from as early as 1613, contain a remarkable level of detail about Young's daily life over forty years. Of course, most witchcraft studies use trial documents. What the present study has been able to do is to supplement these with a variety of other sources. Documents on landholding and financial transactions survive for Dunbar parish, including testaments, conveyancing documents (charters and instruments of sasine), maps and baron court records. It is possible to reconstruct formal landholding and financial relationships between many of the key community players in Young's trial. Events around land, heritability, work and social structure as described in witchcraft documents are remarkably consistent with these other documents.

The valuable combination of surviving documents pertaining to Isobel Young and East Barns provides rare flashes of ethnographic sensibility into the everyday life of an accused witch – allowing for a deeper, more nuanced understanding of the connections between the structures of everyday practices and witchcraft belief. These flashes reveal the ways that witchcraft was experienced in and through Young's daily interactions with the people in her life, and how her community and those closest to her slowly turned against her.

The timeline of Young's life and slowly unfolding witchcraft reputation reveals distinct household patterns to how the specific content of the witchcraft accusations alleged against Young match up with her physical and verbal work as the wife of a head of household in East Barns. Reconstruction of the life of a witch suggests that witchcraft was, in part, a language and practice through which people articulated and influenced their daily domestic arrangements, particularly women's roles in managing competition and co-operation within and between households in the context of a tenant farming community.

II

I want to start with a word (or two) about my use of anthropological theory in this analysis. Anthropological theory has provided a fertile ground for the historiography of witchcraft and historical methodologies in general to explore matters of culture and belief in the past.[2] Alan Macfarlane used functionalist anthropology developed in the study of small-scale societies in the non-western world to help him understand how witchcraft beliefs might function within small villages in England.[3] Whether we agree or disagree with conclusions drawn from this cross-disciplinary pollination, the use of anthropology in historical inquiry has fuelled debate and opened new avenues of exploration.

Likewise, many anthropologists have sought inspiration from an understanding of historical trajectories, seeing culture as part of an arc through time rather than as a static, fully formed and closed system in the present. Historicity allows us to break apart the seemingly coherent culture-present which masks the processes over time through which meaning is created, often through struggle, contestation and loss.[4] Here I am not seeking a cross-cultural definition of witches or witchcraft. Rather, the goal is to apply a particular strand of cultural theory, developed in anthropology, to the study of witchcraft.

I think it is worth stepping out of early modern Scotland and witchcraft, for a moment, to highlight a few components of the theoretical lens used in this study. My approach to witchcraft documents is derived from two anthropological tenets: a focus on small groups as the object of study and recent understandings of 'culture' as a struggle over meaning rather than a finished product. Both of these insights are linked to the historical formation of the discipline of anthropology as rooted within European colonialism and subsequent disciplinary critiques, as well as a deliberate use of theory related to political economy and culture.

A focus on small groups stems from the discipline's birth in its study of so-called 'primitive' or small-scale societies. This early anthropology suggested that the boundaries of 'culture' – seen as a static system of symbols, meanings, rituals, beliefs and life-ways – adhered to the boundaries of whatever group, or 'people', was being studied.[5] Most modern anthropologists, however, would reject an easy linkage between a group of people and 'their' culture, as a product of past colonial encounters that saw so-called primitive people as having simple cultures in contrast to the perceived complexity of European nation-states.[6]

The study of small groups of people, referred to in modern parlance as 'communities' or 'the local', remains one of the hallmarks of anthropology. But now, communities are studied with respect to the larger structures in which the local context forms and is shaped. As the anthropologically-minded historian David Sabean has written: 'The local is interesting precisely because it offers a *locus* for observing relations.'[7] The places that people live, in this view, present vantage points from which to view the concrete workings of larger processes.[8] However, a balance needs to be struck: 'too one-sided a concentration on the larger structures and their lived reality tends to disappear; too exclusive a focus on particular lives and we lose the connections with the larger realities in which those lives are embedded'.[9]

Finally, my approach is attentive to connections between language, power and the construction of meaning through and within the practices of daily life. Culture and language are seen as a practical activity in which meaning is shifting and contingent depending on contexts, rather than a static system of signs and referents with fixed meanings.[10] The anthropologist William Roseberry suggests that 'interpretation cannot be separated from what people say, what they do, what is done to them, because culture cannot be so separated'.[11] This anthropological perspective sees power, domination, hierarchy and social systems of inequality as part of the context that shapes meaning.[12]

I am not the first anthropologist or historian to notice the connections between witchcraft, neighbours and community contexts; nor am I the first to look at witchcraft related to gender and ideology.[13] Anthropology is a varied discipline that offers many different theories and approaches. Here I seek to offer a fresh approach, zeroing in on several key relations that are highlighted through a particular anthropological reading of the documents. It is my hope that through a rich understanding of Isobel Young and her community of East Barns we can see something new in neighbourhood disputes and quarrelsome witches. Young's case highlights how the meanings of witchcraft, and its connections to how early modern people lived their lives within their communities and households, both challenged and reaffirmed the structures of everyday work and social life.

III

We begin with a sketch of Young as a witch. This is, after all, first and foremost what the documents in her case sought to present. A large dossier of documents, created over the course of fifteen years, survives in Young's case, including pre-trial witness statements, interrogatories from interrogations, depositions from Young's defence, a dittay (indictment), trial transcripts, jury deliberation notes and independent verification of her execution in Edinburgh.[14]

Most of the surviving witchcraft documents date the beginnings of Young's reputation for witchcraft to the 1590s, with accusations of magical harm ('malefice') stemming from her long-term quarrels. These quarrels constituted twenty out of the twenty-four accusations in Young's dittay. Neighbours who testified against Young reported that magical harm occurred after a quarrel with Young where she uttered curses or other threatening language and removed her 'couch' (kerchief), sometimes while walking 'withershins' (counter-clockwise).[15] The process of diagnosing Young's harmful magic as the cause of illnesses and other harms in East Barns was helped by several magical healers when they suggested to sick people that Young was the cause of their illnesses.[16] According to witchcraft trial documents, around 1600, Young won a slander case at an unnamed local kirk session against George Sandie, a miller, for publicly calling her a witch. The miller was forced to do public penance. Some time after that, probably before 1613, Young and her sons had a run-in with the kirk session. They were forced to do public penance for engaging in a ritual healing of Young's cattle.

Testimony was taken by the kirk session of Duns from a folk healer named Alexander Fortune in 1619 regarding a small wound that Young had under her left breast. Because he was unable to heal the wound, he surmised that it was a Devil's mark; this was also apparently the topic of rumours in and around the parish of Dunbar.[17] The literature on early modern witchcraft suggests a gulf between so-called popular and elite culture, with the Devil and demonic pacts more prominent in elite beliefs. Documents in Scotland are not clear on how prevalent demonic beliefs were in community and neighbour understanding of witchcraft. This rare document suggests that Young's community was thinking about the Devil, specifically the demonic pact, in relationship to Young's status as a witch. Yet they continued daily interactions with her for another ten years.

On 22 and 24 April 1624 Margaret Melrose and Janet Acheson, two confessed witches from a neighbouring settlement in Dunbar, gave depositions against Young to the presbytery of Dunbar. The hearings were staffed by ministers and a bailie and clerk from the burgh of Dunbar – local men, embedded in the local context.[18] Melrose and Acheson publicly confronted Young, testifying that she had been present at a Devil's meeting with them on the Dunehill of Spot. Most of the witnesses later cited at Young's trial originally provided depositions at these investigations by the presbytery. While most depositions detailed magical harm, many also talked about Young's associations with Melrose and Acheson, alleging that they transformed into animals for meetings.[19]

The central authorities became involved in December 1628 with an order from the privy council ordering her second oldest son, James Smith, to bring Young to Edinburgh to be examined by them. The documents do not make clear why the privy council became interested in Young, but it may have been related to the swell of witchcraft trials in the Lothians between 1628 and 1631. On 26 January 1629, Young was interrogated by Adam Bellenden, bishop of Dunblane, and Alexander Colville of Blair, justice depute.[20] Both men were involved in many other witchcraft cases.[21] Two days later a warrant was issued for Young's arrest, an assize was selected and a trial was set to take place in the justiciary court in Edinburgh.[22] Presumably the council chose to send Young's case to the central justiciary court, rather than issuing a commission for a local trial, because it had already become interested in her case.

Young went to trial in Edinburgh represented by her sons and two well-known Edinburgh lawyers. They constructed an elaborate and reasoned defence against all of the allegations in the dittay. Many of the people who had provided testimony in 1624 journeyed to Edinburgh to testify at her trial, including her husband. The assize was selected from the same community and class as Young. They deliberated on each indictment, finding her guilty of some and not guilty of others. But, in the end, the assize found that Isobel Young had renounced her baptism, entered into the service of Satan, received a Devil's mark, cast 'uncouth and fearful sicknesses on men, women and beasts', and removed her kerchief while she wielded harmful words. Based on this verdict, she was executed.

IV

The witchcraft accusations and case against Isobel Young unfolded and were embedded in the context of her everyday life, household and community. Malefice, quarrels, curses and even magical happenings played out while Young worked, struggled and interacted with other households and her community. Neighbours who testified against Young marked their allegations with reference to calendar customs, seasonal work patterns (such as the Dunbar herring drove, harvest and market days) and household life cycles. When all the witchcraft documents are aggregated, reviewed for evidence of daily life and supplemented by other documents, the arc over time of Young's life and household emerges.

Young's life prior to marrying George Smith and setting up a household in East Barns is murky in the surviving documents. But it is possible to sketch her early years and to speculate about her place of birth, family of origin and household. Following early modern Scottish custom, Isobel retained her own surname. Her father's surname would have been Young. The first step in finding Young's possible roots is to locate men with the surname of Young who were tenant farmers with heritable or similar types of lease in or near the parish of Dunbar, where Young spent the vast majority of her adult life. Two such men were found living in Belhaven, both of whom also occupied land in West Barns: James Young (1582) and William Young (1596).[23] It is possible that James Young was Isobel's father and William Young her brother. Isobel Young's second son was named James, and it was customary to name the second son after the maternal grandfather. Both men were of similar social standing to George Smith, Isobel Young's husband, and Belhaven and West Barns were very near to East Barns in the parish of Dunbar. No other men with the surname Young were found in or around Dunbar in surviving landholding documents. According to witchcraft documents, Isobel Young also had at least one younger brother named Thomas who worked for the Young and Smith household as a shepherd and odd jobber.

Young was probably born in the 1560s.[24] She married George Smith and moved to East Barns, most likely around 1582 when Smith first appears as a 'portioner' there.[25] East Barns was an old estate that had been divided into sixteen portions that were held by heritable feu-ferme tenure.[26] In 1581, the sixteen portions of East Barns were divided into eleven holdings – five men held two portions and six held only one portion. Landholding was remarkably stable from then until 1622, with a father generally passing their portion to their eldest son.[27]

While Smith held only one portion of East Barns, Young and her family began the 1590s with promise. The portioners were at the top of the local hierarchy. Through George Smith, the family and household held a heritable title to land, and they had the labour-power of children and servants. With luck and proper management, land was a source of wealth and security. At least one portion of East Barns passed from George Smith through eldest sons for at least four generations.

Young's witchcraft reputation started in the 1590s and 1600s, when Young's household was at its peak strength in labour-power. All of Young's four sons were of working age, possibly married and still living at home. Smith rented two cottars' houses from a neighbour; these were occupied by married couples and their children who worked for the household. The household also had at least eight unmarried workers: three female servants and three male servants as well as Smith's nephew and Young's brother.

Descriptions of their farm and household in witchcraft documents tell us something about how they lived. Neighbours and witnesses described a house with a locked front door. The household buildings also included at least one barn filled with grain, a byre for animals that included dairy cows, horses, oxen, swine and sheep. The household also had some quantity of cloth, milk products and access to a plough and ploughshare.

In addition to their portion of East Barns, Smith and Young also informally occupied land through leases. Property and informal land use often show up in the documents surrounding death, wills and testaments, but none survive for Smith or Young. However, William Meslet, another portioner of East Barns, died on 9 September 1579 leaving a testament.[28] Of roughly similar social and economic standing to Smith and Young, his inventory suggests the types of moveable goods that Young's household might have had. Meslet's testament listed crops in the barn and the field (wheat, rye, peas, oats and bere), six oxen, one heifer and cow with calf (probably for milking), three horses, eleven ewes, nine hoggs (yearling sheep) and one little hogg, and five varieties of woollen and linen cloth. He also owed servants wages, feu-duty to the king and a tithe to the parson of Pinkerton. Testaments from other households in East Barns from the 1600s show that webs of money-lending, credit and mortgaging of land bound portioner households of East Barns and across the parish of Dunbar to each other in complicated financial arrangements. For example, the testament of Margaret Home in Pinkerton showed that she and her husband owed Young's husband £100 at her death in 1601.[29]

In 1613, Young's eldest son John acquired one portion of East Barns from another portioner. John's acquisition of land, prior to inheriting his father's portion, moved the two Smith households up in combined status by occupying two portions of land. When one family rises, another falls. Mobility in landholding, while rare among the portioners of East Barns during this period, tended to be downward. Witnesses testified that Young told those present to call her 'Lady Home', because she believed that her son would soon acquire some land held by the household of Thomas Home. The tone and intent of Young's comment are hard to interpret. Was she being humorous, self-deprecating or threatening? Since it was recounted in trial documents, it seems that either at the time or in hindsight her comment was viewed as threatening. This was a topic of community discussion and gossip.[30] Rumour was further fuelled by Young's use of curses, kerchief removal and walking withershins.

So far, the documents describe Young as a female head of household, managing, overseeing and conducting a range of productive activities. Documents specifically describe her role in dairying, marketing of household goods and products, cloth production and sale, money-lending, animal husbandry, oversight of sub-leased land, and more. These activities are described in witchcraft documents as the subjects or backdrops of quarrels and altercations that led to magical harm. Young's work also involved what I refer to as 'verbal work'. This included bartering, making deals, harassing people for repayment of loans, beating a competitor to a lease or purchase, and discrediting an unskilled craftsman for his bad products.[31] Other scholarly work on early modern households suggests that she would also have overseen washing, cooking, gathering fuel and child-rearing among other things. Perhaps she helped with planting and harvesting of crops as well.[32]

Several witnesses described Young's household as having odd magical characteristics. Two of Young's servants said that her oxen could speak; one heard one of her oxen cry, 'oh God, oh God, o God'; another said that Young's ox had asked him what ailed him.[33] Several people witnessed Young controlling the weather, conducting magical healing and shape-shifting. And others saw her creeping around in the dark on other people's land and conducting strange rituals.

In fact, Young's household, while economically successful, was riven with internal conflict. Young's husband, George Smith, testified against her in 1624 before the presbytery and again at her trial in 1629, although he must have known that she faced execution. Smith accused Young of attempting to kill him with magic after quarrelling about an unsavoury house guest. Smith claimed to have seen Christian Grintoun, a known witch and associate of Young's, leave his house in the shape of a cat. After a spousal quarrel Young supposedly cursed her husband, saying, 'gudeman, I rew I saw that sight for it will be worse for you hereafter'.[34] Smith then collapsed while ploughing his fields the next day, in front of seven witnesses including their neighbour William Meslet. Young consulted Grintoun on healing her husband and ended up inadvertently transferring the illness to William Smith (George's nephew), who then died. Young claimed that she was a good wife and that Smith had tried to stab her with a sword.[35] Young was found guilty on this charge.

The documents present rich and dense portrayals of economic strife, long-term disputes, and other incidents between Young and other households in the East Barns community. All but four of the seventeen portioners in East Barns testified against Young in 1624 or at her trial in 1629. Three birlawmen of Broxmouth (William Nisbet, Patrick Bryson younger and William Smith), who were responsible for regulation of farming and communal property, also testified against Young.[36] So did many other prominent local people and their children, relatives and servants.

The long-term disputes in which Young engaged with her neighbours are an important link between her daily life and her developing witchcraft reputation – particularly when her household was thriving. These disputes, believed to be the root of harmful magic, also reveal Young in action in her community. Young did not deny that the disputes occurred or the bare facts as described by neighbours. On the other hand, nor did she confess to witchcraft. Rather, Young's defence reinterpreted the quarrels as regular and everyday disputes between neighbours. A few examples are explored below.

Six accusations against Young sprang from a long-term quarrel with three generations of members of the household of Patrick Bryson who in 1581/1582 occupied two portions of East Barns. The Brysons were portioners of higher social standing than Young and Smith within the community of East Barns. By 1600, Patrick was replaced by his eldest son John in landholding documents; Patrick Bryson either died or transferred his land, making John de facto head of that household.[37] Young's eldest son married one of John Bryson's daughters, so perhaps those households were close in life-cycle age.

Disputes began, according to Patrick, around 1595 after he cut Young's swine tether. Young supposedly threw the cut tether into the doorway of Bryson's house while uttering threatening words. Thresholds and doorways held great symbolic import. Bryson claimed that he then lost the power of his right side. He consulted a healer named 'Dame Bet' before determining that his illness was caused by Young. Over the next two decades, roughly nine people connected with the Bryson household claimed to have been injured or killed by Young. Members of the Bryson household engaged in a pattern of quarrels over work and money followed by curses from Young, several allegedly resulting from Young's revenge for calling her a witch in public. Meanwhile, however, Young's eldest son married Patrick Bryson's granddaughter. John Smith and Margaret Bryson lived in Young's household until 1613 when John became a portioner and formed his own household. John Smith stood by his mother, acting as part of her defence team; there is no indication of how Margaret Bryson felt. Young was found guilty of many of these instances of magical harm.

A cluster of quarrels with Thomas Home and his household led to four accusations.[38] After 1600, Home owned the largest share of East Barns. This was bound to cause conflict. Smith and Young apparently wanted to buy a piece of land in East Barns that had become available for the sum of 2,000 merks. Home purchased that land 'over their heads'.[39] The land dispute took a more sinister turn after Young and unknown others were seen walking around Home's dovecote at midnight just before all the doves flew out in a great rush.[40] A dovecote was a symbol of status, but also a potential source of friction between neighbours, because the birds ate grain in the surrounding fields.

After this dispute, Thomas Home and his household claimed that they suffered major losses, including twenty-seven horses, oxen and cows, pains throughout his entire body, and Home's eventual death in Prestonpans, a town northwest of Dunbar parish and closer to Edinburgh. Eventually the Homes lost two of their three portions of East Barns, and John Smith acquired one of those portions.[41] This was seen as the culmination of Young's attempt to acquire their land. Throughout these conflicts, Young and Smith continued to rent some land and borrow animals from Home, and they lent *him* money.[42] The assize found it believable that Young would use magical means to get the Homes' land for her son. She was found guilty of this accusation.

In her quarrels with Bryson and Home, Young was seen to attack wealthier households. With the Homes, whether she used magic or not, she apparently won. But Young also quarrelled with social equals. Smith and Young entered a bidding contest with their neighbours and social equals, William Meslet and Margaret Ogill. Both sought to purchase a wadset, the temporary use of land in return for a loan, from George Home of Meikle Pinkerton.[43] Young's household was short of ready cash, and Meslet and Ogill successfully purchased the wadset for £400. What annoyed Young was that £200 of this sum had been borrowed from Young's household. Meslet and Ogill's failure to repay this loan meant that Young's household could not compete for land. These were the same neighbours who shared plough oxen with Smith and helped him when he collapsed in his fields after quarrelling with his wife. Young believed that Meslet and Ogill improperly took possession of that land – and she said so in public, using threatening words while removing her kerchief and walking withershins. Meslet and Ogill testified that after this quarrel, they started losing animals, their crops were less productive and their whole household fell into decay. Young was found guilty of these charges.

Young was also accused of wielding her considerable powers against those below her. Her cottars, George Umpherston and Janet Hodge, testified that she damaged their butter after Umpherston took the head shepherd's job in East Barns away from Young's brother Thomas. Young's defence testimony asserted that because Umpherstoun and Hodge were her servants, she owned all that they had; it was illogical that she would destroy her own butter. Cuthbert Simpson, a chapman, testified that Young destroyed his livelihood in revenge for her dissatisfaction with a piece of linen he had sold her.[44] Finally, Young was accused of destroying the cattle and worldly goods of Andrew Morton and his family because they were unable to repay a debt to Young when she came to collect.

The documents do not show how Young viewed her own 'powers' at the time. Many of the specifics of her behaviour pointed to maleficent magic and potential witchcraft. Young must have known that the incidents, words and deeds described by her neighbours – walking withershins, loose hair, curses and threats – were provocative. She may have been invoking the power of witchcraft in her everyday life. In a small community, she undoubtedly knew about her growing reputation as a witch. Her hint or wink to her potential power as a witch may have helped her get her way in disputes.

V

Young's case tells us much about household and community in early modern Scotland. The quarrels, words and magically-tinged deeds merged as part of a complex web of female-directed inter-household relations that intertwined economic, social, co-operative and competitive relations. The disputes occurred around the boundaries and interstices between households where status and wealth, co-operation and competition sat uneasily with each other. These disputes reveal a tantalising glimpse into the connections between the social and cultural milieu of East Barns and the witchcraft case made against Young.

The quarrels that began as disputes between individuals rapidly expanded to engulf their spouses, children and servants. Young did not simply attack individuals; she was accused of magically battling whole households. In the accusations alleging misfortune suffered by the households of social superiors and equals, Young was mostly found guilty. However, when accused of harming social inferiors, she was acquitted. It is not clear why the assize found testimony by social inferiors less compelling. It seems that the assize, local men from East Barns and its environs, thought Young most potent as a magical threat when engaged in household battle with other comparable households. Witchcraft victims were identified, not as individuals, but through their position in webs of family and household.[45]

Witchcraft harm was experienced as intimate violence. Young knew her victims very well indeed – they were her husband, her in-laws and people with whom she dealt every day. Very few witches in Scotland were accused of causing large-scale harm such as hailstorms, drought or other bad weather, natural disasters, plague or famine.[46] Typically, in the rare instances where a witchcraft suspect was accused of this kind of generalised harm, their motive was perceived as intending to harm a specific victim. In Young's case she was accused of interfering with the Dunbar herring drove in order to destroy the wealth of George Sandie, the miller.

This intimate violence played out along the rough-edged lines drawn between households around women's work. Accusations against Young revolved primarily around the work for which she herself was responsible. Her quarrels followed her working life and were part of her struggles (as a representative of her household) against other households for a better position and her attempt to maximise her resources. Many disputes occurred within the patterns of women's work – dairying, childcare, ale-brewing and the verbal work of negotiating with other households. Magic, in this case magical harm and beliefs about the Devil, was interwoven with the practices of everyday social and economic life.

Young's accusers portrayed her witchcraft as a magical assault on their households, emphasising links between incidents based on household connections. So, for example, the family and household connections between the Brysons were explained in the documents rather than laid out as totally separate accusations based on individual attacks. Young's own defence testimony hinted at these same social and economic boundaries and relationships imbued within witchcraft belief. The defence, however, argued against a household-structured reading by casting each dispute and misfortune as personal in nature. Disputes with her neighbours were thus moved away from the arena of the social relations of work and household and into a vision of interpersonal, individual psychology and personal responsibility for misfortune. Young's reactions to her neighbours, in her version of the facts, were normal and personal. In her testimony she became the persecuted, honest, honourable, Christian wife and neighbour. Each neighbour's misfortune was variously portrayed as God's judgement, individual laziness or incompetence. So the misfortunes experienced by Margaret Ogill were God's wrath for her covering up the schoolmaster's pre-marital affair; the rash on Lilias Knowis was because she ate raw wort; the Umpherstoun and Hodge butter failing was due to incompetence. By decoupling her neighbours' misfortunes from the social or communal aspects of East Barns life, the defence testimony tried to neutralise the magically charged potential within inter-household relations.

Witchcraft was not simply an interpretation of, or commentary on, daily life. It also influenced how people lived – their work, alliances and disputes – and how they thought about their troubles and other people's successes. Neighbours' experience of witchcraft harm created, enacted and upheld small chains of interpersonal domination that were lived in thought and practice. Young's work – the work of a female head of household – became imbued with magical harm. The widely held beliefs about magic and witchcraft made her everyday work stronger and more potent within her community. Here Young's intimate and everyday practices shaped community belief about her, her work, witches and witchcraft. The local experiences and practices as described in Young's trial partook of and helped to shape people's understandings about witchcraft and magic that were shared across Scotland.

Quarrels followed by harm arose from the practical, day-to-day experiences of households. Young's supposed magical healing, her associations with other known witches, the rumours that she had a Devil's mark, and other magical happenings provided the context in which her quarrelling for land and household gain came to be seen as causing magical harm to her neighbours. Domestic arrangements, particularly of middling peasants such as Young, structured the cultural content of witchcraft accusations and community witchcraft beliefs. The intimate details, both magical and ordinary, of witchcraft accusations in Young's case were clearly drawn from her daily life as the wife of a portioner and a female head of household. These local-level accusations dovetailed with elite theology and understandings of the demonic pact. Further, they wrapped around and reinforced the construct of the domestic – marriage, household and community. A similar pattern can be found in other Scottish witchcraft cases pertaining to wives and widows of middling peasants and mid-level inhabitants of towns and burghs.[47] The argument made here is different from the idea that witches were quarrelsome neighbours. Young's physical and verbal work, as the female head of household, structured both the quarrels that resulted in witchcraft accusations and the supposed objects of her malice and revenge. Much of this work brought Young out of her home, into fields, villages and other people's homes. Local witchcraft accusations revolved around the practical aspects of Young's domestic arrangement as she lived it: production and consumption of goods, the running of her household, raising children and co-operating with neighbours. Individual households were viable economic and social units only through intense, and often tense, links with other households, the larger community, landlords and state institutions. Witchcraft accusations demonstrate that women played a key role in maintaining, or sabotaging, those connections.

Witchcraft highlights the ways that household configurations structured daily life and the ways that people's lived lives expanded outside their households. Households were deemed vulnerable to witchcraft, as if their necessary connections to the community were the very thing that could let in harm. Young's defence arguments were structured against a reading of East Barns's misfortunes as patterned by household, instead presenting misfortunes as random and individual, and denying her agency. The accusations against Isobel Young simultaneously talk about witchcraft and the structures of everyday life.

Notes

1. Elizabeth Ewan, ' "Many injurious words": defamation and gender in late medieval Scotland', in R. A. McDonald (ed.), *History, Literature, and Music in Scotland, 700–1560* (Toronto, 2002); Laura Gowing, *Domestic Dangers: Women, Words and Sex in Early Modern London* (Oxford, 1998), 268.
2. Ronald Hutton, 'Anthropological and historical approaches to witchcraft: potential for a new collaboration?', *Historical Journal*, 47 (2004), 413–34.
3. Alan Macfarlane, *Witchcraft in Tudor and Stuart England: A Regional and Comparative Study* (London, 1970). For further discussion, see Lauren Martin, 'The Devil and the Domestic: Witchcraft, Women's Work and Marriage in Early Modern Scotland' (New School for Social Research PhD dissertation, 2004), 42–4.
4. See, for example, Gilbert Joseph and Daniel Nugent (eds.), *Everyday Forms of State Formation: Revolution and the Negotiation of Rule in Modern Mexico* (Durham, NC, 1994).

5. Raymond Firth (ed.), *Man and Culture: An Evaluation of the Work of Bronislaw Malinowski* (New York, 1957). See also Adam Kuper, *The Invention of Primitive Society: Transformations of an Illusion* (New Brunswick, NJ, 1988).

6. Talal Asad (ed.), *Anthropology and the Colonial Encounter* (London, 1973), 9–19; Kate Crehan, *The Fractured Community: Landscapes of Power and Gender in Rural Zambia* (Berkeley, Calif., 1997). Frances Dolan places this understanding of culture within the discipline of cultural studies, although it also has roots in the anthropological colonial critique: Frances E. Dolan, *Dangerous Familiars: Representations of Domestic Crime in England, 1550–1700* (Ithaca, NY, 1994), 4.

7. David W. Sabean, *Property, Production and Family in Neckarhausen, 1700–1870* (Cambridge, 1990), 10.

8. Crehan, *Fractured Community*, 2, 227–32.

9. Ibid., 9.

10. William Roseberry, *Anthropologies and Histories: Essays in Culture, History and Political Economy* (New Brunswick, NJ, 1991); Raymond Williams, *Marxism and Language* (Oxford, 1977), 27–36.

11. William Roseberry, 'Balinese cockfights and the seduction of anthropology', in his *Anthropologies and Histories*, 29.

12. A distinction between 'culture' and 'conduct', or 'thought' and 'action', in anthropology suggests that culture provides the road map and structure for action. This has been a common way that language and practice have been understood in anthropological thought. See, for example, Clifford Geertz, *The Interpretation of Cultures* (New York, 1973); Richard A. Barrett, *Culture and Conduct: An Excursion in Anthropology* (Belmont, Calif., 1984), ch. 3.

13. See, for example, Robin Briggs, *Witches and Neighbours: The Social and Cultural Context of European Witchcraft* (2nd edn., Oxford, 2002); Annabel Gregory, 'Witchcraft, politics and "good neighbourhood" in early seventeenth-century Rye', *Past and Present*, 133 (November 1991), 31–66; Lyndal Roper, *Oedipus and the Devil: Witchcraft, Sexuality and Religion in Early Modern Europe* (London, 1994); Stuart Clark, *Thinking with Demons: The Idea of Witchcraft in Early Modern Europe* (Oxford, 1997).

14. *SJC*, i, 96–120 (books of adjournal); *RPC*, 2nd ser., iii, 4, 540; Edinburgh City Archives, town treasurer's accounts, vol. 5 (1623–1636), p. 598 (record of execution); NRS, Tyninghame kirk session minutes, CH2/359/1, fo. 60r.; NRS, JC26/9, 'Issobell Young' bundle, nos. 1–15 (pre-trial witness depositions, a dittay, interrogatories, witness lists, Young's statement).

15. See Martin, 'Devil and the Domestic', 202–4, 289–95, for full description and implications of kerchief removal.

16. *SJC*, i, 97–100; NRS, JC26/9/1, item 1. Briggs, *Witches and Neighbours*, 174–9, documented a similar pattern of witchcraft diagnosis conducted by folk healers, whom he called 'witch-doctors'.

17. NRS, JC26/9/12.

18. NRS, JC26/9/1.

19. Ibid., item 5.

20. NRS, JC26/9/4. The interrogatory for this 'interview' survives.

21. Bellenden was involved in at least eleven other documented witchcraft cases during 1629–1631. He was assigned as an investigator (read interrogator) and commissioner to cases in the central and southeast of Scotland (Stirling,

Haddington, Berwick and Perth). Colville was involved in ten documented cases as an investigator and commissioner to cases from the central and southeastern areas of Scotland (Clackmannan, Perth, Edinburgh, Fife and Haddington). He was involved in cases from 1629 to 1662. These figures probably under-represent their full involvement.

22. *RPC*, 2nd ser., ii, 540; iii, 4.
23. *RMS*, v, 357; vi, 490; *Exchequer Rolls of Scotland*, xxiii, 144.
24. Witnesses suggest that Young's witchcraft reputation probably started after her marriage. The average age of women's first marriage was the mid-twenties: R. A. Houston, 'Women in the economy and society of Scotland, 1500–1800', in R. A. Houston and I. D. Whyte (eds.), *Scottish Society, 1500–1800* (Cambridge, 1989), 127; Deborah Symonds, *Weep Not for Me: Women, Ballads, and Infanticide in Early Modern Scotland* (University Park, PA, 1997), 99. Since her reputation spanned forty years, she was probably at least 65 years old at the time of her execution.
25. *RMS*, v, 369. Marriage and occupation of land tended to occur around the same time for men in early modern Scotland: Houston, 'Women', 126–7.
26. For further discussion, see Martin, 'Devil and the Domestic', 255–9.
27. Martin, 'Devil and the Domestic', 248.
28. NRS, CC8/8/8 fol. 205–7. His son worked with Smith and testified against Young.
29. NRS, CC8/8/37, 623–5.
30. NRS, JC26/9/5; see also *SJC*, i, 96–120 (books of adjournal).
31. Martin, 'Devil and the Domestic', 307–8.
32. For fuller accounts of women's work, see Symonds, *Weep Not for Me*, ch. 4; Houston, 'Women'; Margaret H. B. Sanderson, *A Kindly Place? Living in Sixteenth-Century Scotland* (East Linton, 2002), ch. 8.
33. NRS, JC26/9/1.
34. Ibid.
35. Kirk session records contain many references to marital violence: Margo Todd, *The Culture of Protestantism in Early Modern Scotland* (New Haven, Conn., Mass., 2002), 284–90.
36. NRS, Original Courtbooks of the Baron-baillie of Broxmouth and Pinkerton from 1620 to 1649 and from 1735 to 1764, GD100/289.
37. Martin, 'Devil and the Domestic', 248.
38. NRS, JC26/9/3. The Home quarrel consisted of charges 9 and 15–18.
39. NRS, JC26/9, document 1. The timeline for this dispute is roughly confirmed by charters in the Great Seal register: *RMS*, vi, 907.
40. In a separate charge, Young was accused of conducting a magical protection ritual for her cattle near the Home dovecote.
41. NRS, JC26/9/9.
42. Thomas Home's widow Lilias Knowis testified that her husband 'cost' with George Smith for two cottar's houses and one rig of land: NRS, JC26/9/9. Cost means 'payment in kind for rent, dues or wages': *Concise Scots Dictionary*.
43. NRS, JC26/9, document 1.
44. NRS, JC26/9 item 1; *SJC*, i, 118. Cuthbert appeared personally at her trial.
45. Lauren Martin, 'Scottish witchcraft panics re-examined', in Julian Goodare, Lauren Martin and Joyce Miller (eds.), *Witchcraft and Belief in Early Modern Scotland* (Basingstoke, 2008), 119–43; Scott Moir, 'The crucible: witchcraft

and the experience of family in early modern Scotland', in Elizabeth Ewan and Janay Nugent (eds.), *Finding the Family in Medieval and Early Modern Scotland* (Aldershot, 2008), 49–59.

46. Julian Goodare, 'Scottish witchcraft in its European context', in Goodare, Martin and Miller (eds.), *Witchcraft and Belief*, 26–50, at pp. 28–30.

47. For instance, the cases of Janet Cock (1661), Agnes Finnie (1644) and Margaret Oswald (1629): SSW.

5
Witch-Hunting in Scotland, 1649–1650

Paula Hughes

The dramatic political events in Scotland during the 1640s may seem to give an air of inevitability to the witch-hunting that broke out in 1649–1650. Supporters of the revolutionary National Covenant, and later the Solemn League and Covenant, had gained firm control of Scottish political and ecclesiastical institutions. The National Covenant of 1638 was a contract between the Scottish people and God, in which those who subscribed to it promised to behave in a godly manner. The Solemn League and Covenant of 1643 further cemented this and laid foundations for exporting the 'perfect' model of presbyterian church government to England. In the autumn of 1648, after the collapse of the moderate covenanters' Engagement with Charles I, the radical wing of the covenanting movement seized power. By 1649, protection of the sanctity of the covenants was at the top of the agenda for the regime.

I

Throughout the 1640s the kirk became increasingly concerned about sinful behaviour. It was a regular topic of discussion for the kirk's central bodies – the general assembly and the commission of the kirk – and, in the localities, kirk sessions and presbyteries. Witchcraft and superstition were among the most serious of these concerns. Charming was the practice of using magical objects, spells or prayers to cure ailments or for personal gain; this had been treated hitherto as an ecclesiastical offence but never as a criminal offence.[1]

During 1643–1644, presbyteries dealt with an increased number of charmers.[2] In 1646, the commission of the kirk petitioned parliament to criminalise the practice of charming and consulting of witches and charmers.[3] This became linked with a debate about 'consulters' with charmers and witches. The original 1563 witchcraft act included a directive against consulters with witches, but even by 1567 it had been recognised that this provision was a dead letter. Witches, in the usual official sense of maleficent magical practitioners who made a pact with the Devil, did not really have 'consulters' anyway.[4] Nevertheless, parliament eventually responded, and on 1 February 1649 issued a new act against witches:

> The estats of parlement &c, understanding that there are some persons who consult with devills and familiar spirits who, notwithstanding of the 73 act of Queene Marie [i.e. the 1563 act] quhairby it is ordained that all witches sorcerers necromancers and consulters with them are to be punished by death, doe yet dreame to themselffis impunity becaus consulters are not expresslie mentionat in the said act: doe thairfor for further clearing theirof declare and ordaine that whatsoever persone or persons shall consult with devillis or familiar spirits are lyable to the paines contained in the said act and shall be punished by death; and the saids estats ratifies and approves all former acts made aganst witches, sorcerers necromancers and consulters with thame in the haill heads, articles and claussis thairof.[5]

This thus ratified the act of 1563 and sought to clarify the position of 'consulters', but instead of criminalising consulters with charmers, or even consulters with witches, it condemned 'persons who consult with devills and familiar spirits' – a phrase that would normally have been understood to mean necromancers. The act's statement that 'consulters are not expresslie mentionat' in the 1563 act sits oddly with the mention, a few words earlier, of the fact that consulters had indeed been mentioned in it. Indeed necromancy had also been mentioned in the 1563 act. Thus, the new act did not go as far as the general assembly and the commission of the kirk had expected. On the surface it looked as though it clarified the position of 'consulters', but it did not really do so. Perhaps as a result, there is no evidence of any charmers, or consulters with witches or charmers, being prosecuted under the new act in 1649–1650. Nor for that matter were 'familiar spirits' mentioned in the prosecutions, though the Devil was certainly prominent. All cases that went through to the central authorities to request a commission for trial involved the straightforward crime of witchcraft.

The radical regime believed that Scotland was experiencing a second Reformation in 1649. The regime demonstrated its godliness in a number of ways, especially the removal of the ungodly from government and the army. But to demonstrate its godliness, the new regime also undertook a broader campaign of moral reform. In the early months of 1649 parliament passed twelve acts concerning morality, including acts against fornication, adultery, incest, blasphemy, drunkenness, swearing and profanity and witchcraft.[6] Betrayal of the covenants came in many forms, from the mass betrayal of the covenants through the Engagement in 1647 to personal acts of betrayal by those acting in an ungodly manner. Suspected witches fell into the latter category. The act of becoming a witch involved renouncing baptism and entering into a pact with the Devil, which was the ultimate betrayal of the Scottish people's covenants with God.

What happened in 1649–1650 was a culmination of ten years of dominance of political and religious life by presbyterian radicals with apocalyptic visions and an impending sense that the nation's troubles resulted from the scourge of the ungodly threatening to subvert a covenanted and godly nation.[7] In 1649–1650 many charges of witchcraft noted that the suspected witch had entered into a 'covenant' with the Devil as opposed to the more conventional 'pact'. The main features of the pact, for example renouncing of baptism, receiving the Devil's mark and a new name, and consummation of the pact, remained key features in confessions. However, the substitution of the term 'covenant' for 'pact' is not to be taken lightly.

II

The evidence for witch-hunting comes from several different stages of the process. In the early, pre-trial stage, local church courts – kirk sessions or presbyteries – were often involved. The kirk session was often the first official body to hear of an accusation of witchcraft, when a parishioner or group of parishioners complained to it about a suspected witch. Stuart Macdonald has argued that the kirk sessions were instrumental in bringing suspected witches to the notice of the authorities.[8] This is true to the extent that kirk sessions, and presbyteries, carried out a key function in the pre-trial stage by helping to gather evidence against suspects and putting that evidence forward to apply for a trial. However, the initial accusation or report of witchcraft in a chain of accusations came from the local community.

In rare cases a minister might write to a neighbouring kirk session to inform them that a suspect had named a parishioner in a confession, or a presbytery would write to a neighbouring presbytery upon hearing of a case of witchcraft to enquire whether any of their own residents had been named.[9] These interactions could be important when chain-reaction witch-hunting was occurring. By that time, most suspects were generated not by neighbourhood accusations but by confessing witches. However, before that stage, the vast majority of initial accusations were brought to kirk sessions' attention either by ordinary folk complaining of an act of witchcraft or by a counter accusation of slander if someone had been called a witch.

Macdonald's interpretation thus sees the kirk sessions as being proactive in hunting for witches. However, in 1649–1650 the local authorities reacted to reports of witchcraft from the community and from other parishes. Once a report had reached a session it would appeal for witnesses and evidence. Macdonald appears to have interpreted this as the first step in searching for witches in the community, placing the initiative in the hands of the kirk session.[10] However, the kirk session was reliant on residents to inform and bring information about their neighbours to the kirk session. Occasionally, even the accused would bring the case to the session by complaining of slander. In any such case, the session would appeal for witnesses, examine evidence and inform the presbytery.

Once evidence was compiled, the presbytery evaluated and 'attested' the evidence as to whether it was sufficient for 'suiting' or requesting a commission for a trial from the central institutions. In 1649–1650, presbyteries acted as important intermediaries between the local investigation and the official trial. Almost all of the commissions granted by the committee of estates in 1649 referred to the suspects as belonging to presbyteries as opposed to parishes, counties or burghs.

Evidence found in local church court records includes measures taken to imprison and interrogate suspected witches, confessions of accused witches, witness testimonies and accounts of previous behaviour of witchcraft suspects.[11] In some cases, kirk sessions or presbyteries would bring in a witch-pricker to gather evidence of the witch's mark. This locally-compiled material was then taken to the central authorities in Edinburgh. If the evidence was satisfactory, the authorities would grant a commission of justiciary to a group of local men, authorising them to conduct a criminal trial in the locality.[12] In some periods of Scottish witch-hunting, trials could also be held in the central justiciary court in Edinburgh, but there appear to have been no instances of this in 1649–1650.

Most of the surviving evidence for the 1649–1650 witch-hunt comes from central records of the granting of these commissions. Most commissions were for trying of several witches, which is symptomatic of 'chain-reaction' witch-hunting – searching for suspects and apprehending them if named by a confessing witch. Commissions were granted to a small group of commissioners, usually between five and nine, usually with a quorum of three or four. Some commissioners were named repeatedly. Of the eleven commissions granted for the presbytery of Haddington, James Skirving, Richard Skirving and Alexander Borthwick were each named on five.[13] Each commission empowered the commissioners to convene a court and hold a trial for the named witchcraft suspects. Evidence of the outcome of the trial rarely survives, but there are strong indications that the acquittal rate was low.[14]

Witch-hunting was thus co-ordinated centrally. The covenanting revolution made significant changes to the political framework in Scotland. Parliament was placed firmly at the head of political life and was in session much more often than before. During parliamentary recesses the executive government was headed, not by a privy council appointed by the king, but by a committee of estates appointed by parliament.[15] The privy council would normally have been responsible for granting commissions to try witches, but in 1649–1650 the council had been reduced to a nominal institution and did not grant any commissions.[16] Instead, the committee of estates acted as the co-ordinating body when parliament was not in session.

Like parliament, the general assembly of the church became more institutionalised and met more frequently. The general assembly consisted of representative ministers and lay elders. Although the church was no longer represented in parliament, the general assembly influenced political life through the commission of the kirk. This governed the church when the assembly was not in session, just as the committee of estates governed the country when parliament was not in session.

The wordings of trial commissions indicate that each commission was issued on its own merit. For example, of the five commissions issued on 4 December 1649, only one commission contained the order to take an inventory of the accused's belongings.[17] Such an order may indicate that some of the witches to be tried may have been known to possess property worth confiscating. Forty-seven of the commissions noted that the depositions against and confessions of the witches were either subscribed, attested or revised by the presbytery – a further indication of presbyteries' significant role in the pre-trial stage of the prosecution of witches in 1649–1650.

An unusual general commission was granted on 4 December for the trial of people in the presbytery of Biggar, who had been accused of witchcraft by Janet Coutts from Peebles.[18] This offered the local authorities *carte blanche* to try any suspects named by Coutts. The commission included some procedural guidance, instructing that she was to be confronted with those she had accused of witchcraft and that those whom she then confirmed as witches were to be tried. It was the only general commission granted in 1649–1650; all others were restricted to named individuals. The central authorities were usually cautious in their proceedings. Requests for commissions were carefully considered before they were granted by the committee of estates, and clear instructions were given to the commissioners on how to proceed. Less information was recorded about commissions granted by parliament, but given parliament's concern at the potential use of torture to extract confessions and the clear remit it gave to the May 1650 committee (to be discussed below), it is likely that parliament gave the same level of consideration and instruction in each case that the committee of estates did.

Parliament and the committee of estates were sometimes appealed to in cases of mistreatment of suspected witches. Bessie Masterton and Marjory Durie petitioned the committee of estates, complaining against the treatment they received at the hands of the presbytery of Dunfermline during their incarceration. There is no evidence that their petition was successful, but there are no further references to them in the official records.[19] The nature of their mistreatment was not specified, but it most likely refers to the common practice of sleep deprivation and 'watching', where suspects were watched by ministers or elders to extract confessions.

Handling requests to try suspected witches could be a lengthy process. Margaret Finlayson's confession and the depositions against her were dated February and March 1650. The application for a commission to try her was addressed to the 'rycht honorabill committee of estates of parliament or the Lords of the Secret Counsall' on 21 March 1650. Her case was passed to the sub-committee set up by parliament to consider papers concerning witches in May 1650. The committee did not hear her case until 29 June 1650, when it recommended the justice depute to consider the case and report back.[20]

Finlayson's case also indicates local uncertainty about the changing nature of central government: Which body was responsible for granting commissions to try witches? Another such case had occurred in September 1649 when the presbytery of Glasgow sent witness testimonies and a supplication to 'the rycht honorable Comite of Estaites or Lords of His majesties Priwie Counsil' requesting a commission to try Maud Galt.[21] There is no evidence that a commission was granted for her trial.

III

Defining an exact number of witches who were accused is problematic due to the nature of record-keeping and the survival and condition of records.[22] The Survey of Scottish Witchcraft can produce a figure for exactly 800 people accused of witchcraft in 1649 and 1650. This figure is made up of 557 named individuals and additional entries for 243 unnamed persons. The latter figure is imprecise, since most of these unnamed persons come in groups of unknown size, where the Survey had to make an estimate of their numbers. This often occurred with the commissions granted by parliament, which contain little detail. They give the name of the parish or presbytery in which the suspected witch was to be tried but no names of suspects or names of commissioners to try them. This commission granted on 5 July 1649 is typical:

> THE QUHILK DAY Comissioun wes grantit be the Parliament to cer-taine persouns for administrating Justice vpon some persons guiltie of the cryme of witchcraft within Aberdour and Innerkeithin Haymouth and Dirltoun.[23]

In such cases, when parliament issued a commission for the trial of 'some persons' or 'certain persons' in a given parish or presbytery, the Witchcraft Survey treated that as being 3 persons. If the 'certain persons' were stated to be from more than one parish, that was treated as 3 from each parish. This method of counting is imprecise and there is a danger of double counting if (for instance) named witches found in presbytery minutes are the same ones for whom parliament later issued a commission naming no names. The Survey adjusted for all known instances of this, but there may be others. On the other hand, some of the groups of unknown size were probably larger than 3, sometimes much larger. In one case in the presbytery of Biggar, the names are unknown but the presbytery record states that Janet Coutts had named 48 witches.[24] Commissions too could encompass sizeable numbers. One commission to interrogate suspects in Peebles, dated 6 November 1649, named 39 suspects;[25] if this had been a parliamentary commission, this number would not have been mentioned and the Survey would have treated it as a group of 3. Finally, some reports of extensive witch-hunting are almost impossible to quantify. The unnamed Scottish witch-pricker, who extended his activities to northern England in 1649, claimed that he had been responsible for two hundred executions in Scotland and England – probably mostly in Scotland.[26] It was claimed that Janet

Coutts named approximately 88 suspected witches across the borders region, encouraged by the deal she had struck with the witch-pricker George Cathie. These figures possibly include the 39 suspects to be tried in Peebles by the commission granted by the committee of estates on 6 November 1649, but the remaining names are difficult to trace. Some of them may appear in the Survey's statistics, but probably not all of them do.

Figure 5.1 shows a chronological distribution of the 557 individuals named as accused witches in 1649–1650. Lauren Martin has recently warned against the pitfalls of 'suspect counting' using disparate evidence from different dates.[27] These figures are of witches who were named on supplications for commissions, and they are listed at the date of the commission granted for their trial, a standard record (usually the last) of official involvement. In the case of individuals whose accusations were not pursued, the date of their appearance is used. This chart is based on records of accused witches compiled from the Witchcraft Survey, and cross-referenced with accused witches named on commissions granted by the committee of estates and accused witches named in the records of kirk sessions and presbyteries within the synod of Lothian and Tweeddale.

As can be seen from Figure 5.1, there was a large wave of prosecutions in the second half of 1649, with two distinct peaks in July and October–November. Prosecutions continued at a lower level for the first few months of 1650 before rising to a third, smaller peak in June. Significant

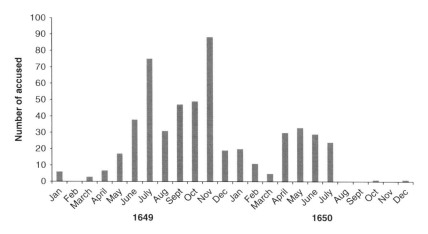

Figure 5.1 Accused witches in Scotland by month, 1649–1650

prosecutions continued into August 1650 but then dropped suddenly in September to almost nothing. The overall high point of accusations was in November 1649, when 87 people were accused.

The first recorded witchcraft accusations in 1649–1650 occurred in January 1649 in the presbyteries of Cupar and Dunfermline in Fife.[28] In January 1649, there were six recorded cases: two in Cupar, three in Dunfermline and one in Haddington. Despite these initial cases, the witch-hunt did not gather momentum until May 1649. Accusations then continued throughout December, into January, February and March, with a slight dip in April, culminating in another peak in accusations from May until July. Witch-hunting in 1649–1650 comprised a series of local hunts that spread into one another as accusations crossed parish, town and county borders. Macdonald describes a 'massive hunt' in the presbytery of Dunfermline in 1649–1650 and tells of how the presbytery 'fought... to maintain control of both the process and the incarcerated suspects', a situation which was to be repeated throughout the areas most affected by witch-hunting in 1649–1650.[29]

Witch-pricking fuelled the process, as local authorities sought to supplement the usual evidence against witches (confessions and neighbours' statements) with evidence of the Devil's mark. Several professional prickers operated during the 1649–1650 witch-hunt.[30] The most interesting was George Cathie, from Tranent, who travelled between many parishes in central and eastern areas of the country during the course of the 1649–1650 witch-hunt. He was called upon by the presbytery of Peebles in September 1649 to search Janet Coutts.[31] Coutts had attempted to flee after she had been apprehended, and those involved in her interrogation had trouble in bringing her to a confession. After Cathie had found the mark on Coutts, her interrogators reported to the presbytery that she had confessed and named around 80 other witches in Peebles, Lanark, Biggar and Jedburgh. She was transported to Biggar and Jedburgh to be further examined about the individuals that she had named in those areas.

However, on 4 January 1650 the presbytery of Biggar wrote to the presbytery of Peebles informing them about Coutts's 'inconstancie in delateing and passing from her delateiouns' against individuals she had previously named when confronted with them. The brethren at Peebles responded by 'exhorting' the commissioners who had been appointed to try Coutts 'to tak speedie course for execution of justice upon her, as one desperatlie sent to the devil'. Further correspondence between the presbyteries led to scrutiny of Cathie's role in bringing Coutts to a confession and naming of other witches.[32] The brethren at Jedburgh passed this information on to Cathie's home presbytery of Haddington, and he was called to appear before them on 17 April. He did not appear, and the presbytery sent one of the ministers to Tranent 'to deall with the civil magistrate' to ensure his attendance. He eventually appeared before the presbytery on 1 May and denied that he had struck a deal with Coutts that she would name other witches 'so that he might get his implyment'.[33] The presbytery ordained that James Smith, one of the elders at Tranent, was to deal with the bailies of Tranent to bring Cathie to appear before the presbytery of Peebles. There is no further record of Cathie, but it would be a fair assumption that this incident put a stop to his career. Those whom Coutts had falsely accused were exonerated, but she was still sent to the stake.

By the spring of 1650 the committee of estates was concerned with the more pressing matters of negotiating with the exiled Charles II, a royalist rising led by the earl of Montrose and a breakdown in relations with the English government led by Oliver Cromwell. On 12 April 1650, it created a sub-committee to deal with granting commissions to try witches until parliament reconvened and came up with a more permanent solution.[34] Parliament then, on 18 May, created another committee to consider witchcraft cases and to devise a more permanent method for dealing with witches.[35] Unfortunately no records of either the sub-committee of the committee of estates or the parliamentary committee survive. The loss of these records may mean that there were further witches about whom no evidence survives. Some evidence does survive, however, in local records, of cases that would have gone to the committees. Finally, a new committee of estates was appointed to rule from 5 July until 26 November 1650, granting only two further commissions to try witches.

IV

Witch-hunting was unevenly spread across the country. The following statistical analysis uses the method developed by Lauren Martin to analyse the regional intensity of Scottish witchcraft panics.[36] She divided Scotland's thirty-four counties into ten regional groups and worked out how many witchcraft suspects were recorded for each one in the Witchcraft Survey. This exercise can be carried out for 1649–1650, and the results are shown in Table 5.1. There were 555 suspects whose county of residence was recorded and these counties are arranged in the table by region, with the regions listed in descending order of number of suspects. The locations of these counties are shown on the map on p. xiii above. As will be seen from the table, the largest numbers of suspects were recorded in the regions of Lothian, East Borders and Strathclyde.

Table 5.1 Numbers of suspects by region and county, 1649–1650

Lothian	264	
Edinburgh		79
Haddington		160
Linlithgow		25
East Borders	98	
Berwick		19
Peebles		44
Roxburgh		29
Selkirk		6
Strathclyde	79	
Argyll		0
Ayr		38
Bute		5
Dunbarton		10
Lanark		14
Renfrew		12
Fife	71	
Fife		71
Kinross		0
Tayside	17	
Forfar		16
Perth		1
Dumfries and Galloway	16	
Dumfries		9
Kirkcudbright		0
Wigtown		7
Grampian	5	
Aberdeen		4
Banff		1
Elgin		0
Kincardine		0
Central	3	
Clackmannan		0
Stirling		3
Highland	1	
Cromarty		0
Inverness		0
Nairn		0
Ross		1
Sutherland		0
Far North	1	
Caithness		0
Orkney		1
Shetland		0
TOTAL	555	

Source: SSW.

Martin's method then asks how these crude figures might be translated into accusations per capita of population. A pioneering census was conducted in Scotland in 1755. The population probably increased somewhat between 1650 and 1755, but the regional distribution of the population probably changed little (unlike in the following century when the distribution was affected by industrialisation and emigration). The proportion of suspects in a given region can thus be related to the proportion of the population in that region. The results of such a calculation are shown in Table 5.2. The crucial figures are in the column 'Suspect: population intensity 1649–1650': the larger the figure, the more intense the prosecution in that region. A figure of 1.0 in that column would indicate that prosecutions in that region were at an average intensity for 1649–1650. The right-hand column, 'Suspect: population intensity 1563–1736', shows Martin's figures for the Scottish witch-hunt overall. These allow comparisons to be drawn with 1649–1650.

Table 5.2 shows that the area categorised by Martin as Lothian, which included the presbytery of Haddington, produced 48 per cent of the suspects in 1649–1650. This is staggering considering that the area represented only 11 per cent of the overall population at the time. The region which produced the next highest proportion of suspects was the East Borders; this included the presbytery of Peebles, which produced many suspects due to the activities of George Cathie and Janet Coutts.

Table 5.2   Intensity of prosecution by region, 1649–1650

Region	Suspects (%)	Population (%)	Suspect: population intensity 1649–1650	Suspect: population intensity 1563–1736
Lothian	48	11	4.4	3.0
East Borders	18	6	3.0	1.5
Fife	13	7	1.9	1.7
Strathclyde	14	20	0.7	0.7
Dumfries and Galloway	3	6	0.5	0.7
Tayside	3	15	0.2	0.4
Central	1	4	0.2	0.5
Grampian	1	16	0.1	0.4
Highland	0	11	0.1	0.5
Far North	0	5	0.1	1.0

Source: Table 5.1 above, combined with data from Martin, 'Scottish witchcraft panics re-examined', 125. Some figures are affected by rounding.

Administratively, these regions were covered by the synod of Lothian and Tweeddale. The synod acted as a regional assembly, covering seven presbyteries: Biggar, Dalkeith, Dunbar, Edinburgh, Haddington, Linlithgow and Peebles. These were close to Edinburgh where local witch-hunters had easy access to the parliament and committee of estates.[37] The concentration of cases in Haddington in 1649–1650 is also not surprising given that this area experienced intense witch-hunting in the previous witch-hunts of 1590–1591, 1597 and 1628–1631; the 1660–1661 hunt would also be concentrated there.[38] Table 5.2 shows, however, that 1649–1650 was Haddington's most intense period of witch-hunting overall.

There were also other areas with intense witch-hunting in 1649–1650. The Strathclyde region produced 14 per cent and Fife produced 13 per cent of suspects. For Strathclyde, its large population reduces the per capita intensity to below the average for 1649–1650, but Fife was well above the average per capita intensity. Stuart Macdonald has recently written that the 1649–1650 witch-hunt was concentrated in Fife and the Lothians. Macdonald claims that the cases that occurred outside this area after the main outbreak of witch-hunting occurred in Fife and the Lothians were 'aftershocks'.[39] A clearer conclusion, however, would be that the witch-hunt was concentrated in the Lothians.

V

The 1649–1650 witch-hunt came to an abrupt end due to the souring relations between Cromwell and the Scottish parliament. Negotiations with Charles II and another royalist rising led by Montrose diverted the regime's attention away from the pursuit of witches. This is evident in the lack of quantitative evidence of commissions being granted. However, it is apparent that witch-hunting was still going on because there are references to commissions being granted. A warrant was issued in March 1650 to send Alexander Colville of Blair, one of the justice deputes, to Galloway to try suspects there.[40] As we have seen, two committees were created in April and May to consider evidence against witches and grant commissions for the trial of witches. By June, the regime was concerned with purging the army and preparing for an anticipated invasion by Cromwell's forces after the latter's conquest of Ireland.

By July 1650, Cromwell's forces had crossed the border and passed into the Borders and Lothian regions where witch-hunting had been intense. The presence of enemy troops in these localities provided the ordinary folk with a more tangible and immediately dangerous enemy than witches. Moreover, some presbyteries had to abandon their meetings, removing the most important local administrative unit in combating witchcraft. Up to 17 July the presbytery book for Haddington recorded dealings with suspected witches alongside the organisation of supplies and the arrival of troops ready to defend against Cromwell's forces. After that date, the presbytery did not meet again until 13 August 1651 'in respect of the present troubles and violence of war'. Once normal business was restored, no more witchcraft accusations were recorded.[41]

Occasional cases still reached the central authorities. The committee of estates granted two further commissions to try witches, on 8 August and 12 November 1650.[42] Christine Clerk petitioned the committee of estates in November; she had been imprisoned for witchcraft but had not confessed, nor had any witnesses testified that she was a witch. The committee ordered her to be liberated upon caution.[43] When parliament reconvened on 26 November it ordered the committee for bills to consider outstanding requests for commissions to try witches. The last commission to be granted in 1650 was granted by parliament on 2 December for the trial of John McWilliam, Margaret McInlay and Margaret McMurich in Dumbarton.[44] This was far from the heartland of the witch-hunt, but it was an area that the Scottish government still controlled.

VI

This chapter has discussed the 1649–1650 witch-hunt from a top-down perspective. The church pressured the central authorities throughout the 1640s for action to be taken on the threat of witchcraft in the country. The 1649–1650 witch-hunt has been described 'from above', examining the way in which commissions to try witches were granted and the role of the presbytery as an intermediary in the processing of suspected witches, bridging together the local experience of apprehending and interrogating a witch and co-ordinating requests for trials to the central authorities. The 1649–1650 hunt was not a continuous nationwide hunt; rather it was a series of localised hunts mainly concentrated in the Lothians and Tweeddale, which spread to neighbouring areas.

When the witch-hunt broke out in the spring of 1649 it did not turn into the free-for-all that one might have expected, given the pressure exerted by the church. This was largely due to the orderly response of the central institutions in making sure procedures were followed, issuing timely reminders that 'mistreatment' was not to be used in extracting confessions, and hearing petitions from those who claimed mistreatment. Unofficial torture, usually in the form of sleep deprivation, was regularly used in extracting confessions of witchcraft. Pricking was supposed to find the Devil's mark, but it could also be connected with pressure to confess. In April 1650, the chancellor, the earl of Loudoun, asked that suspects renew their confessions in front of trial commissioners, indicating concern over how confessions were being obtained.[45] This letter was sent just as the hunt was escalating in its final peak before it was cut short by the arrival of Cromwell's forces.

The way the central authorities attempted to deal with the outbreak of witch-hunting in 1649–1650 reflects a more long-term trend of dealing with large-scale witch-hunts and a more deep-rooted concern over existing procedure, which extended further back than 1649. This indicates that the central authorities' 'readiness to panic'[46] over witchcraft could result in an inability to cope with the demand for witchcraft commissions. The central authorities had to deal with the influx of applications for commissions from the localities and had to manage the demand by trying to find ways to organise their response. This in turn led to temporary measures to deal with the problems, especially in times when more general political or diplomatic crises occurred. I believe that the prosecutions of 1649–1650 can be categorised as a panic rather than a hunt in the initial stages, as the term 'hunt' implies proactive seeking of witches. On the surface it looks like a hunt with its co-ordination and discussions taking place at high level, but it was all reactive measures, both by the local and central authorities. The commission of the kirk and general assembly had pushed for a witch-hunt by pressing parliament for legislation, but even these steps were reactions to news that reached them from the localities.

It may be argued that the 1649–1650 witch-hunt was inevitable because of the church's campaign throughout the 1640s for action to be taken on witchcraft. This chapter has discussed how attempts were made in 1649 to change both the legislation against witchcraft and the procedure for dealing with witches. The witch-hunt can be divided into two phases. The first phase was from May to December 1649, when responding to the outbreak of witchcraft accusations was a pressing concern for the radical regime, as is evident by the stringent record-keeping and intensity of demand for commissions to try witches. The second phase was from January to July 1650 when the breakdown in relations with Cromwell, negotiations with Charles II and Montrose's rising diverted the regime's attention away from the pursuit of witches. This is evident in the lack of quantitative evidence of commissions being granted – though these conclusions are rendered tentative by the scarcity of evidence of the activities of the central sub-committees of April and May. By June 1650, the regime was distracted by war. However, this only tells one side of the story. The steps taken to control the number of witches being prosecuted and the strict guidelines given to commissioners named to carry out trials indicate that the central authorities were moving towards taking measures to bring the witch-hunt to a conclusion. If Cromwell's forces had not crossed the border in 1650 the witch-hunt might have continued in the localities, but it is possible that it would have run out of steam, given that the central authorities were already showing concern that it was getting out of hand.

Notes

1. Joyce Miller, 'Devices and directions: folk healing aspects of witchcraft practice in seventeenth-century Scotland', in Julian Goodare (ed.), *The Scottish Witch-Hunt in Context* (Manchester, 2002), 90–105; Owen Davies, 'A comparative perspective on Scottish cunning-folk and charmers', in Julian Goodare, Lauren Martin and Joyce Miller (eds.), *Witchcraft and Belief in Early Modern Scotland* (Basingstoke, 2008), 185–205.

2. *Records of the Kirk of Scotland, Containing the Acts and Proceedings of the General Assemblies, 1638–1649*, ed. Alexander Peterkin (Edinburgh, 1843), 354.

3. *Records of the Commissioners of the General Assemblies of the Church of Scotland*, 3 vols., eds. Alexander F. Mitchell and James Christie (SHS, 1892–1909), i, 44, 64; cf. Miller, 'Devices and directions', 91.

4. Julian Goodare, 'The Scottish witchcraft act', *Church History*, 74 (2005), 39–67, at p. 65.

5. *APS*, vi, II, 152, c. 44 (RPS, 1649/1/62).

6. RPS, 1649/1/118, 119. See also Paula Hughes, 'The 1649–50 Scottish Witch-Hunt, with Particular Reference to the Synod of Lothian and Tweeddale' (University of Strathclyde PhD thesis, 2008), 28.

7. For the context of godly discipline and witchcraft in Scotland during the 1640s, see John R. Young, 'The covenanters and the Scottish parliament, 1639–51: the rule of the godly and the "Second Scottish Reformation"', in Elizabethanne Boran and Crawford Gribben (eds.), *Enforcing Reformation in Ireland and Scotland, 1550–1700* (Aldershot, 2006), 131–58; John R. Young, 'The Scottish parliament and witch-hunting in Scotland under the covenanters', *Parliaments, Estates and Representation*, 26 (2006), 53–65.

8. Stuart Macdonald, *The Witches of Fife: Witch-Hunting in a Scottish Shire, 1560–1710* (East Linton, 2002), 169–78.

9. For example, upon hearing of the arrest of Jean Craig in Tranent, the presbytery of Peebles wrote to the interrogating minister Robert Balcanquall on 31 May 1649 to find out whether Craig had named residents of Peebles as fellow witches. NRS, Presbytery of Peebles, 1644–1649, CH2/295/3, p. 114.

10. Macdonald, *Witches of Fife*, 175–8.

11. For a detailed study of such material, see Anna Cordey, 'Reputation and witch-hunting in seventeenth-century Dalkeith', Chapter 6 in this volume.
12. Julian Goodare, 'Witch-hunting and the Scottish state', in Goodare (ed.), *The Scottish Witch-Hunt in Context*, 122–45.
13. NRS, PA11/8, fos. 101, 115, 144; PA11/9, fo. 5.
14. Liv Helene Willumsen, *Witches of the North: Scotland and Finnmark* (Leiden, 2013), ch. 3.
15. During this period, parliament was in session during the following dates: 4 January 1649 to 16 March 1649, 23 May 1649 to 7 August 1649, 7 March 1650 to 8 March 1650, 15 May 1650 to 5 July 1650. The committee of estates was in session: 14 March 1649 to 23 May 1649, 7 August 1649 to 7 March 1650, 7 March 1650 to 15 May 1650 and 5 July 1650 to 26 November 1650.
16. The modern editors of the privy council records printed several commissions in their edition of privy council papers, but in fact these were mostly commissions that were granted by parliament in June and July 1649. For instance, the confessions of Isobel Brown and Helen Taylor, both from Eyemouth and who were accused alongside Elspeth Smith, are dated 2 July and 8 July 1649 respectively, but a note was added to Brown's confession dated 5 July saying that the estates 'grant commission' to try her: *RPC*, 2nd ser., viii, 195.
17. NRS, PA11/9, fos. 3r.-6r.
18. Ibid., fo. 3r.
19. See NRS, PA11/8, fos. 135, 185; PA12/4, September warrants; and PA7/6, paper 148. It is possible that Durie and Masterton were included in the commission granted by parliament on 31 July 1649 for the apprehension of some of the wives of some of the magistrates and others in Inverkeithing. See *APS*, vi, II, 510 (RPS, 1649/5/309). For more on this case, see Louise Yeoman, 'Hunting the rich witch in Scotland: high-status witchcraft suspects and their persecutors, 1590–1650', in Goodare (ed.), *The Scottish Witch-Hunt in Context*, 106–21, at pp. 118–19.
20. *RPC*, 2nd ser., viii, 211–35.
21. Ibid., 198–204. For the intersection of witchcraft and lesbianism in this case, see Julian Goodare, 'Maud Galt (fl. 1648–1649)', in Elizabeth Ewan *et al.* (eds.), *The Biographical Dictionary of Scottish Women* (Edinburgh, 2006), 131.
22. Lauren Martin and Joyce Miller, 'Some findings from the Survey of Scottish Witchcraft', in Goodare, Martin and Miller (eds.), *Witchcraft and Belief*, 51–70, at pp. 55–8.
23. *APS*, vi, II, 463 (RPS, 1649/5/198).
24. SSW, case reference C/JO/2860. These 48 were counted, because the numbers were known. The Survey of Scottish Witchcraft estimated that Coutts named about 88 people altogether in early 1650; the remainder were allowed for elsewhere in the Survey's figures.
25. Hughes, 'The 1649–50 Scottish Witch-Hunt', 189–90.
26. Brian P. Levack, 'Witch-hunting in revolutionary Britain', in his *Witch-Hunting in Scotland: Law, Politics and Religion* (London, 2008), 55–80, at p. 74.
27. Lauren Martin, 'Scottish witchcraft panics re-examined', in Goodare, Martin and Miller (eds.), *Witchcraft and Belief*, 119–43, at p. 123.
28. SSW.

29. Macdonald, *Witches of Fife*, 108, 113.
30. See in general W. N. Neill, 'The professional pricker and his test for witchcraft', *SHR*, 19 (1922), 205–13.
31. NRS, CH2/295/3, p. 121a.
32. Ibid., pp. 114–15.
33. NRS, CH2/185/6, pp. 114–15.
34. NRS, PA12/5.
35. *APS*, vi, II, 564–6 (RPS, M1650/5/6).
36. Martin, 'Scottish witchcraft panics re-examined', 123–5.
37. Larner cited this as a reason why the witch-hunt as a whole was concentrated in this area: Christina Larner, *Enemies of God: The Witch-Hunt in Scotland* (London, 1981), 80.
38. Martin, 'Scottish witchcraft panics re-examined', 124–5.
39. Macdonald, *Witches of Fife*, 25; cf. Larner, *Enemies of God*, 80–8.
40. NRS, PA12/5, March minutes.
41. NRS, CH2/185/6, p. 124.
42. NRS, PA12/5, November warrants.
43. Ibid.
44. *APS*, vi, II, 614 (RPS, M1650/11/18).
45. Goodare, 'Witch-hunting and the Scottish state', 122.
46. Ibid., 136.

6

Reputation and Witch-Hunting in Seventeenth-Century Dalkeith

Anna Cordey

The witch's reputation in the community is a well-established theme, but still capable of further development with the aid of detailed studies. Many studies of 'reputation' have focused on the question of how people came to be suspected of witchcraft by their neighbours – a vital question, but nevertheless one that tends to focus on certain types of witches. Such witches certainly existed in Scotland. It is not always clear how a decision was taken to prosecute a neighbourhood witch, but records of Scottish prosecutions often show neighbours contributing to the process, testifying to quarrels, curses, bewitchments, enmities and reconciliations – sometimes going back for several decades. It is easy to see these witches' reputations as the mainspring that drove their prosecution. However, in Scotland as in many other places, a reputation for witchcraft among neighbours was not the only driving force for prosecutions; people could also be named by another confessing witch. It has not always been clear whether such people had reputations or not.

This chapter conducts an in-depth examination of the nature and functions of reputations for witchcraft in Scotland. It is based on a case-study of the presbytery of Dalkeith, a group of sixteen parishes near Edinburgh, in the period 1649–1662 when there were two significant witchcraft panics (1649–1650 and 1661–1662). As will be seen, the study embraces witches who had reputations among their neighbours and witches who did not. It makes suggestions on how to prove that a given witch did not have a prior reputation. It also argues that a few of the 'reputations' that appear to emerge from the records can be seen, on closer inspection, to be illusory.

I

Witches usually acquired reputations by being seen to cause misfortunes. Misfortunes, however, were not randomly attributed to the nearest witch, merely because they were inexplicable to the people of the seventeenth century. Robin Briggs has shown that peasants did not believe witches to be randomly cruel: they chose their targets.[1] Alan Macfarlane was the first to show in detail that the association of a misfortune with witchcraft would tend to follow a quarrel where the suspected witch had been treated badly. The person who had abused the witch, violating the duties of good neighbourhood, would feel a sense of guilt. This guilt, combined with fear if the woman (and it was usually a woman) already had a reputation for witchcraft and had cursed them, could lead to the desire to blame them for any misfortunes. The feeling of guilt was transferred and the victim–bully roles reversed.[2] David Sabean saw this model at work in Germany and wrote about it in terms of power relations, with the weak being feared by the strong.[3]

Women's tongues often got them into trouble. Curses and threats uttered in the heat of anger at an injustice could backfire if the person they were aimed at suffered in some way afterwards. There is rarely a sense in the trial records of which cases caused a reputation to begin, which cases were remembered differently once a reputation had grown and which cases added to this reputation. Clive Holmes has commented that many charges presented in court in England were for crimes which had supposedly taken place many years before, but had not been reported at the time.[4] The most we can expect from trial records is an idea of the general circumstances surrounding the growth of reputation. However, parish records can sometimes give us an idea of how a suspected witch had behaved in the years leading up to an official accusation.

Where future witches appeared in kirk session records before their official accusation, it was almost always in cases involving words. They were either being punished for scolding or cursing, or they were pursuing a slander case against another member of the community. The fact that witches were often women with short tempers and sharp tongues has been noted in many studies. Christina Larner wrote that having a 'ready, sharp and angry tongue' was a major characteristic of the witch: 'No cursing: no malefice: no witch.'[5] John Harrison's work on the use of branks as a punishment for scolding women is also useful. He shows that the social profile of the 'scold' in Stirling was similar to the profile of the Scottish witch. She was an established member of the community, yet was generally poor and she scolded others of around the same social status. Harrison comments that the branks were used most often at the times of greatest concern with witchcraft in Scotland. These women, he concludes, *could* have become witches, but were not suspected of witchcraft because their curses and threats did not appear to come true.[6]

Several women in Dalkeith were charged with serious cursing during this period, but were never accused of witchcraft. Marion Leach, in Newbattle, was charged with 'bid[d]ing the devill rugg [i.e. tear] the heart out of Elspeth Sympsoun'. Marion Wilson, in Dalkeith, got into trouble for saying that she would give herself to the Devil to have amends of Alexander Calderwood and Alexander Dickson.[7] These women were all felt deserving of punishment and correction, but despite their entreaties to the Devil, they were not suspected of witchcraft. Their threats were not believed to have taken effect.

The family feud between Isobel Ferguson and her son, which ended with his death in 1661, began similarly, but then took a more sinister turn. Ferguson first got into trouble with the session in September 1658. She was charged with swearing, 'saying to her daughter in law god put her sonne and her together but shoe should mak the devill separat them'. The shocked session warned her that they would 'see what her cariag sall be hearafter'.[8] This was recalled in 1661, when it was further alleged that she had threatened her son. He had gone on a trip, 'and hee not taken leave of his mother'. Ferguson went to his house and told her daughter-in-law that, because of his slight, there would be no joy in his homecoming – 'and [it] was well known that fell so out, for he came home that night exceeding sick and continued grievouslie tormented till he died'.[9] Ferguson's first appearance in front of the kirk session aroused attention, but was not followed by a misfortune. The second threat seemed to predict the death of her son, which did occur; this pointed to witchcraft.

Curses by suspected witches could take a variety of forms. There were specific predictions that precise things would happen, such as death or paralysis or loss of wealth. Often, threats were generalised, such as a promise that a person would regret saying or doing something that had hurt the witch. Isobel Ferguson's threat against her son was like this. In some cases, the witch would shout, perhaps clapping her hands. In others, she would walk away muttering.

Yet there are several cases which cannot be explained by the reversal of guilt. Occasionally there is no record of a quarrel, but an indication that victims believed the witch to be acting out of malice or jealousy. Ferguson's neighbours commented that they had been poorer since they had lived next to her. She said that they would get even poorer before they grew richer and, over the next two years, five of their horses died. In another example, Margaret Erskine commented on Bessie Bell's good health. Bell immediately began to experience chest pains, her body swelled up and she collapsed.[10]

II

Cursing was not the only suspicious activity by which a person could acquire a reputation for witchcraft. Attempting to flee when accused, or even beforehand, as in the cases of Christian Wilson and Janet Watson, were signs of a guilty conscience.[11] Several other causes for suspicion can be mentioned more briefly, such as a victim dreaming of the witch, seeing her at a sickbed or deathbed, or as they died, calling on surviving relatives to bring to justice the witch responsible. Jean Forrest fell out with Janet Cock, and Jean's child died that night. Forrest cried, 'Alace that ever I had to doe with that witch Janet Cock, for she has bein at my bed syd all this night standing and I could not be rid of her and behold the [*illegible*] of it my child is dead.'[12] William Richardson, who killed Christian Wilson's hen, saw Wilson by his bedside 'in the likenes of ane Gray Catt'.[13] These nocturnal visions look like cases of sleep paralysis.[14] James Douglas was so certain that Janet Cock was the cause of his death that he was even reported to have said, 'Lord forgive my friends if they doe not garre [i.e. cause] burne her, for under god said he schoe is the cause of my death and I leave it upone her.'[15] The importance of the spoken word in early modern society gave these words real potency.[16]

Other kinds of reputation-creating behaviour could occur after the death of a possible victim. Christian Wilson was suspected for causing the death of her brother because she had frequently argued with him, showed no grief at his death and refused to visit the body. When she was eventually forced to do so by the bailie and minister, she went reluctantly and reportedly shook all the way. She was compelled to touch the body in a ritual known as bierricht. When she did so, blood rushed out of his wounds, though there had been no 'apeirance of a spot of blood either upone his bodie or nigh to it' before.[17]

Similar to suspicion aroused by a lack of grief was a refusal to be reconciled with a neighbour after a quarrel. Reconciliation rituals were important. Janet Cock refused an offer 'to make agriement' as follows: 'Malitiouslie and bitterlie giurning and gnashing your teith, and beating your hands upon your knees said O! them that called me a witch.'[18] If Cock had agreed to a reconciliation, this would have formed part of a pattern that often led to the victim of witchcraft being cured of their illness. When a woman agreed to cure somebody believed to be bewitched, it was often assumed that she was either taking responsibility for the bewitchment or she was confirming that she had the power to remove such maladies. This could assist the growth of a reputation in the long term, even though it defused the immediate quarrel.

III

This leads on to the issue of 'charmers' in the sense of people who offered their services as healers and diviners. Charmers were distinct from witches; they were self-professed, whereas witches were labelled by others. For most people, the local healer or charmer offered the only medical attention they could ever hope to receive. Nevertheless, a charmer could sometimes acquire a reputation for witchcraft. Space precludes a full discussion of this topic, which has been covered by others from other angles.[19] Here it seems more appropriate to focus on one particular type of healer: the midwife.

David Harley has stressed that midwives were vital members of the community and would normally have been respected, rather than feared as witches.[20] Harley's arguments have effectively undermined the idea that charmers and midwives were systematically targeted during witch-hunts. Yet, it is possible to move too far towards the other extreme. In Dalkeith, it is clear that the authorities saw charming as suspicious: scratch the surface and it was likely that something more damning was going on. And charming and midwifery seem to have been linked.

This can be illustrated from the cases of two witches. In the first, Agnes Johnstone was accused of two counts of charming. When Agnes Alexander was having trouble giving birth, Johnstone put salt in her mouth and said, 'Our Ladie said, and sooth she said, that after birth salt never hade'. Johnstone was also accused of curing Thomas Thompson's bad eye with a stone.[21] Questioned, both of Johnstone's clients refused to take any responsibility. Alexander claimed that she was in so much pain that she did not know what she was doing. Thompson said that he did not know whether it was the stone that had healed his eye, but that he would have nothing to do with Johnstone ever again. The session eventually passed on her details to the 'civill magistrate' who they hoped 'wold lay hands on hir for witchcraft'.[22] The attitude of Johnstone's clients hardly points to a loyal regard for their local midwife and healer. In the second case, Beatrix Leslie was also suspected of using charming in the birthing chamber. William Young and Agnes Acheson were terrified of her after their friendship with her broke down; both had nightmares that she was devouring them. The fact that Leslie had been Acheson's midwife did not make them trust and respect her once the relationship had failed; rather, it caused further unease because they were aware of her abilities.[23] Again, sleep paralysis seems to have been involved.

The last major factor which could lead to the creation of a reputation was being known to be associated with an existing witch. There are several cases, particularly in the kirk session records, which demonstrate how dangerous it was to be a witch's friend or relative. Larner saw the accusation of 'witch's get' as a common first stage in the labelling process.[24] However, there were only two instances in Dalkeith where association with known witches led to a formal accusation by a neighbour. The first was that of Margaret Walker and her daughter Janet Currie.[25] The other was that of Agnes Hill, accused because of her friendship with the witch Agnes Lawson; she visited Lawson in prison.[26] The inhabitants of Dalkeith presbytery probably did believe in this kind of guilt by association, but they had few opportunities to articulate it. Usually, kirk sessions treated such accusations as slanders. In both Newton and Inveresk, sessions issued warnings to their parishioners that people labelled 'witch's get' would be protected by the church and that those doing the labelling would be harshly dealt with.[27]

IV

Women who were called witches by their neighbours, even in a fit of passion, were frequently not content to let the matter lie. To allow such a slur to pass would be to acquiesce in the name of witch. In London, Laura Gowing has found that an individual would be assumed guilty until they had publicly proven their integrity. A case of slander was not a private affair. A woman who had been accused of being a whore or a witch wanted her accuser to be rebuked publicly, so that the whole community could take note and gossip accordingly. To bring a slander case was to change the dynamics of the quarrel.[28]

There were several different types of slander case in Dalkeith. The first was the isolated incident, when, during a quarrel or when drunk, one member of the community called another a witch. When that person complained to the session, these incidents usually ended with the guilty person apologising. One such case occurred in Newton in 1661, when Margaret Adams complained that John Wilson had called her a witch and had also uttered 'abominable oaths'. When he appeared before the session, he expressed his sorrow, explaining that he was drunk at the time.[29] Such isolated cases, where the complainer never appeared in the records again and where the slanderer meekly faced the music, ended perfectly for those whose good names had been restored.

The second type of slander case was where the litigant appeared several times. It seems that when a person was often called a witch and complained to the session, mud was eventually bound to stick. This was probably what happened to Janet Cock. She complained in 1645, 1655 and 1659 that neighbours had called her a witch, and the session found in her favour each time, but she was still ultimately tried for witchcraft in 1661. There seems to have been a shift in the session's attitude. In 1655, they dealt harshly with Walter Lithgow, who was made to acknowledge 'that he had scandalized Jonet Cocks good name' and gave 'signes of his sorrow for the same'. By 1659, however, Helen Wilson confessed that she had called Cock a witch, but there is no record of any 'good name' or any particular outrage at what she had done.[30] It is possible that Cock's reputation had grown by this stage and that the session were becoming uneasy.

Bringing a case to the kirk session was to announce publicly that you had been called a witch, and this could attract unwelcome attention. Geillis Chartes pursued a slander case against John Lawrie, but unfortunately for her, Isobel Ferguson was questioned before the same meeting for witchcraft. Ferguson named Chartes as a co-conspirator, probably because her name was fresh in her mind in association with the word 'witch'. Chartes was arrested, pricked for the mark and imprisoned, the clerk noting perhaps redundantly that she had lost her case against Lawrie.[31] Meg Shanks chastised her daughter, Margaret Erskine, for going to the session as she was just drawing attention to herself.[32] There was a fine line between upholding a good reputation and undermining an already shaky one.

None of the witnesses in Erskine's case actually acknowledged that they had called her or thought her a witch. They were, however, willing to cast suspicion upon her in a roundabout way by relating strange tales about sinister events which had occurred around her. This is the third type of slander case, where witnesses essentially said, 'no, but' to the session when asked if they had called a person a witch. Both Bessie Bell and Isobel Watt related tales of sudden illnesses which passed only when Erskine touched them. Aware that her case was going badly, Erskine attempted to deflect suspicion of witchcraft onto another woman, Elspeth Scott, who, Erskine said, had made her ill for two weeks.[33] Another example took place in Penicuik in 1661. Three women, Christian Purdie, Agnes Elphinstone and Marion Tweedie complained to the kirk session that John Louvine had been calling them witches. He denied the charge, but he did recount a suspicious story, telling of how he had arrived home late one night on his horse. He claimed to have gone to investigate a fire in a field and to have seen the women dancing around the fire, waving handkerchiefs. He added that he was ill that night and that his horse died two days later.[34] Why were these people casting suspicion without being prepared to go the whole way and accuse a suspected witch in front of the session?

V

It seems clear that in these cases, the witnesses did believe that the women were guilty. There are several possible reasons why they refused to voice their suspicions. Robin Briggs found that peasants might not be willing to go to the authorities because they mistrusted central courts and felt cheated if a witch was found innocent.[35] This is possible, but no Dalkeith evidence supports it directly. David Sabean suggests that in some cases, peasants would not call someone a witch before the authorities because the witch was too powerful within the community. Only when she had lost some power or position would others be prepared to attack.[36] This could be applied to Janet Cock, who appears to have had some standing in Dalkeith as a healer and petty trader. She was called a witch informally by neighbours at least seven times over the years. Yet until 1661, there was no official investigation of her. What, if this was the case, could have caused the sudden shift in power relations? A possible explanation is the involvement of a central figure of authority who altered the dynamics of power at work in the community.

A reluctance to accuse a neighbour at the kirk session may seem like a denial of the legitimacy of the court. Were the peasants making the point that they did not want these people burnt at the stake – that it was just going too far? Stuart Macdonald notes that people in Fife were willing to testify in a trial, but would not initiate proceedings.[37] This seems to have been the attitude in Dalkeith too. Where there were specific accusations for witchcraft or charming to a kirk session, they almost always came from session elders rather than ordinary villagers, even though there was no shortage of witnesses once a trial got under way. It is possible that a shift in the balance of power was caused by the involvement of the elder.

It seems that peasants had their own ways of dealing with witches and that they generally felt no real *need* for official punishment. Robin Briggs suggests that some people were reluctant to admit their suspicions because they still hoped for reconciliation within the community.[38] The methods used to manage neighbourhood witches in Dalkeith tend to match those used across Scotland and elsewhere.[39] There are examples of attempting to avoid her, appeasing her with gifts of food, confronting her aggressively and demanding that she or another witch remove an illness. Added to this was the insidious power of gossip and rumour to undermine the position of a suspected witch. As Briggs writes, witches were a part of everyday life in the early modern period: they were just another hazard which people had to deal with. Trial records show only a small part of this.[40] After all, peasants did not believe in witches only during the panics – they lived with them day in, day out. There were probably witches in many parishes who never came to trial at all, but lived out their lives with a reputation. The local people would realise the danger and deal with it in their own way.

In general, the people of Dalkeith needed to be galvanised into action, and there were plenty of men in positions of power who were willing to take on this role. The active witch-hunters of Dalkeith are beyond the scope of this chapter, but it is clear that the region cannot fit Briggs's model in which, once a panic was under way, almost all cases were initiated by the peasantry.[41] Both Christina Larner and Julian Goodare have opted for a more complex interpretation, essentially focusing on the co-operation between central and local elites and emphasising the involvement of all levels of society.[42] While central authorities provided the system with which to prosecute witches, local authorities initiated proceedings, and the peasantry provided evidence and the base belief in witches which fuelled the whole process. However, without pressure from their social superiors, the peasantry would not take their grievances about witches to the kirk session. In general, as in Margaret Erskine's case, they would even be slow to admit *suspecting* witchcraft in a neighbour.

VI

This suggests that the importance of reputation may have been over-emphasised. Returning to the question of the evidence on which 'reputation' is based, further reasons may be suggested to question its importance. Those suspects who had long-term reputations attract more attention because they generated the most paperwork. It is clear, however, that many witches in Dalkeith had no prior reputation, but were swept up in the panics of the time, their convictions based on confessions of demonic pacts. Moreover, the concept of 'reputation' itself is not a simple one; it requires careful scrutiny.

There are three main types of evidence for the existence of a reputation. Firstly, and best known, there are witness statements, in pre-trial or trial records, where neighbours testify to past events. Secondly, there are previous slander cases. These are particularly useful in not being coloured by hindsight, but need to be treated carefully as evidence for community attitudes. If the record shows a kirk session decreeing that someone should not have been called a witch, this evidence does not usually tell us whether the wider community agreed or not, though indications can be gleaned from repeated slander cases. Thirdly, witches' confessions frequently recorded how long ago she or he had made the demonic pact. A suspect who was known to have a reputation would probably have been encouraged by an interrogator to name a date which took this reputation into account. By contrast, if a suspect had no known reputation, this would imply that the pact was likely to have been recent and a date a few months earlier would be given. Janet Cock, Isobel Ferguson, Christian Wilson, Beatrix Leslie and Janet Peaston, who can all be seen to have had reputations, admitted to pacts lasting twenty-four, forty, thirty, seven and four years, respectively.[43] Such women tended to be accused and investigated first in a hunt. It was then that chain accusation began to become an issue.

Confessing witches often named others who already had reputations, but not always. Figure 6.1 shows a chain of accusations in diagram form. The accusations begin with Isobel Ferguson; she names three others, two who seem to have had reputations – Geillis Chartes and Beatrix Leslie – and one who probably did not – Christian Paterson. Paterson confessed only to having been the Devil's servant for a few months.[44] However, in her confession she did name other witches, including Chartes and indeed Ferguson; such mutual accusations seem to have been thought to add weight to the case against all those involved. Reputation and 'ill fame' were helpful in securing a conviction at trial, but it was not vital. This was, after all, a secret crime and lack of reputation was no proof of innocence. The confession, on the other hand, was extremely important in the trial process. Brian Levack has found that a trial commission was almost impossible to gain if the suspected witch had not confessed beforehand.[45] Where there was no reputation, the confession was even more significant.

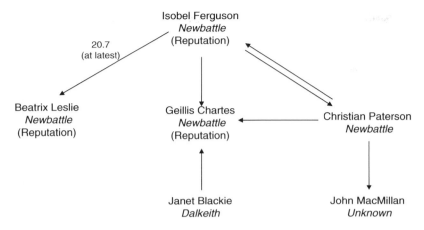

Figure 6.1 Chain of accusations, Newbattle, 1661

Of the twenty-four people for whom investigation and confession documents exist from 1661, only four appear not to have been taken to trial. Eight certainly had reputations, three may have done and thirteen almost certainly did not. Only one of these thirteen, William King, never confessed – and he was never tried. Two others withdrew their confessions, Agnes Thomson stating that she had been lying and Margaret Stevenson claiming to have been tortured; they too were not tried.[46] This leaves nine people who seem to have had no reputations who still confessed and were tried. Many of them had been named by other confessing witches, and they in turn named several others.

A different story is told by a more wide-ranging chain, shown in Figure 6.2. Accusations frequently cross parish boundaries; here there are witches from two adjacent parishes, Newton and Inveresk. Moreover, the web is not self-contained. Janet Dail, David Johnstone, William King, Agnes Johnstone, Janet Lyle and Elspeth Haliburton are its main constituents, but the panic spreads more widely when Margaret Ramage begins to name further witches.

This web is also interesting as it spreads widely over time as well as space, giving insight into how social memory worked. In her confession in 1661 Janet Dail mentioned that she had been in a house with Margaret Barbour and Agnes Anderson when she made the pact. These two women had been tried by commission in 1649.[47] Dail may have made this claim either because it made her story appear more realistic or because she had a reputation based on her association with

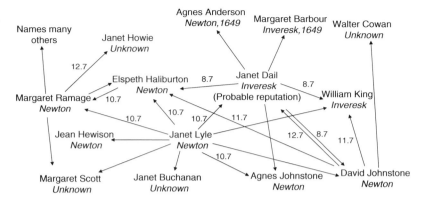

Figure 6.2   Chain of accusations, Newton and Inveresk, 1661

these two known witches.[48] Margaret Bannatyne (not a member of this group) illustrates another aspect of social memory. She was from Crichton and was mentioned as Agnes Williamson's accomplice in 1662. Williamson was from Haddington, and there is no record of any proceedings against Bannatyne during the 1661–1662 hunt. However, she appeared again in 1678 as an accomplice to various witches from Crichton and Haddington, and was made to confront several of them.[49] This shows how easy it was for reputations to be created and to stick, even for seventeen years.

Several conclusions suggest themselves in the light of these examples of chain accusation. The first is that merely to be accused by a confessing witch was extremely dangerous. The witch at the start of a chain or web frequently had a reputation. Being named could lead to arrest, interrogation, confrontation, pricking and confession. The practice of making witches confront each other was certainly important here. This took place on many occasions in Dalkeith. The action of making the accused face the confessing witch and being challenged forcefully in front of witnesses must have been dramatic and compelling. The confrontation would often be followed by pricking, and these two events together would be enough to convince witnesses of her guilt. Even if the case was dropped later, the local population would always think of her as a witch. Sir George Mackenzie highlighted the dread that seized one accused woman, who said that she would rather die than go back into society now that she had been imprisoned for witchcraft. She told him that she had not confest because she was guilty, but being a poor creature, who wrought for her meat and being defam'd for a Witch she knew she would starve, for no person thereafter would either give her meat or lodging, and that all men would beat her, and hound Dogs at her, and that therefore she desired to be out of the World.[50]

Mackenzie was active in the Dalkeith and Musselburgh areas in 1661 and the manuscripts show that he interviewed several accused witches in the Musselburgh tolbooth. The woman whom he described was probably Janet Dail. She mentioned that she was terrified, though not of the justices. She said that she had refused to confess at first, 'for fear of shame of the world'.[51]

The second point about chain accusation was that, as several people were all naming each other, this gave added weight to the case against each of them. Janet Watson named three other people. After pricking, they in turn named her.[52] This would seem to be a far more compelling case in court or in a request for a commission. Thirdly, accusation chains undoubtedly added to fears of the witchcraft conspiracy. Julian Goodare has also come to this conclusion, seeing the naming of accomplices as promoting the belief that there was an underground movement of witches.[53] Lastly, the phenomenon meant that the role of the peasant was practically removed from the equation. They were not involved in interrogation and the demand for more names from accused witches. The responsibility for this must lie with the local elites – the men who were also primarily responsible for producing suspects.

VII

Much has been said about witches with long reputations. Robin Briggs has written: 'Alleged lengths of reputation are more accurate than not, although it is hard to see how this could be proven.'[54] It would certainly be desirable to find a way of evaluating the long reputations which appear, retrospectively, in the trial records. The Dalkeith evidence cannot answer this question conclusively, but some questions can be posed and answers suggested.

After a person with no reputation had been named by a witch, been interrogated and had confessed, was it possible that an 'instant reputation' could build up around her with the aid of hindsight? Could 'ill fame' be created at will? This question is extremely difficult and, in relation to Dalkeith, impossible to answer definitively. However, some clues are suggestive. One is the way in which the words 'ill fame' or 'notorious witch' were used. These words would seem to indicate a long-standing reputation, but in fact they could be used to describe individuals who had simply been named by one or more confessing witches and had then confessed themselves. This process made them into 'notorious witches' overnight. Bessie Moffat, who confessed that she had made the pact only a couple of months before, was mentioned in a list of 'notorious witches' in Elspeth Graham's indictment. William King was listed as one of a number of 'notorious witches' in the Musselburgh meeting of the justiciary court on 28 July 1661, even though he had refused to confess and was never actually tried. It is likely that once this had happened, the community would then begin to remember misfortunes and interpret them with hindsight into instances of bewitchment. The accused witch could then be fed more directly into the flow-chart of reputation and accusation. Janet Dail's fearful attitude certainly suggests that people would now consider her a confirmed witch.

Another way in which 'instant reputation' may have occurred was through the intervention of local figures of authority. Mary and Janet Colden, Janet Cock's daughters, wrote to the justice general and his deputes, begging for justice for their mother, who they claimed was being framed for witchcraft by William Scott, the bailie of Dalkeith. He was single-handedly turning everybody against their mother and dragging up old arguments; people were complying because they were frightened of him. He had apparently taken all her money and property, and was going round town to all Cock's former friends and getting them to tell stories about her. They said that the whole town was 'afraide of him because he is heids man in the town'. Furthermore, they suggested that his determination was down to a personal grudge as he blamed Cock for the death of one of his children, although Mary and Janet pointed out that five of his other children had died too.[55]

If there is any truth in this letter, and we must allow for exaggeration, the implications are extremely interesting. There can be no doubt that Janet Cock had a long-standing reputation. However, if Scott was visiting people with whom Cock had solved her differences and getting them to testify against her by remembering quarrels and misfortunes in new ways, it is possible that this aggravated her reputation as it ultimately appeared. There are in fact some inconsistencies between the indictments and witness statements, suggesting that whoever provided information for the indictment – in which Scott had a role – had seriously exaggerated some of the evidence. In court, witnesses were unwilling to testify to these embellished accounts. The dittay (indictment) for Cock's second trial said that James Ritchie was ill for six months after a dispute with her. In court, he said that he did not become ill at all, he only lost some money. Robert Hardie said that William Hardie, who it was claimed had become ill straight away and then died, had only become ill two to three weeks after the dispute and had lived for six years afterwards.[56]

Janet Cock's case is unusual in that there is so much paperwork surviving and that the prosecutors had so much personal enmity towards her. How often this sort of behaviour occurred cannot be estimated. However, the fact that it happened at all means that it may have done so again. To be a woman with a reputation was undoubtedly dangerous, but it is also clear that many of those formally accused did not have a reputation and that a damning case could be built around almost anybody.

VIII

This study has allowed a detailed view of the conflicts and exchanges which occurred in day-to-day village life. The development of reputation was a complex business, of which the documents can show us only a small part. However, a local study has meant that individual people have been examined, along with their relationships and activities in order to gain a fuller picture. Here, general ideas about witch-hunting may be put to the test. The situation in Dalkeith has particularly highlighted the fact that the peasantry were specific in whom they believed to be a witch. Witches were rarely, if ever, randomly cruel, and misfortunes tended to follow quarrels, where a specific curse or threat had been uttered.

Dalkeith people did not fear witches because they were allied with the Devil, but because they were able to cause misery and distress. The witch of Dalkeith, although powerful and able to cause disease, death and the disruption of household activities, did not have the huge and devastating ability of some other Scottish and European witches. If she damaged crops, it was only a small area or amount, rather than the food for an entire settlement. Dalkeith witches did not control the weather, as many European witches were believed to do. Other forms of witchcraft, such as the evil eye and demonic possession, occurred rarely, if ever.

Neighbours certainly recognised particular individuals as witches and engaged in familiar strategies of conciliation and avoidance. They rarely initiated prosecutions, however, preferring to leave this to the church elders. They were often willing to testify against known witches once prosecutions had begun, but in some cases they can be seen attempting to avoid doing this. Moreover, it can be argued that the witches with reputations were only a minority of those accused. Most witches were caught up in chain-reaction hunts in which a confessing witch named accomplices. In these, accusations by other witchcraft suspects did not usually rest on a prior reputation among the community. Some 'reputations' appear to have been created by the process of accusation, since some of those accused escaped prosecution during one panic, only to be arrested again during another, without any indication of neighbours' testimony against them. And when neighbours were invited to reinterpret earlier events, as in Janet Cock's case, we can see how an 'instant reputation' could be created.

There was, therefore, a link between reputation and witch-hunting – but only an indirect one. Witches were often *assumed* to possess 'ill fame'. Some people who had existing reputations for witchcraft were prosecuted for it. Quite possibly, however, some people with reputations for witchcraft escaped prosecution; this is inherently hard to prove, and the Dalkeith records are no more than suggestive. What the records do show more clearly is that during the panics, when chain-reaction hunts occurred, numerous people *without* reputations were dragged in, being named by another confessing witch. It was this, rather than existing reputations, that drove the panics.

Notes

1. Robin Briggs, *Communities of Belief: Cultural and Social Tension in Early Modern France* (Oxford, 1989), 74.
2. Alan Macfarlane, *Witchcraft in Tudor and Stuart England* (London, 1970), 196.
3. David W. Sabean, *Power in the Blood: Popular Culture and Village Discourse in Early Modern Germany* (Cambridge, 1984), 148, 153. Cf. Briggs, *Communities of Belief*, 108.
4. Clive Holmes, 'Women: witnesses and witches', *Past and Present*, 140 (August 1993), 45–78, at p. 55. Briggs has also identified difficulties with evidence given in retrospect: Robin Briggs, *Witches and Neighbours: The Social and Cultural Context of European Witchcraft* (2nd edn., Oxford, 2002), 17.
5. Christina Larner, *Enemies of God: The Witch-Hunt in Scotland* (London, 1981), 97. Cf. D. E. Underdown, 'The taming of the scold: the enforcement of patriarchal authority in early modern England', in Anthony Fletcher and John Stevenson (eds.), *Order and Disorder in Early Modern England* (Cambridge, 1985), 116–36, at p. 120; Macfarlane, *Witchcraft*, 158–9; Briggs, *Witches and Neighbours*, 23.
6. John G. Harrison, 'Women and the branks in Stirling, *c.*1600 to *c.*1730', *Scottish Economic and Social History*, 18 (1998), 114–31.

7. NRS, Newbattle kirk session minutes, CH2/276/4, 27 November to 29 December 1661; Dalkeith kirk session minutes, CH2/84/3, 16 July to 13 August 1661.

8. NRS, Newbattle kirk session minutes, CH2/276/4, 26 September 1658, 10 October 1658.

9. NRS, Newbattle kirk session minutes, CH2/276/4, 3 July 1661.

10. NRS, HCP, JC26/27/9, item 18; Newbattle kirk session minutes, CH/276/4, 1 November 1654.

11. NRS, HCP, JC26/27/9, items 2, 5.

12. NRS, books of adjournal, JC2/11, fos. 46v., 43r.

13. NRS, HCP, JC26/27/9, item 2.

14. See Margaret Dudley and Julian Goodare, 'Outside in or inside out: sleep paralysis and Scottish witchcraft', Chapter 7 in this volume.

15. NRS, HCP, JC26/27/3, item 12.

16. Cf. Larner, *Enemies of God*, 143.

17. Another incident occurred with Beatrix Leslie. Two girls who had angered her were killed by a falling roof in a coal pit. Neither body bled until Beatrix was brought to their bodies. See NRS, HCP, JC26/27/9, items 2, 7, 19.

18. NRS, books of adjournal, JC2/11, fo. 43r.

19. Joyce Miller, 'Devices and directions: folk healing aspects of witchcraft practice in seventeenth-century Scotland', in Julian Goodare (ed.), *The Scottish Witch-Hunt in Context* (Manchester, 2002), 90–105; Owen Davies, 'A comparative perspective on Scottish cunning-folk and charmers', in Julian Goodare, Lauren Martin and Joyce Miller (eds.), *Witchcraft and Belief in Early Modern Scotland* (Basingstoke, 2008), 185–205.

20. David Harley, 'Historians as demonologists: the myth of the midwife-witch', *Social History of Medicine*, 3 (1990), 1–26.

21. NRS, Newton kirk session minutes, CH2/283/2, 11–18 August 1661. For magical use of stones, see Joyce Miller, *Myth and Magic: Scotland's Ancient Beliefs and Sacred Places* (Musselburgh, 2000), 109.

22. NRS, Newton kirk session minutes, CH2/283/2, 15 September 1661.

23. NRS, HCP, JC26/27/9, item 19.

24. Larner, *Enemies of God*, 99.

25. *RPC*, 3rd ser., i, 74. Little more is known of them as their trial was by commission.

26. NRS, Dalkeith kirk session minutes, CH2/84/3, 30 July 1661. Hill was eventually tried by commission: *APS*, vii, 283.

27. In Carrington, the minister and elders attempted to make peace between two couples who had fallen out after one man had called another 'witch's get' and refused to withdraw his claim: NRS, Carrington kirk session minutes, CH2/62/1, 15 September to 24 November 1661.

28. Laura Gowing, *Domestic Dangers: Women, Words and Sex in Early Modern London* (Oxford, 1996), 135.

29. NRS, Newton kirk session minutes, CH2/283/2, 25 August to 20 October 1661.

30. NRS, Dalkeith kirk session minutes, CH2/84/2, 5–17 July 1655, 6 March to 2 May 1659.

31. NRS, Newbattle kirk session minutes, CH2/276/4, 23 June to 10 July 1661.

32. Ibid., 1–22 November 1654.

33. Ibid., 1–29 November 1654.
34. NRS, Penicuik kirk session minutes, CH2/297/1, 29 December 1661 to 12 January 1662.
35. Briggs, *Communities of Belief*, 43.
36. Sabean, *Power in the Blood*, 109.
37. Stuart Macdonald, *The Witches of Fife: Witch-Hunting in a Scottish Shire, 1560–1710* (East Linton, 2002), 177.
38. Briggs, *Witches and Neighbours*, 67–8.
39. Julian Goodare, 'Women and the witch-hunt in Scotland', *Social History*, 23 (1998), 288–308, at p. 298; Macfarlane, *Witchcraft*, 103–10; Briggs, *Communities of Belief*, 26.
40. Briggs, *Communities of Belief*, 28, 63.
41. Ibid., 63.
42. Larner, *Enemies of God*, 83–5; Julian Goodare, 'Witch-hunting and the Scottish state', in Goodare (ed.), *The Scottish Witch-Hunt in Context*, 122–45, at pp. 138–9. There has been debate over the respective roles of central and local elites, but that is a separate issue. See Brian P. Levack, 'Absolutism, state-building, and witchcraft', in his *Witch-Hunting in Scotland: Law, Politics and Religion* (London, 2008), 98–114.
43. NRS, books of adjournal, JC2/11, fo. 35v.; HCP, JC26/27/9, items 17, 2, 9, 5.
44. NRS, HCP, JC26/27/9, item 13.
45. Brian P. Levack, 'Judicial torture in Scotland during the age of Mackenzie', *Miscellany of the Stair Society*, iv (2002), 185–98, at p. 195. Cf. Macdonald, *Witches of Fife*, 134–6.
46. NRS, HCP, JC26/27/2, item 6.
47. Ibid., item 5; NRS, register of the committee of estates, PA11/8, 16 October to 20 November 1649.
48. NRS, HCP, JC26/27/9, item 13. Christian Paterson (Chain 1) mentioned John MacMillan in her confessions as having been at meetings with her, although he had been executed over four years before she made the pact at Martinmas 1660.
49. SSW.
50. Sir George Mackenzie, *Laws and Customes of Scotland in Matters Criminal* (Edinburgh, 1678), 87. This passage has been much quoted ever since Sir Walter Scott drew attention to it in *Letters on Demonology and Witchcraft* (London, 1884; first published 1830), 237–8.
51. NRS, HCP, JC26/27/2, item 6.
52. NRS, HCP, JC26/27/9, items 5, 8, 10, 13; NRS, papers of the Society of Antiquaries of Scotland, depositions against witches, GD103/2/3/11, 21–26 July 1661.
53. Goodare, 'Witch-hunting and the Scottish state', 137.
54. Briggs, *Witches and Neighbours*, 17.
55. NRS, HCP, JC26/27/9, item 20.
56. NRS, books of adjournal, JC2/11, fos. 45v., 46r.

7

Outside In or Inside Out: Sleep Paralysis and Scottish Witchcraft

Margaret Dudley and Julian Goodare

These two stories may seem to have little in common – especially since the people who tell them are separated by some three centuries:

> Once every month since then, the Devil appeared to you, sometimes in a house, and sometimes in the fields, in various shapes and likenesses; sometimes in the shape of a beast, and sometimes in the shape of a man; and made you kiss him in several places, and worship him on your knees as your lord.[1]

> I went to bed and lay down and felt a tickling up my side; had a flash, a vision of the following scene. I was standing in the kitchen and I opened the door, and there he stood. A tall alien in a blue and black wet suit. He was skinny, bald, with a narrow head, big eyes, and light skin. He scared me profoundly.[2]

The first story is an extract from the dittay (indictment) of Marion Grant who was executed for witchcraft in Aberdeen in 1597. The second story was related by an anonymous person claiming contacts with UFOs, and describes an alien abduction experience. Both describe beings that are outside our modern scientific understanding of proof. Throughout recorded history people have made claims of contact with superhuman or non-human entities. Modern claims, and the experiences prompting them, are classed as anomalous phenomena. This chapter is about the culturally specific narrative clues that bridge these testimonies, pointing to a common psychological explanation. People experienced entities that approached them from the Outside-in, but the psychological interpretation shows the experiences coming from the Inside-out.

121

The most likely experience behind both these testimonies is sleep paralysis. This has been thoroughly investigated in a seminal paper by Owen Davies.[3] Davies ranges over the whole of Europe and demonstrates a number of common factors that reflect the universality of the experience. What we can offer here is a case-study of a single country – a case-study that does two things in particular. Firstly, it confirms Davies's findings and illustrates how his methodology can be applied. Secondly, it offers a shift of emphasis, at least for Scotland, picking up on one of Davies's own suggestions to argue that there is more than one way to interpret the effect of sleep paralysis on early modern witchcraft. But before such interpretations, the sleep paralysis experience must first be explained.

I

Sleep paralysis is a medical condition related to narcolepsy (a form of epilepsy which induces sleep without warning). Sleep paralysis is milder and much more common; between 25 and 40 per cent of the population have experienced it.[4] It occurs during the 'rapid eye movement' (REM) phase of sleep. Sleep is caused by the inhibitory action of REM-off cells in reciprocal interaction with REM-on cells. This symbiotic process prevents motor output (paralysing the body to prevent the acting out of dreams causing injury to self or others) and blocks sensory input, while providing the forebrain with internally generated activity which leads to dreams. REM sleep occurs several times in a night and usually passes unnoticed, though dreaming is more common and more vivid in this phase. It has been called the 'paradoxical' stage, as the brain is more active but less accessible to external stimuli.[5] The condition is commonly labelled as sleep paralysis, or perhaps more fully 'awareness during sleep paralysis', although full consciousness is rare. Little is known about the actual physiology of sleep paralysis, but its symptoms come in a now well-recognised sequence of episodes.

The symptoms can be frightening, especially for the first-time experient. The experience tends to happen when the subject is about to fall asleep or about to wake, usually while lying on their back. The subject wakes up feeling paralysed and sensing a presence in the room with them. Although they are consciously aware of their environment, they are unable to move – except for their eyes – or to speak. The sensation of a presence induces fear or even terror. A feeling of levitation or flying is sometimes described. Some relate seeing balls of light, or being in unusually light surroundings. A visible or invisible entity may seem to sit on their chest, shaking, strangling or prodding them. Visual hallucinations can include lights, animals and figures. Auditory hallucinations have been described as heavy footsteps, a buzzing noise or the sound of heavy objects being moved.

One neurological model suggests three sets of experiences in sleep paralysis.[6] The first set of experiences is the 'Intruder'. This may be due to the activation of the amygdala, situated in the brain, which is involved in normal fear reactions. With sensory input and output blocked, the process of analysing the source of the fear may last several minutes instead of the usual fraction of a second, allowing increasingly elaborate interpretations to be made. Such interpretations can be informed by stimuli received during the period, either from outside (such as external sounds) or from inside (middle ear activity). These result in auditory or visual hallucinations.

The second sleep paralysis experience is labelled the 'Incubus'. This is the phase, noted above, when the subject feels pressure on their back or chest. It may be due to the subject's efforts to control their breathing, not understanding that their body remains paralysed; their lack of success is interpreted, by the brain, as pressure or feelings of being crushed or choked.

The third and final phase, which occurs only in a minority of cases, has been termed 'Unusual Bodily Experiences'. This includes the sensations of floating or flying, and out-of-body experiences. As the subject is paralysed and cannot receive feedback, any vestibular (inner ear) activity is interpreted by the brain as floating or flying. This produces a distinct type of experience; people who have reported out-of-body experiences sometimes interpret them as a form of life-altering spiritual elevation of body and soul. They are sometimes happy about the experience, unlike those who perceive a terrifying 'intruder'. We have largely omitted discussion of this type of experience, as it is distinct from the others. Out-of-body experiences are discussed in another chapter of this book.[7]

Overall, then, sleep paralysis produces vivid and often terrifying experiences, although it is physically harmless. It is not the same as a bad dream, even a 'nightmare' in the modern usage of this term to mean an anxiety dream. It does, however, constitute the likely reality behind the original term 'night-mare'.[8] It is particularly common in the 'hypnagogic' and 'hypnopompic' phases of sleep, respectively the phases of gradually falling asleep and gradually waking up. Pre-industrial sleeping patterns may have made people particularly prone to sleep paralysis. They habitually woke up, at least partially, for an hour or so around midnight, in between periods known as 'first sleep' and 'second sleep'. The end of the 'first sleep' was a period of particularly vivid dreaming.[9]

Sleep paralysis does not directly cause people to see witches, demons or aliens; the 'intruder experience' is no more than a vague sensation. People have to *interpret* their terrifying experience retrospectively. In the cases with which we are concerned, they conclude that the anomalous experience must have been due to witches, demons or aliens. This involves constructing false memories – which is remarkably easy, as a number of studies have shown. Many people are suggestible, and complex memories of non-existent phenomena can be created retrospectively. In one experiment, respondents were asked about their memories of the media's coverage of a recent aeroplane crash; over half came to 'remember' some details of a television film of the crash, even though no such film existed.[10] Once someone has had a terrifying nocturnal experience involving an intruder in their room, they need to explain it. Their search for an explanation may well include the creation of a 'memory' of a more detailed view of the intruder – especially if the search is assisted by an interested expert like a witchcraft prosecutor. This 'memory' will contain the kind of beings that people think likely to have been assaulting them: aliens today, witches or demons in the early modern period.

II

The symptoms of sleep paralysis, and the anomalous phenomena they produce, appear to be a universal experience, but interpretations of them vary from culture to culture. What were the dominant cultural interpretations of the sleep paralysis experience in early modern Scotland? Here we must visit some of the testimonies found in Scottish witchcraft trials, beginning with statements by accusers of witches.

One such incident can be seen in the trial of Janet Lucas, an accused witch in Aberdeen in 1597. Her dittay included an accusation from the goodman (tenant) of Petmurchie, who witnessed the Devil in his room at night. He claimed that Janet, who was sleeping in the same room but in a separate bed from Petmurchie and his wife, must have summoned the Devil as there were only the three of them in the house. His wife was lying ill with a fever next to him, and all the doors and windows were locked.

> The Deuill thy maister, com to the[e], and thow, be his instigatioune and thy inchantment, the gudwyf beand lyand seik, the parpan

[i.e. partition] wall of the hous schuik and trymblit, and made sic ane dwne and noyis as [if] the same haid bene halelie fallin.... At this same nicht that the wall trimblit and shuik be thy deuilische inchantmentis, the Deuill thy maister, appeirit to the[e] in the said gudwyf of Petmurchieis chalmer, quhair the gudman him self was lyand, in the forme of ane four futit beist.[11]

Some classical symptoms of sleep paralysis are evident here. Petmurchie hears loud noises, feels vibrations and senses a four-footed beast. He gets out of bed to light a candle. He complains, when Lucas asks him what the matter is, 'I trow the Deuill is in the hous, for I can nocht lye in my bed for feir.'[12] Petmurchie's intense fear is a common emotion for sleep paralysis sufferers. He also appears to be able to recall the incident remarkably well, although no indication is given as to how long ago it occurred.

Another likely episode of sleep paralysis, from the same group of Aberdeenshire trials, is that of Helen Gray. She was accused that 'thow com to William Chalmeris hous in Clochtow, on the nicht, the durris being clos, and yeid [i.e. went] up and doun the fluir, and thaireftir past out at the window in the lyknes of ane dog, quhilk the said William ratefies, and apprewis on his consciens, that he saw the same'.[13] Fewer details are given here, but the motif of the closed doors is a recurring one that seems to have been a standard way of reporting an anomalous nocturnal episode.

Women with children in the bed with them may have had a particular propensity to experience visions of an assaulting witch. In 1661, when a Dalkeith woman was lying in bed with her child, Janet Cock 'and many utheris came in and lay above her, and they all drew at her chyld: and shoe having said, "the Spirit of Grace be in this house," they went all out of the glasse window with a noise.' When a mother in Dundas lay 'in chyld-birth with her young chyld besyd her, in the night-tyme, the doore being locked,' Janet Millar, 'with uther notorious witches, who are since brunt, blew up the doore, and came in upone her, essayed to tacke the young chyld from her, bot not having the power, went to the doore in a confusione'.[14] Rosina McGhie, in Dumfries in 1671, having quarrelled with the accused witch Elspeth Thomson, feared that Thomson might attack her young child; she 'took an extraordinary sickness and swelling herself, Qch she thought was occasioned by ane other fear, That she visibly saw Elspit thomson come to her bed, endeavouring to destroy her and her chyld'. Thomson's husband, William McGhie, also experienced episodes of what appear to have been sleep paralysis, according to two neighbours who related what he had told them: 'yr came one tyme a great heaviness over him, and yt the devil came like a rat, and bet his left arme', and 'one morning in his bed, he saw ye devil looking in his face, and being terribly affrighted, his wife griped him fast, and sd qt neided him to be so feared, for she was not feared for all that'.[15] It is ironic that Thomson's attempt to reassure her husband seems to have led him to conclude that she was to blame for his terrifying experience.

Several likely sleep paralysis cases show the experient as seeing, not the witch, nor the Devil, but an animal that they believed to be the witch – often a cat or sometimes a dog (as in Helen Gray's case above). Margaret Duncan, Janet Gentleman and Marion Ure, in Glasgow in 1699, were accused by William Scott of having 'appeared in the chamber where the said William Scot was lying in the bedd betwixt two and three hours in the morning in the likeness of ane sow, ane catt and ane ape, and danced in the rome before his bed, he being waking at the tyme and verry sensible of ther being present; and after a litil tyme they all three vanished'.[16] Beatrix Leslie in 1661 had a quarrel with William Young's wife, 'and that same verry night, the said William Young awakened out of his sleep, in a great affrightment and sweat, crying out, that she with a number of catts wer devouring him'.[17] Probably not all cats were manifestations of sleep paralysis, though. The cat that insisted on sharing the bed of Katherine Ewen and Ambrose Gordon for twenty nights, and bit Gordon's arm, was probably a real cat, though their belief that the witch Janet Wishart had sent it is less credible.[18]

III

People experiencing sleep paralysis would be particularly likely to construct a false memory of having seen a witch if they were concerned about the witch's reputation, and especially if they had had a quarrel with the witch. Petmurchie's experience involved both. The case of Agnes Finnie, tried in Edinburgh in December 1644, provides another example. On one day in June 1643, John Cockburn had quarrelled with Finnie's daughter Margaret Robertson, and the alleged incident occurred that night.

> Litle rest gat he that nycht bot having gottin his first sleip and awaiking furth thereof being struckin in great feir and amaisement, he saw and evidentlie perseaved, all the durris and windowis of his hous being fast cloised, yow the said Agnes Fynnie, with yor dochter

Margaret Robertsone, bothe sitting one his bedside, fearcelie ruging at his breist; and being in excessive feir with that villent rugging and vexing him in a manner foirsaid, he cryed out all that tyme: 'God be in this hous. I ken yow weill aneughe. God be in this hous.'[19]

Here the violent 'ruging' (tugging) of Cockburn's chest relates easily to the sensations of pressure or choking in the 'incubus' phase of sleep paralysis. The feeling of fear comes across strongly, and also the sensation of a presence in the room. Cockburn's cries woke his wife and apprentice, who confirmed his state of fear. Finnie had had a reputation as a witch for almost thirty years, and Cockburn's quarrel with her daughter would have worried him. Stress is a predisposing factor to sleep paralysis. Cockburn's experience also occurred at the end of his 'first sleip', which, as we have seen, was often a time of vivid dreams.[20]

This case is also interesting for the way that Cockburn's anomalous experience was interpreted by the authorities. Finnie's trial occurred in the central justiciary court, with highly-trained advocates on both sides. The accusation terminated with two alternative interpretations of the event: 'Quhilk feirfull apparitione was ather the devill himselff or your selffis, brocht thair be his devillische illusiones and be your procurement.'[21] Cockburn himself seems to have been sure that his assailants had been Finnie and her daughter, but the prosecutors thought that it could have been the Devil. Indeed the phrase 'devillische illusiones', applied to both of the possibilities, indicates that they thought that if the apparition was not actually the Devil, then the Devil at least played the key role in bringing it about – something that Cockburn himself did not mention. The defence could have argued that if what Cockburn saw was really an illusion brought by the Devil, then Finnie was perhaps not responsible for it; but this possibility does not seem to have been entertained.[22]

Historians discussing contemporary interpretations of demonic apparitions have tended to focus on cases of demonic possession.[23] England and New England sometimes saw a distinction between guilty 'possession' and innocent 'obsession', but this distinction does not seem to have been drawn in Scotland.[24] Moreover, the cases under discussion here were not straightforwardly cases of 'possession'; the apparition seen by Cockburn remained external to him. As for the question of whether the Devil could counterfeit the appearance of an innocent person, this became a matter of debate in the Salem trials but was rarely discussed in Scotland.[25] We need more study of the intellectual interpretation of apparitions in early modern Scotland, although this would take us well beyond the experience of sleep paralysis and indeed beyond witchcraft.[26]

IV

The material that we have discussed so far confirms Davies's findings. Some people in Scotland, as elsewhere, suffered from sleep paralysis and interpreted their anomalous nocturnal experiences as attacks by a witch. However, these findings can be extended. It was not just accusers of witches who described experiences of sleep paralysis: some witches also did so themselves. These cases are less common, but they exist, as Davies suggested that they might.[27] They deserve careful attention.

Scottish witchcraft suspects were often asked about their encounters with the Devil. Coercive interrogation made it essential for them to answer this question somehow. They did not necessarily talk about the Devil; some talked about fairies.[28] What we are mainly looking for here are cases in which the witchcraft suspect had experienced sleep paralysis symptoms, and talked about the 'intruder' in such a way as to enable the interrogators to conclude that this was the Devil. Possibly they already believed that they had truly had some contact with otherworldly beings, or possibly the process of interrogation persuaded them of this. We will come back to the dynamics of interrogation; but first, some likely cases.

Marion Grant's dittay, quoted at the head of this chapter, goes on to give greater detail of her visits from the Devil:

> The Devill apperit to the[e], within this auchteine dayis or thairby, quhome thou callis thy god, within the said James Cheynis pantrie, about ane hour in the night, and apperit to the[e] in ane gryte man his likness, in silkin abuilzeament, with ane quhyt candill in his hand.[29]

A good deal of detail is evident here. The time is known, one o'clock in the morning, and a light anomaly is also in evidence, 'with ane quhyt candill in his hand'. This is strongly indicative of sleep paralysis.

Detecting sleep paralysis symptoms experienced by accused witches is not as obvious as it is for the sleep paralysis symptoms related by the accusers. In the case of Andrew Man, in Rathven in 1598, no time of the day or night was mentioned. We are told that the first visitation from the Devil occurred in his mother's house and that the visits continued for 'the space of threttie twa yeris sensyn or thairby'. Sleep paralysis can be a prolonged condition, with attacks becoming more frequent during times of stress. The hour of the visit was apparently less important to the interrogators. Most dealings with the Devil were associated with night-time, so perhaps this was taken for granted. Another item of his dittay reads: 'Thow saw Christsonday cum owt of the snaw in the liknes of a staig, and that the Quene of Elphen was their, and vtheris with hir, rydand vpon quhyt haiknayes.'[30] Light and light colours feature in this passage, as they do in many sleep paralysis episodes.

Man's much-discussed and extraordinary case has many unusual features; he is certainly not a *typical* Scottish witch. In searching for sleep paralysis among Scottish witches, should we be mainly looking at the unusual cases like Man's? Not necessarily. Let us take the case of Agnes Pogavie, in Liberton in 1661. Pogavie was caught up in a group prose-cution during a major panic, and her confession was brief and heavily demonic, with stereotypical renunciation of baptism, sex with the Devil, Devil's mark and financial reward that turned to a 'sclait stone'. This is standard material in Scottish witchcraft cases, and all of it could have come straight from leading questions under torture. Yet Pogavie began with what looks like a sleep paralysis experience: 'as she was lying in her bed, as she thought waking, she thought her spirit was carried away, she said the[y] say the divel his a bell that he rings'. Neither spirit flight (out-of-body experience) nor the Devil's bell (anomalous sounds) were part of the standard repertoire of demonic confessions as sought by inter-rogators, so they are likely to have represented something like Pogavie's real experience.[31]

The 'incubus' phase of the sleep paralysis experience, with something pressing on the chest, appears in several witches' testimonies. Thomas Black, one of Pogavie's co-accused, confessed that the Devil appeared to him in the night, 'the doores being fast locked', and that the Devil 'lay heavie on' him.[32] Helen Wilson, in Prestonpans in 1659, experienced the Devil coming to her as a rat. She chased the rat away, but the Devil then changed into a man and lay heavy on her as she slept.[33] Janet Paiston, in Dalkeith in 1661, was lying in bed one night after her hus-band had beaten her, and 'ther came as shoe thoght a heavie spirit wpon hir which maid hir to say the beleif and the Lords prayer and yet shoe could not be red thairof'.[34]

Another motif to watch for is unaccounted-for or missing time. Time runs at a different pace in fairyland, and the same is reported by alien abductees. A sleep paralysis episode can give the impression of a great deal of time passing when in fact it may only last a few seconds. This phase of REM sleep can allow for extended interpretations of what is happening to the experient. Andrew Man told of such an encounter:

> Thow grantis the elphis will mak the[e] appear to be in a fair chalmer, and yit thow will find thy self in a moss on the morne; and that thay will appear to have candles, and licht, and swordis, quhilk wilbe els bot deed gress and strayes.[35]

This episode may well feature some sleep paralysis symptoms. As well as the unusual passage of time, Man describes the interior lighting of the chamber; similarly, alien abductees describe the interiors of spacecraft as luminous. Light anomalies feature in many sleep paralysis episodes.

V

Was there a sexual element to sleep paralysis as it manifested itself in Scottish witchcraft? Some modern women (though not men) experiencing sleep paralysis have reported that aspects of it resembled sexual assault.[36] This seems to have been behind a number of cases discussed by Davies.[37] Many Scottish witches were accused of having sex with the Devil, and this may provide some relevant evidence.

One possible explanation of sleep paralysis involved the incubus and succubus, male and female demons respectively, who were said to enter the victim's room at night and have sexual intercourse with them. Incubi and succubi do not seem to be mentioned by name in Scottish witchcraft trials, although incubi had been encountered in the twelfth century.[38] This may be because they were thought to have a natural cause. Davies cites a number of naturalistic interpretations of incubi, including one Scottish example: James VI, in his *Daemonologie* (1597).[39] An earlier Scottish example is the canon lawyer William Hay, in the 1530s:

> People who suffer the incubus sometimes think they are oppressed by a man known to them, sometimes by a woman with whom they have had intercourse, and associate them with anyone whose eyebrows meet together. In fact there is no truth in this at all, for this is either caused by the pressure of blood round the heart when sleeping on one's back or by a slight exhalation arising to the head, which oppresses and interferes with the sense organs. When these things occur in sleep it is quite obvious that they are not real.[40]

However, this remarkable description of sleep paralysis was almost a throwaway comment, in the middle of a discussion of the Canon *Episcopi* – the famous tenth-century law concerning women who were deceived by demons into believing that they were transformed into animals and carried long distances.[41] Neither Hay nor James gave clear directions for distinguishing between natural and demonic experiences, beyond rejecting the actual term 'incubus'. Sleep paralysis, although widespread, is not common knowledge among the general population today. If naturalistic interpretations of the 'incubus' were common in our period, then sleep paralysis may actually have been better known then, but evidence for this is scanty. Partly this may be because a sleep paralysis experience that *was* interpreted naturalistically would be unlikely, by definition, to be recorded in a witchcraft trial, concerned as this had to be with demonic intervention. In practice, people who had anomalous sleep experiences were readily able to opt for a demonic interpretation, or to have one suggested to them.

There was, of course, a great deal of demonic sex reported in Scottish witchcraft trials. It was normal for women, at any rate, to be asked about sex with the Devil. Much of the material thus obtained was stereotyped, deriving from the authorities' interest in deviant sex rather than from the witches' real lives. The church courts, which often identified witches and orchestrated their prosecution, spent most of their time disciplining fornicators and adulterers.[42] The mixture of stereotyped and individual detail is characteristic of witches' confessions.

One witch who seems to have interpreted her experience of sleep paralysis in sexual terms was Elizabeth Crockett, in Alloa in September 1658:

> In Lentron last bypast, shoe lying in hir bed in the dawing found ane come in to hir bed and lye in hir right arme, and thairat shoe thocht he had carnell copulatione with hir, and that he wes nether cold nor hott, and declared that shoe knew not when he come in nor when he went away.

The interrogators then seem to have persuaded her that this had been the Devil. Asked about the Devil's mark, she continued: 'shoe knew not whether the Devill gave hir ane mark or not that night he lay with hir, but if it wer found wpon hir, shoe should be content to die the death of a witch'. Later that day she added a further detail, still ambiguous: 'the said Elisabeth did confess that if shoe had the Devills mark it was on hir privie member'. Interrogated again in March 1659, she omitted the sexual element but added some further details:

> In Lentron last, shoe being lying in hir bed wnwell in the dawning of the day, found ane thing come on hir in the bed wnder the clothes and lay above hir very heavie, having nether armes nor legs, hot nor cold as shoe thought, clothed with old gray clothes, but shoe saying (as shoe affirmed) Christ be heir it evanished away and shoe knew not how it come nor how it went away.[43]

Crockett was clearly a confused and desperate woman, pressed hard by her interrogators; they may have forced her to add the sexual element. But this merely underlines that that was how these confessions were constructed. Crockett's original experience, though vivid, was probably inchoate – a thing without arms or legs, pressing her chest as she was waking in the early morning. It was during the interrogation itself that she came to reinterpret it in demonic and sexual terms.

VI

Both alien abduction narratives and witchcraft trial narratives are related through the process of answering questions posed by someone in authority. For the alien abductee, the person in authority is a therapist – someone claiming authoritative knowledge of alien abductions, who can confirm that the subject's anomalous nocturnal experience was indeed an abduction by aliens. For the accused witch, this person was their interrogator – someone claiming authoritative knowledge of the Devil, who could confirm that the subject's anomalous nocturnal experience was indeed the Devil. Scottish witchcraft suspects were often interrogated coercively, including the use of torture. What implications does this have for the way in which episodes of sleep paralysis were recorded?

Sleep paralysis experients sometimes recall specific details of their experience – sights, sounds, lights. Some experients, however, wake up feeling that something terrifying and profound has happened to them, but with no clear memory of any details. Some alien abductees base their claim entirely upon their memory of having felt terrified during the sleep paralysis episode and have no conscious recollection of actual contact with aliens. This is because the ufologists have disseminated the idea that symptoms of sleep paralysis are indicative of abduction by aliens.[44]

How can a false memory be created in either of these circumstances? False memories, as we have seen, can be generated by many people; there is no pathological condition involved. Studies have identified personality types who are particularly prone to false memories, though it would be hard to link these with early modern witches, about whose personalities we usually know little.[45] It is more relevant that a trance-like state similar to hypnosis can be produced from the pressures of interrogation. Memories 'recovered' from trance-like or hypnotic states are notoriously unreliable; memories can be changed and even completely created in these states.[46] Whole episodes of information can be suggested to people, retained and repeated.

Under conditions of coercion, some people will 'confess' without fully believing that what they are confessing is true. There are immediate benefits to them: cessation of questioning or pressure, approval from the interrogator. These can easily outweigh the long-term disadvantages: punishment for the crime, which to an innocent person may seem an improbable prospect. This type of confession has been called 'pressured-compliant'. But some people will go further and will come to believe what they are confessing – creating what has been called a 'pressured-internalized' confession.[47] Various types of pressure can be effective, but one is particularly significant: sleep deprivation, for one or two nights, causes people's suggestibility to increase markedly.[48] This is something to which Scottish witches were often subjected. Such conditions were highly likely to produce false memories.[49]

The kind of questions that could have been put to the suspects include: 'Where and when did you meet the Devil? What happened when you met him?' These are fairly open questions. But the interrogators also asked more specific, less open, questions. For women at least, these might include: 'Did you have sex with the Devil? What was that like? Was the Devil's body cold?' This last question, which derived from elite demonological ideas, seems to have been common.[50] Leading questions under pressure can easily make people suggestible. Questions like these, to someone who had had an anomalous nocturnal experience, could have triggered the creation of a false memory.

Diane Purkiss makes the important point that people talk about what they know, rather than what they do not know. Some accused witches will have drawn their confessions from stories that they had heard as fictions; to stave off the pressure of questioning, 'a woman might drag a folktale from her memory to make silence rather than to break it'. This, however, is more convincing than the inference that she draws – that 'the early modern populace did not "believe" in fairies and they did not disbelieve'.[51] Today, we read fictional stories about imaginary humans, but this does not call the existence of real humans into question. The early modern populace may have known that a particular folktale about fairies was a folktale, but there is no evidence that they doubted the actual existence of fairies. The extraordinary and vivid reality of the sleep paralysis experience was, for some, confirmation of their existence.

This may even apply to the case that Purkiss discusses in most detail, that of Elspeth Reoch, in Orkney in 1616. Reoch confessed that the 'farie man' who became her spirit guide had assaulted her sexually: he 'delt with you [i.e. Reoch] tua nychtis and wald never let her sleip', urging her to have intercourse with him, promising rewards and saying that she should henceforth be dumb, to protect the prophetic gifts that he was conferring on her. In Reoch's tale, she eventually succumbed to his assaults: 'And upoun the thrid nycht that he com to hir she being asleep and laid his hand upoun hir breist and walknit her, and thairefter semeit to ly with her.'[52] After this she was indeed dumb for a long time. Sleep paralysis is probably not the whole explanation for this story, which appears to be a fantasised reworking of some trauma – rape, perhaps, or failed courtship.[53] But the final phrase here, 'semeit to ly with her', along with the pressing on the chest, may well indicate that one or more episodes of sleep paralysis were woven into Reoch's agonised recollections.

VII

Overall, the material reviewed in this chapter reveals an important psychological dimension of Scottish witchcraft. It is well known that some Scottish witches made fantastical confessions of encounters with uncanny beings. Here it can be seen that for some of these witches, sleep paralysis was probably at the core of the experiences they related. Not all the anomalous phenomena in the confessions can have originated with this condition, but we have isolated a group of examples for which the condition is the best explanation.

The universal, medically-recognised symptoms of sleep paralysis, combined with historic and culturally specific forms of description, provided two sets of narratives for early modern Scottish folk: one in which the 'intruder' assailing them was a malevolent witch, and the other in which the 'intruder' was a more benevolent fairy or other such being for which they themselves were responsible. The first narrative was that of a victim of witchcraft; the nocturnal apparition was a witch, often someone with whom they had previously quarrelled. The second narrative was that of a witch; the nocturnal apparition, originally interpreted as a fairy, was reinterpreted under interrogation as the Devil.[54] Both of these narratives were thus reinterpreted by the authorities as demonic, but in different ways. In the first narrative, the authorities had to question whether the witch was an autonomous agent in sending an apparition of themselves to assault the victim, or whether she or he was in fact exploiting demonic agency. The apparition could really have been the Devil, and indeed perhaps was probably the Devil. Witches' confessions are complex narratives that contain more than one voice and one set of beliefs. In the second narrative, the authorities had a more straightforward interpretative task: the benevolent fairy was really the Devil. This was an easy deduction to make because it was usually assumed that fairies were really demons. But there remained a crucial difference between the two narratives. The first experient was a victim of someone else's witchcraft: the second was a witch.

These narrative threads can both be paralleled in modern cases of alien abduction. Most abductees feel themselves to have been assaulted in an unwelcome way, just as the accusers of witches did. But some feel that there were positive aspects to their experience, and this may more closely parallel the experience of some witches who had apparently experienced sleep paralysis. One abductee claimed to have been given a book of universal truths and secrets that she had in her possession for several days.[55] This is comparable to the way in which some witches gained magical powers from the fairies – Andrew Man and Elspeth Reoch, for instance.

The best examples of sleep paralysis in early modern Scotland are seen in the testimonies of the accusers of witches, who were convinced that the witch or the Devil had entered their rooms at night and frightened the life out of them. The recurrence of standard phrases in witnesses' testimony, like 'the doors and windows being closed', may indicate that there was a recognised repertoire of ways to describe the sleep paralysis experience. Some experients had others to confirm the reality of their experience. John Cockburn's wife and apprentice confirmed his state of fear; probably they also agreed with him that his experience should be attributed to witchcraft, and if so, this could have had a reinforcing effect. The creation of false memories can be encouraged by peer pressure, when someone else claims to 'remember' the non-existent phenomenon.[56]

Sleep paralysis is harder to find in the confessions of accused witches, but we have identified quite a few examples. Some accused witches did believe, or came to believe, that they had been involved with Satan or otherworldly creatures. In some cases, their beliefs originated with visual and auditory hallucinations experienced during sleep paralysis. Both for the accused witch and the accusers, these events were experienced as coming from the Outside-in, as an external force that manipulated them. They could never have been aware, in their early modern society and culture, where the Devil, his demons and human agents were thought of as a real threat to Christianity and society, that the origin of their belief was internal, caused by a psychological condition that produced anomalous phenomena which came from the Inside-out.

Notes

1. *Spalding Misc.*, i, 171 (modernised). We would like to thank Dr Louise Yeoman for helpful guidance in the initial stages of our research.
2. Nicholas P. Spanos, Patricia A. Cross, Kirby Dickson and Susan C. DuBreuil, 'Close encounters: an examination of UFO experiences', *Journal of Abnormal Psychology*, 102 (1993), 624–32, at p. 627.
3. Owen Davies, 'The nightmare experience, sleep paralysis, and witchcraft accusations', *Folklore*, 114 (2003), 181–203.
4. Katharine J. Holden and Christopher C. French, 'Alien abduction experiences: some clues from neuropsychology and neuropsychiatry', *Cognitive Neuropsychiatry*, 7 (2002), 163–78, at pp. 166–70.
5. Celia Green and Charles McCreery, *Lucid Dreaming: The Paradox of Consciousness during Sleep* (London, 1994), 5.
6. J. Allan Cheyne, Steve D. Rueffer and Ian R. Newby-Clark, 'Hypnagogic and hypnopompic hallucinations during sleep paralysis: neurological and cultural construction of the night-mare', *Consciousness and Cognition*, 8 (1999), 319–37.
7. Julian Goodare, 'Flying witches in Scotland', Chapter 9 in this volume.
8. Davies, 'Nightmare experience', 182–3.
9. A. Roger Ekirch, 'Sleep we have lost: pre-industrial slumber in the British Isles', *American Historical Review*, 106 (2001), 343–86, at pp. 363–74, 382.
10. Krissy Wilson and Christopher C. French, 'The relationship between susceptibility to false memories, dissociativity, and paranormal belief and experience', *Personality and Individual Differences*, 41 (2006), 1493–1502.
11. *Spalding Misc.*, i, 148.
12. Ibid., 149.
13. Ibid., 127.
14. Quoted in J. G. Dalyell, *The Darker Superstitions of Scotland* (Glasgow, 1835), 584.
15. 'Unpublished witchcraft trials, part 2', ed. A. E. Truckell, *Transactions of the Dumfriesshire and Galloway Natural History and Antiquarian Society*, 3rd ser., 52 (1976–1977), 95–108, at pp. 101–2.

16. Hugh V. McLachlan (ed.), *The Kirk, Satan and Salem: A History of the Witches of Renfrewshire* (Glasgow, 2006), 359.
17. Quoted in Dalyell, *Darker Superstitions*, 8.
18. *Spalding Misc.*, i, 91; cf. Davies, 'Nightmare experience', 196.
19. *SJC*, iii, 642.
20. His case is cited by Ekirch, 'Sleep we have lost', 366, though Ekirch does not discuss sleep paralysis.
21. *SJC*, iii, 642.
22. It might have been worthwhile for the defence to attempt to exploit the prosecution's expressed uncertainty, to argue that the nocturnal assault could not be proved if they did not prove whether the assailants were the Devil or Finnie, and to argue that if it was the Devil, then this need not have been Finnie's responsibility. However, they instead attempted a naturalistic defence: the apparition was a 'fantasticall dreame', and it was impossible for a real being to enter when the doors and windows were closed. The prosecution felt it unnecessary to reply to this in detail: *SJC*, iii, 655, 659.
23. Moshe Sluhovsky, *Believe Not Every Spirit: Possession, Mysticism, and Discernment in Early Modern Catholicism* (Chicago, IL, 2007).
24. David Harley, 'Explaining Salem: Calvinist psychology and the diagnosis of possession', *American Historical Review*, 101 (1996), 307–30; Brian P. Levack, 'Demonic possession in early modern Scotland', in Julian Goodare, Lauren Martin and Joyce Miller (eds.), *Witchcraft and Belief in Early Modern Scotland* (Basingstoke, 2008), 166–84.
25. James VI was interested in what kind of people could see demonic apparitions, but not in who the apparitions might represent: James VI, *Daemonologie*, in his *Minor Prose Works*, ed. James Craigie (STS, 1982), 33, 43–4.
26. The materials for such a study would include George Sinclair, *Satans Invisible World Discovered*, ed. Thomas G. Stevenson (Edinburgh, 1871), and Robert Wodrow, *Analecta: or Materials for a History of Remarkable Providences*, 4 vols., ed. Mathew Leishman (Maitland Club, 1842–3).
27. Davies, 'Nightmare experience', 197–9, mentioning the *benandanti* of Friuli.
28. Lizanne Henderson and Edward J. Cowan, *Scottish Fairy Belief: A History* (East Linton, 2001), ch. 4.
29. *Spalding Misc.*, i, 172.
30. Ibid., 121.
31. Quoted in Christina Larner, Christopher H. Lee and Hugh V. McLachlan, *A Source-Book of Scottish Witchcraft* (Glasgow, 1977), 257.
32. Ibid.
33. SSW.
34. G. F. Black (ed.), *Some Unpublished Scottish Witchcraft Trials* (New York, 1941), 45–6.
35. *Spalding Misc.*, i, 121–2.
36. Cheyne *et al.*, 'Hypnagogic and hypnopompic hallucinations', 330.
37. Davies, 'Nightmare experience', 190–3.
38. Julian Goodare, 'Scottish witchcraft in its European context', in Goodare, Martin and Miller (eds.), *Witchcraft and Belief*, 26–50, at pp. 34–5. The concern was usually with women's relations with incubi; succubi were rarer.

39. Davies, 'Nightmare experience', 186–8. For the reference to James, see his *Minor Prose Works*, 48.

40. William Hay, *Lectures on Marriage*, ed. John C. Barry (Stair Society, 1967), 127.

41. For the Canon *Episcopi*, see Alan C. Kors and Edward Peters (eds.), *Witchcraft in Europe, 400–1700: A Documentary History* (2nd edn., Philadelphia, PA, 2001), 62–3, and Walter Stephens, *Demon Lovers: Witchcraft, Sex, and the Crisis of Belief* (Chicago, IL, 2002), 126–37.

42. Julian Goodare, 'Women and the witch-hunt in Scotland', *Social History*, 23 (1998), 288–308, at pp. 294–7; Christina Larner, *Enemies of God: The Witch-Hunt in Scotland* (London, 1981), 149.

43. BL, Egerton MS 2879, fo. 5r.-v. The scribe first wrote 'found ane come on hir', implying a person, and then added the word 'thing'. The phrase 'hot nor cold' is evidently a confused answer to a standard leading question about the coldness of the Devil's body. The vanishing at the name of Christ may be a folkloric motif, also found in the case of Janet Cock above.

44. Holden and French, 'Alien abduction experiences', 170.

45. Christopher C. French, 'Fantastic memories: the relevance of research into eyewitness testimony and false memories for reports of anomalous experiences', *Journal of Consciousness Studies*, 10 (2003), 153–74.

46. Susan Blackmore, 'Abduction by aliens or sleep paralysis?', *Skeptical Inquirer*, 22:3 (May–June 1998), http://www.csicop.org/si/ (accessed 27 May 2010).

47. Gisli H. Gudjonsson, *The Psychology of Interrogations and Confessions: A Handbook* (Chichester, 2003), ch. 8.

48. Gudjonsson, *Psychology of Interrogations and Confessions*, 389–90.

49. Alternatively to the concept of false memory, the phenomenon of 'false belief' has been posited, arising from loss of confidence in one's real memories under stress: Gudjonsson, *Psychology of Interrogations and Confessions*, 212–13.

50. Goodare, 'Women and the witch-hunt', 295.

51. Diane Purkiss, 'Sounds of silence: fairies and incest in Scottish witchcraft stories', in Stuart Clark (ed.), *Languages of Witchcraft: Narrative, Ideology and Meaning in Early Modern Culture* (London, 2001), 81–98, at pp. 83–4.

52. 'Acts and statutes of the lawting, sheriff and justice courts within Orkney and Shetland, 1602–1644', *Maitland Miscellany*, ii (1840), 189.

53. Or, as Purkiss speculates, incest – Reoch being one of two 'women who *talk about* incest and fairies in the same breath': Purkiss, 'Sounds of silence', 91 (emphasis in original). But Reoch did not talk about incest; she merely reported encountering a 'blak man' who 'callit him selff ane farie man quha wes sumtyme her kinsman callit Johne Stewart': *Maitland Miscellany*, ii, 189. Quite apart from the fact that he was dead, the distancing phrase 'callit him selff' shows that Reoch herself did not entirely believe that he was her kinsman. Such a doubtful relationship could hardly have been so close as to fall within the forbidden degrees of incest. The original trauma seems more likely to have been connected with James Mitchell, father of Reoch's recently-born child, than with the 'blak man'.

54. Witches' visions were often of more benevolent figures, but for evidence of their moral ambiguity, see Emma Wilby, *Cunning Folk and Familiar Spirits:*

Shamanistic Visionary Traditions in Early Modern British Witchcraft and Magic (Brighton, 2005), ch. 7.
55. Peter M. Rojcewicz, 'Between one eye blink and the next: fairies, UFOs and problems of knowledge', in Peter Narváez (ed.), *The Good People: New Fairylore Essays* (Lexington, KY, 1991), 479–514, at pp. 489–90.
56. Matthew B. Reysen, 'The effects of social pressure on false memories', *Memory & Cognition*, 35 (2007), 59–65.

8

'We mey shoot them dead at our pleasur': Isobel Gowdie, Elf Arrows and Dark Shamanism

Emma Wilby

The four confessions given by Isobel Gowdie in Auldearn, Nairnshire in 1662 are consistently cited as the most extraordinary on record in Scotland. In remarkable detail and with inimitable style they cover a diverse range of folkloric and demonological subject matter, from stereotypical pacts with the Devil to feasting under hills with the fairy king and queen. Arguably the most striking of all the passages in the confessions are those depicting elf-arrow shooting. In her first confession, Isobel claims that she and the other members of her coven

> vold flie away q[uhe]r ve vold be ewin as strawes wold flie wpon an hie way, we will flie lyk strawes q[uhe]n we pleas wild strawes and corne strawes wilbe hors to ws q[uhe]n ve put th[e]m betwixt owr foot, and say hors and hattok in the divellis nam, and q[uhe]n any sies thes strawes in whirlewind, and doe not sanctifie them selves, they we mey shoot them dead at our pleasur....[1]

Having established her power to shoot and kill people, Isobel then provides a grim roll-call of the arrow-slain. This passage, from her third confession, runs to over 200 words, beginning:

> th[a]t q[uhi]ch trowbles my concience most is the killing of sewerall persones, with the arrowes q[uhi]ch I gott from the divell, the first voman th[a]t I killed wes at the plewgh landis, also I killed on in the east of murrey, at candlmas last, at that tyme bessie wilson in aulderne killed on th[e]r, and margret wilson ther killed an uth[e]r, I killed also James dick in conniecavell, bot the death th[a]t I am

most of all sorrie for, is the killing of william Bower in the miltowne of moynes, margret brodie killed an vowman washing at the burne of tarres, Bessie wilsone killed an man at the bushe of strutheris Bessie hay in aulderne killed an prettie man, called dunbar at the eist end of the towne of forres as he wes coming out at an gaitt . . . [2]

I

As many commentators have noted, these passages have links with fairy lore. The fairy host was believed to roam the countryside, sometimes using plant stalks as steeds, in search of sustenance. In addition to stealing milk and taking the 'foyson' (nutritive quality) of the grain, they killed humans and animals with 'elf arrows', tiny projectiles identified with the prehistoric arrowheads found in many parts of Scotland. If the humans who crossed the fairies' path did not 'sain' (bless) themselves, the fairy darts would cause them to sicken or die.[3] It was also believed that humans could be called upon to function as fairy archers, with Welsh cartographer Edward Lhuyd noting in 1699 of the Highlanders that 'their Opinion is that the Fairies (having not much Power themselves to hurt Animal Bodies) do sometimes carry away Men in the Air, and furnishing them with Bows and Arrows, employ them to shoot Men, Cattle, &c.'[4] Similarly, variations on Isobel's 'hors and hattok' anthem appear in a number of sources as a fairy levitation cry.[5]

Although Isobel's arrow-shooting passages were clearly rooted in fairy lore, we still need to explain why she stood up in the Auldearn tolbooth before a crowd of local ministers and townsfolk and confessed to having shot elf arrows herself. While it is one thing to say that a figure of legend or gossip, such as the weaver from the Bridge of Awe, travelled in a fairy whirlwind and killed his neighbour with an elf arrow, it is another thing to claim that '*I* flew in a fairy whirlwind and killed my neighbour with an elf arrow.'[6] We cannot postulate simplistic elite superimposition – as we may reasonably do with regard to Isobel's demonic pact accounts – for the idiosyncratic and folkloric nature of the arrow-shooting passages strongly suggests that Isobel took an active role in their creation. We can speculate that her claims were the result of disorientation brought on by pressures of imprisonment and interrogation. Mid-seventeenth-century Auldearn was a hotbed of covenanting fundamentalism and social unrest. Harry Forbes, the minister who led Isobel's questioning, was not only a religious extremist, but was also obsessed with the threat of witchcraft and believed himself to have been a victim of maleficent magic. In addition, several relatives of Isobel's primary named victim, John Hay of Park, attended her interrogations in the belief that the deaths of three family members had been caused by *maleficium*.[7] There would have been plenty of reason for Isobel's prosecutors to question her coercively and suggestively, with research suggesting that she is likely to have woven fairy beliefs into false memories produced in response to close questioning about *maleficium* and the witches' coven.[8]

But we may be jumping to conclusions if we assume that this was all there was to it. The strangeness of Isobel's arrow-shooting claims is ameliorated by the fact that they were not wholly unique. Other witches confessed to shooting elf arrows. In a few cases their narratives hint at fairy host-related activity, with Bute witch Margaret NcLevin's claims that she and her companions 'went to Birgadele broch and in a window [where] Margret NcWilliam shot James Androws son and that Marie More NcCuill was appointed by them to take away the body and leave the stoke of a tree in his place' clearly referring to the same nexus of belief.[9] Over 150 years later, outside the interrogatorial arena and after all the hubbub about witches had died down, perfectly sane and ordinary Highlanders were still claiming to have shot elf arrows in the company of the fairy host. The following anecdote, recorded by nineteenth-century folklorist John Francis Campbell, is one of many from the period:

> An old highlander declared to me that he was once in a boat with a man who was struck by a fairy arrow… [later] a man, whom the fairies were in the habit of carrying about from island to island, told him that he had himself thrown the dart at the man in the boat by desire of *them* [the fairies]: "*they made him do it.*" My informant evidently believed he was speaking truth.[10]

Of course, these examples do not obviate the possibility that Isobel's arrow-shooting passages may have been some kind of false confession – but they do raise the possibility that there may have been more to her claims than meets the eye. And in order to explore this possibility, we must now turn to shamanism.

II

In his pioneering work, *Ecstasies*, Carlo Ginzburg argued that shamanistic beliefs and practices contributed to ideas surrounding the witches' sabbath.[11] He distinguished two traditions: *warrior* shamanism (involving aggressive rites designed to combat enemy persons and spirits) and following-the-goddess shamanism (involving processional rites, rooted in devotion to a supernatural female figure). Although in practice this distinction is often blurred, and although Ginzburg's asserted links between following-the-goddess traditions and a pre-Christian 'pan-Eurasian' goddess figure have been criticised, his early modern evidence does help us to articulate a polarity that emerges from the records.[12] Clear examples of *warrior* shamanism can be found from early modern Friuli, where the *benandanti* believed that on certain nights of the year, while lying in bed, they engaged in visionary rites that involved fighting enemy witches for the fertility of local fields.[13] Following-the-goddess shamanism, alternatively, is epitomised in seventeenth-century Sicily where, as Gustav Henningsen has shown, women who termed themselves the *donas de fuera* believed that on certain nights of the week they joined a group of women, under the auspices of a female authority figure, while in some kind of dream state. In this company, they engaged in fairy-like activities, such as feasting and dancing in house-to-house processions, to generate prosperity and gain healing skills.[14] Although it has generated opposition and controversy, Ginzburg's 'shamanistic hypothesis' has since been supported and developed by a number of scholars who have been able to avoid many of its more controversial claims.[15]

Ginzburg argued that Isobel Gowdie's claims to have feasted under local hills with the fairy king and queen, along with similar testimony from Aberdeenshire cunning-man Andro Man (1597), suggest that following-the-goddess traditions may have been extant in early modern Britain.[16] Certainly, among contemporary historians and folklorists, the Scottish fairy queen is agreed to represent a version of the 'European nocturnal goddess'.[17] Like her variants on the Continent, she progressed through the countryside with her train of spirits (identified as fairies or the dead), feasting and dancing in house-to-house processions and remote countryside locations. She also attracted human followers, with the early modern Scots believing that by joining the fairy queen and her train an individual could acquire magical benefits. Several kirk session records and witch testimonies contain references to people who, like Marion Or in 1602, professed to 'ride with the fair folk and to have skill'.[18]

Although Ginzburg focused on Isobel's descriptions of feasting under sacred hills with the fairy queen, other aspects of Isobel's confessions also suggest following-the-goddess themes. Isobel frequently mentions the fact that she and her coven 'wold goe s[eve]rall howses in the night tym'. At Robert Donaldsone's house they 'went in at the kitchen chimney, and went down wpon the crowk' in order to feast on 'beiff and drink'; at Grangehill, they 'got meat and drink enough'; at the earl of Moray's house they 'gott anewgh ther and did eat and drink of the best, and browght pairt w[i]th ws'; and at Bessie Hay's house in Auldearn they consumed an ox that they had killed previously, presumably with elf arrows. Although Isobel does not make specific reference to these house-to-house visits conferring prosperity, they seem to have been generally benign. Not only does she fail to report the performance of any *maleficium* at these events, but her claim that 'q[uhe]n ve goe to any hous we tak meat and drink, and we fill wp the barrellis w[i]th owr oven pish [i.e. piss] again', could be interpreted as a reference to the female group leader's powers of magical increase, reflecting the fact that in Nairnshire, as in other places that hosted the fairy cavalcade, 'no one noticed any decrease in the food supplies' after its visit.[19] Also compatible with the following-the-goddess nexus is the fact that, although she does not overtly link her abilities to the fairy queen, Isobel seems to have acted as a healer. She provides her interrogators with three long and detailed healing charms, and describes how she and her coven performed rituals to heal bewitched children.

In addition, in keeping with similar groups throughout Europe, Isobel's feasting companions were ontologically diverse. There were non-human spirits (the fairy monarchs, the elves, the Devil); the dead (the 'bodies' that 'remain with us' after they have been shot and killed by elf arrows); and the living (Isobel and her neighbours). Even Isobel's use of the term 'coven', which has been taken up by scholars to denote a stereotypical group of malevolent witches, echoes the references to 'companies', 'societies' and 'troupes' found in Continental following-the-goddess traditions.[20] When interpreted through the lens of the shamanistic hypothesis, these elements invite us to speculate that when Isobel provided her prosecutors with narratives about feasting and dancing with the fairies under hills and in the cellars of houses, she was not just recounting local fairy lore as some kind of coerced fiction, but drawing on memories of shamanistic dreams or trances, consciously undertaken for the benefit of her community, prior to her arrest.

But while this thesis is helpful, it is insufficient. As we noted earlier, Isobel's descriptions of feasting with fairy queens and dancing on hilltops are seamlessly intertwined with equally vivid accounts of performing a wide spectrum of harmful magical acts, of which the elf-arrow shooting forms the apotheosis. For Isobel, the company that feasted under the fairy hill were the same company that travelled in whirlwinds in order to hunt down and kill their neighbours. As we have seen, these references are too divergent from demonological convention to be dismissed as elite superimposition, and too consistent with contemporary folklore to be dismissed as anomalous. Consequently, in Isobel's case, before we can even entertain theories about following-the-goddess visionary traditions, these maleficent elements need to be explained.

We find few answers in the shamanistic hypothesis, as it currently stands. Although there have been many disputes over how the shamanistic experience should be defined, anthropologists and historians agree that one of its core features, and that which distinguishes it from a non-shamanistic visionary experience, is that it involves spirit-contacting rites undergone specifically for the benefit of the community. In other words, however dramatic the voice or the vision, however deep the dream or trance, unless there is evidence of community-benefiting rationale a rite cannot be defined as shamanistic. In their analyses of warrior shamanism in early modern Europe, scholars such as Ginzburg and Pócs have shown that – although violent – the militaristic activities of cults like the Friulian *benandanti* and Hungarian *táltos* fit into this template. Here, aggressive shamanistic rites are played out in the context of epic battles motivated by beneficent aims such as obtaining fertility of the fields or protecting towns from earthquakes.[21]

But these analyses do not seem immediately relevant to Isobel's case. Unlike those of the *benandanti* or *táltos*, her aggressive acts seem hard to justify in this way. While interpersonal tensions may have underpinned her alleged assaults on the few identified victims, such as Harry Forbes and her landlord John Hay, most of her *maleficium* seems disturbingly random and indiscriminately vindictive. In her long lists of the arrow-slain, for example, there is no evidence of any prior grievance and many of the victims are not even named. It is difficult to link Isobel's violent and arbitrary attacks to any kind of shamanistic ethos.

III

However, we can gain new insights into this problem from recent developments in anthropology. In 2004, Neil Whitehead and Robin Wright noted that

> there has been a marked tendency in past two or three decades to emphasize the positive, therapeutic and socially integrative dimensions of shamanism ... [but the] ethnographic experience of

Amazonian dark shamanism pointedly contradicts this imagery and, while issues of the politics of representation cannot be ignored, it is obviously the role of anthropology to provide a more adequate interpretation and presentation of actual Amazonian practices. Although recognized, [until now] the 'dark' side – the shamans' power to destroy or inflict harm through sorcery and witchcraft – has received little in-depth attention.[22]

Whitehead and Wright emphasise that while most shamanistic aggression can be clearly linked to the community-benefit rationale – with protecting the tribe against enemies and healing the sick being the most commonly cited aims – recent fieldwork in Amazonia has uncovered dark shamanistic traditions that are far more difficult to rationalise in this way. Here, the central envisioned rite is that of killing or, as it is often termed, 'ritual predation', and the predator's victims are often targeted in a shockingly indiscriminate way. The practices of the Guyanese *kanaimà* are illustrative. *Kanaimà* shamans ritually stalk, kill and mutilate their envisioned human victims by inserting various objects into their mouth and anus. Then, sometime later, they 'return to the dead body of the victim in order to drink the juices of putrefaction'.[23] This predation is so violent, and its community-benefiting rationale so obscure, that it has traditionally been viewed as a form of revenge-motivated witchcraft, but Whitehead shows that it has a deeper shamanistic purpose. After killing their victims, the *kanaimà* give some of the body fluids to their mentors (*kanaimà'san*) and, by virtue of the latter's special relationship with Makunaima, the creator of plants and animals, this exchange has a protective effect on the community.[24] Similar conclusions have been reached about the dark shamans of the Amazonian Warao tribe.[25]

Kanaimà predation is not, as with the *benandanti* or *táltos*, aimed at specific enemy combatants, but is apparently indiscriminate, with Whitehead emphasising that their 'selection of victims is ultimately a matter of indifference, in the sense that anyone will do'.[26] As a result the *kanaimà* shaman could find themselves targeting members of their own tribe, and even their own family members, with one informant telling Whitehead that 'If you learned to kill you must then kill – they have the urge to kill and it might even be a brother or sister.'[27] Such random predation is in fact an expression of standard shamanistic compulsion. The experience of being taken over by an uncontrollable power is a worldwide feature of shaman narratives. Shamans often depict the visionary impulse as an accumulation of psychological tension that has to be released, by 'shamanizing', in order to restore physiological equilibrium and avoid becoming either physically or mentally sick.[28] Similarly compulsive dynamics have been observed by historians working with early modern material, with Ginzburg noting that the *benandanti* were propelled to go out and perform their envisioned battles in response to an 'irresistible' urge.[29] While shamanistic compulsion has generally been studied in the initiatory context, it has been clearly linked to shamanistic predation in many parts of the world, from Siberia to East Asia.[30] The *kanaimà* who told Whitehead that, while travelling in spirit, 'he killed [a woman] with his hands and stopped her up... he didn't really know what he was doing' was articulating a trans-cultural experience.[31]

IV

These shamanistic perspectives are relevant to Isobel because shamanistic compulsion can also be detected in Scotland's host-related arrow-shooting narratives, as they have emerged from the seventeenth through to the nineteenth centuries. The following Victorian account, told to J. F. Campbell by a local doctor, suggests that the 'call' came through a build-up of psychological tension. Campbell claimed that, after pointing to a particular hill, the doctor told him:

'Do you see that kind of shoulder on the hill? Well, a man told me that he was walking along there with another who used to 'go with the fairies', and he said to him – 'I know that they are coming for me this night. If they come, I must go with them; and I shall see them come, and the first that come will make a bow to me, and pass on; and so I shall know that they are going to take me with them.' 'Well,' said the man, 'we had not gone far when the man called out, "*Tha iad so air tighin*. These are come. I see a number of 'sluagh' the people; and now they are making bows to me. And now they are gone." And then he was quiet for a while. Then he began again; and at last he began to cry out to hold him, or that he would be off.' 'Well,' said the doctor... 'he was fairly lifted up by the "sluagh" and taken away from him, and he found him about a couple of miles further on, laid on the ground. He told him that they had carried him through the air, and dropped him there. And,' said the doctor, 'that is a story that was told me as a fact, a very short time ago, by the man whom I was attending.'[32]

The compulsive quality of host participation is even more evident in anecdotes depicting men or women reluctant to accept their call.

Campbell's contemporary Alexander Carmichael claimed that a Uist woman told him about a Benbecula man to whom the fairies were, unfortunately, 'partial':

> His friends assured me that night became a terror to this man, and that ultimately he would on no account cross the threshold after dusk. He died, they said, from the extreme exhaustion consequent on these excursions. When the spirits [the sluagh] flew past his house, the man would wince as if undergoing a great mental struggle, and fighting against forces unseen of those around him.[33]

The same visionary impulses that drove the Highlanders into trance also seem to have driven them to kill. Those who believed themselves to have been swept up by the fairy host never claimed to have shot elf arrows willingly, but emphasised that they had been forced or commanded to do so by the fairies, with Carmichael noting that the host 'commanded men to follow them, and men obeyed, having no alternative. It was these men of earth who slew and maimed at the bidding of their spirit-masters'.[34] As we have already heard from another of Campbell's informants, one Highlander claimed that he shot an elf arrow at a man in a boat 'by desire of *them*: "*they* made him do it"'.[35]

That this belief was widespread in the early modern period is further supported by the fact that wherever contemporary first-hand accounts of participation in host-related arrow-shooting emerge (which is usually, as we saw earlier, in witchcraft records), the protagonists claim that they were ordered or coerced to shoot and kill their victims by the host or host leader – here generally defined as the Devil rather than a fairy. The power of these visionary impulses, and the degree to which they could subsume personal will, are painfully intimated in the trial dittays (indictments) of Margaret NcWilliam, who, as we have seen, participated in a coven that engaged in host-related arrow-shooting. She claimed that she had killed her own son:

> about 18 yeires syne being dwelling in Chapeltoune the devill apeired to her at the back of the Caleyaird and she haveing sustained losse by the death of horse and kye was turneing to great poverty he said unto her be not affrayed for yow shall get ringes eneugh ... he sought her sone William a child of 7 yeires old which she promised to him and he gave her ane elf arrow stone to shott him which she did ten dayes therafter that the child dyed immediately therafter which grieved her most of anything that ever she did.[36]

Here we can speculate that during a period of intense physical and psychological suffering NcWilliam succumbed to a visionary impulse that caused her to participate in a host-related hunt during the course of which she aimed an arrow at her own son. When she regained normal consciousness, she looked back in horror at what she had done. Although it does not specifically mention arrow-shooting, cunningwoman Janet Traill's account, given to the Perth kirk session in 1623, strongly suggests the same visionary dynamic:

> 'When I was lieing in child bed lair [stated Traill], I was drawn forth from my bed to a dub near my house door in Dunning, and was there puddled and troubled.' Being asked by whom this was done? She answered, 'by the fairy folks, who appeared some of them red, some of them grey, and riding upon horses. The principal of them that spake to me was like a bonny white man, riding upon a grey horse.' She said, 'He desired me to speak of God, and do good to poor folks' ... Being asked the cause why she was so much troubled by them? She answered, that the principal of them had bidden her do ill, by casting sickness upon people, and she refused to do it.[37]

V

These perspectives encourage us to re-evaluate Isobel's arrow-shooting passages. We must of course retain our earlier view that much of her testimony is likely to have been the result of false confession elicited through interrogatorial coercion and suggestion. Similarly, we cannot rule out the possibility that mental illness may have played a role. But we can now speculate that there may have been an experiential component to Isobel's arrow-shooting claims. It is notable that although Isobel's confessions contain indications that she willingly participated in, or even relished, her bloodthirsty experiences, on at least five occasions she specifically states that she had been encouraged or commanded to shoot her arrows by the Devil, with comments like the following appearing in all four confessions: '(the Devil) giwes them [elf arrows] to ws each of vs so mony ... [and] Qwhen [*rest of line missing*] giwes th[e]m to ws he sayes shoot thes in my name' and 'the divell gaw me an arrow, and cawsed me shoot an vowman in that fieldis: q[uhi]lk I did and she fell down dead'.[38]

As with so much of Isobel's testimony, these comments are open to a variety of interpretations, but in the context of our discussion about dark shamanism they could be interpreted as indications that Isobel's arrow-shooting passages may have drawn on memories of compulsive acts of visionary aggression experienced prior to arrest. Like her contemporaries in Bute, and her Victorian counterparts two centuries later, she may have been periodically seized by an irresistible impulse that propelled her into an envisioned bloodlust during which she saw herself as loosing elf arrows at the men, women and animals that became, during the course of her deep dreams or trances, identified as prey. On recovering from these experiences, Isobel may have looked back in horror at what she had done. Certainly, her claim that 'th[a]t q[uhi]ch trowbles my conscience most is the killing of sewerall persones, with the arrowes q[uhi]ch I gott from the divell' suggests genuine remorse.

VI

While these perspectives may give us an insight into the psychological mechanisms that may have propelled Isobel into envisioned arrow-shooting, for her experiences to be defined as 'shamanistic' as opposed to just 'visionary' the question of rationale remains. What community benefit could possibly have emerged from these strange bouts of ecstatic violence?

We can gain some insights into this question from Corsica, where a dark shamanistic cult of allegedly archaic origin – the *mazzeri* – existed until the mid-twentieth century. The *mazzeri* believed that their spirits periodically left their bodies and roamed the countryside hunting animals, 'tear[ing] their prey to death with their teeth, like hounds'. After their quarry had been wounded or killed, the *mazzeri* identified them as a human relative or neighbour in spirit form, and the animal's death almost always presaged the death of its human counterpart. Compulsion is clearly evident in the *mazzeri* sources, with the folklorist Dorothy Carrington emphasising that they were 'called' to kill, 'could not even choose their victims' and bore 'no animosity towards the animal they have to kill, nor towards the human being it represents'. As in other dark shamanistic traditions, this urge to engage in ecstatic violence was so powerful and indiscriminate that, on occasion, the *mazzeri* could be 'ordered to kill those they loved the most'.[39] One *mazzera*, Carrington claimed, informed 'a female member of the family [in the morning] that she had killed her child, that night, in a dream. She regretted what she had done, but it was not she who had committed the act, but something that had entered into her. She would make amends.' The fact that the visionaries did not keep their violent acts to themselves, but informed those they had killed, or seen killed, of their impending death, leads

Carrington to conclude that their rites lifted, for a brief moment, 'a fragment of the veil that covers the mystery of dying' and functioned as a form of death-divination.[40]

Can we suppose that the envisioned arrow-shooting experiences of Isobel and her contemporaries – should they have existed – mirrored the same rationale? That their violent envisioned rites were valued because they offered their communities the opportunity to gain valuable knowledge of those who were about to die? Such a possibility is supported from a variety of quarters. Firstly, it is important to remember that – as in any society where life is precarious – the prediction of future death was a major concern in pre-industrial Scotland. Signs and portents of death were warily watched for: visions of winding sheets, funeral processions or coffins being made; eerie sounds of glasses rattling at wakes; apparitions of the wraiths or physical doubles of the about-to-die; encounters with crows or ravens. Death-divination was a core preoccupation of popular visionaries, from the early modern period through to the nineteenth century, with folklorist Isabel Grant claiming that 'The visions of people who had the Second Sight were largely concerned with a future death.'[41] Similarly, the immediate desire of many clients of magical practitioners was for a prognosis – to be told whether or not they would survive their illness.[42]

Secondly, we have the fact that, with regard to arrow-shooting experiences, there would have been ample opportunity for divinatory discourse. Despite the grisly and sensational nature of their dreams and visions, those who participated in fairy hunts do not seem to have been shy about publicising them. The anecdotes and eyewitness accounts found in the collections of nineteenth-century folklorists make it clear that in this period the men and women who engaged in these activities broadcast their experiences both to their victims and to the community at large.[43] With regard to the early modern centuries, where arrow-shooting accounts generally appear in witchcraft records and could therefore have been alleged, as opposed to confessed, our assessment must be more speculative, but Lhuyd's observation in 1699 that it was widely believed that the fairies abducted humans as archers enables us to assume that something comparable occurred. Certainly, Isobel's claim, in her third confession, that 'Janet breadheid spows to Jon taylor told me a litl befor she wes apprehendit th[a]t margret wilsoen in aulderne shot allexr hutcheon in aulderne' suggests just this.[44]

Thirdly, working with Carrington's theories on the social function of the *mazzeri*, we have the fact that early modern Scottish society nurtured the deeper belief matrices necessary to sustain dark visionary traditions of this kind. Carrington emphasises that the Corsicans tolerated the brutal murders of the *mazzeri* not only because they functioned as a form of divination but also because they believed the visionaries to be innocent of the crimes they committed. For the Corsicans, the shamanistic compulsion was of divine origin. The victims of the *mazzeri* did not die because they had chosen to kill them, but because God himself had decided that it was their time to die. 'God ordained all she did', claims Carrington of one *mazzera*; 'It was He, she believed, who determined the day of the death of each one. She had been chosen to convey this news; she could only submit to His will.' This perspective reflected the 'fatalistic Christianity' adhered to by many Corsicans. As servants or messengers of God, the *mazzeri* functioned as 'instruments of fate'.[45] We find similar attitudes towards dark shamans in indigenous cultures from the Americas and Siberia.[46]

Fatalistic beliefs were strong and widespread in early modern Scotland. They helped people to cultivate the profound acceptance necessary to endure frequent privations and bereavements. Although Protestant theologians would not have wanted to interpret their Christian beliefs in such terms, as defined in their broadest sense fatalistic beliefs – in the form of the doctrines of predestination and providence – were fundamental to the reformed world-view and could have merged relatively harmoniously with the more inchoate Christian fatalism of the fireside. A little over a century after Isobel's trial an observer noted, with regard to the inhabitants of Auldearn: 'the general gloominess of their faith, which teaches them, that all diseases which afflict the human frame are instances of Divine interposition, for the punishment of sin; any interference, therefore, on their part, they deem an usurpation of the prerogative of the Almighty'.[47] Dark Gaelic proverbs like 'No man can avoid the spot, where birth or death is his lot' and 'His hour was pursuing him' are testament to these sentiments.[48] The possibility that fatalistic convictions such as these were powerful enough to enable death-divinatory arrow-shooting traditions to function in early modern Scotland gains support from various quarters. It is notable that even in the seventeenth century seers involved in death-divinations of any kind often seem – outside the Church at least – to have escaped moral censure. Although, like the *mazzeri*, they were often feared, they were not considered to be personally responsible for their grisly visions, or blamed for the grave messages they brought to their fellow men. Indeed, their inability to resist their dark calling seems to have elicited some sympathy, with contemporary minister James Kirkwood claiming of the second sight that 'It's so very troublsome to many, that theyd be gladly free from it.'[49]

Barring accounts appearing in witchcraft records, the same explanatory dynamic appears in sources describing arrow-shooting experiences. From Lhuyd's comments of 1699 through to those of nineteenth-century folklorists like Campbell, it is clear that all the farmers, lairds and weavers who claimed to have been forced to participate in the fairy hunt were considered to be innocent participants who were in no way responsible for the murders they were required to commit: the fairies 'made them do it'. Although the early modern Scots would not necessarily have articulated host-related arrow-shootings specifically as acts of 'fate', taken as a whole the evidence suggests that their tolerance of these traditions was rooted in a profound cultural fatalism. As I have explored elsewhere, the etymological and mythological links between fairies, witches and personifications of fate, like the martial *valkyrja*, support this thesis, and illustrate how, from an early period, following-the-goddess and warrior shamanism themes may have combined.[50] In this context, Isobel's role as fairy-empowered killer need not have been incompatible with her role, delineated earlier, as fairy-empowered healer in a regional following-the-goddess tradition. The intimacy with the fairies necessary to gain healing skills could have demanded an incorporation of their death-bringing aspect.

This tolerance, however, would not have precluded accusations of witchcraft. Even if fatalistic world-views enabled both the fairy hunters and their communities to justify such traditions, the hunters would have been highly vulnerable. Anthropologists have shown that dark shamanistic practices usually occupy an ambiguous position in their host culture. While they may be justified by mythology and by the self-protective or healing skills that they bring to the tribe, the aggressiveness of the practices means that those shamans who, whether deliberately or inadvertently, cause undue offence can be rejected by their communities. If a dark shaman oversteps the mark – perhaps through allowing personal vendetta to be seen to influence his choice of victim – the delicate balance between what the tribe gains and what the tribe loses through his envisioned activities becomes disrupted and the shaman can be ostracised or killed.[51] Whitehead has also noted that under the influence of Christian missionaries the nuances underpinning dark shamanistic practices, like those of the *kanaimà*, can become obscured, with local people who might have previously endured them being encouraged to denounce them in simplistic dualist terms.[52]

Something similar may have occurred in early modern Scotland. Like the early missionaries who travelled to the Amazon, the Scottish reformers strove tirelessly to revise and re-shape the popular world-view; a world-view that was often so alien to them that, as Stuart Clark has pointed out, 'The cultural distance that separated the aims of the religious reformers (and their secular backers among the European states) from the ideas and behaviour of the mass of the laity seemed to be great enough to invite comparison with the colonial confrontations overseas.'[53] Under the acculturating influence of the reformed church, with its stringent 'black and white' and 'of God and not of God' mentality, the moral subtleties that underpinned host-related arrow-shooting divinations (and many other popular beliefs and practices) would have become obscured, while the church's eagerness to prosecute magical activities may have encouraged those less tolerant of these practices to seek redress in the courts. Consequently, however much a woman such as Isobel maintained that she was coerced into performing these violent acts, the fact that she participated in them at all put her in a perilous position. Once she was hauled before the church authorities, the uneasy truce that may have existed in her mind between the folkloric fatalism of the fireside and the godly fatalism of the church would have dissolved under the glare of the interrogatorial spotlight. And there, in an instant, the fairy archer would have been transformed into the witch.

VII

Although our assessments of Isobel's arrow-shooting passages have been brief and highly speculative, we cannot leave them without noting their wider relevance. While there have been various controversies surrounding the shamanistic hypothesis, the core dilemma for many historians has been how far to extend the thesis. While the evidence is strong enough for most to accept that in certain well-defined cases, such as those of the *benandanti* or *donas de fuera*, visionary rites took place, it is harder to assess whether this experiential component existed in relation to the more conventional and demonologically stereotypical accounts of sabbath-like activities found in witchcraft records. While it is generally agreed that these 'sabbath narratives', as we can term the latter here, contain shamanistic themes and motifs of folkloric origin, scholars remain uncertain as to how far these narratives represented experience as opposed to belief.

This problem presents itself most keenly in relation to narratives from western Europe, for two reasons. Firstly, the latter are often heavily demonised, with their high levels of stereotypical content suggesting that interrogatorial influence was strong and that therefore efforts to isolate the voice of the accused are largely fruitless. Secondly, the shamanistic status of these narratives is challenged by the fact that they are usually characterised by arbitrary malevolence. Although, as in Isobel's case, western European sabbath-narratives often contain reference to beneficent activities (such as healing) or neutral ones (such as feasting), they usually feature one or more maleficent – and often inexplicably brutal – magical acts, ranging from the raising of storms to the killing and eating of children. These acts frequently gain a disturbing intensity from seeming to be performed, and the victims targeted, in a chillingly indiscriminate way. Because it is difficult to link these narratives to any kind of community-benefit rationale, and because, as we have seen, they generally carry signs of interrogatorial contamination, few scholars give serious consideration to the possibility that they may have possessed an experiential dimension.

Our analyses of the shamanistic context of Isobel's *maleficium* may shed some light on this issue. Although we have been focusing on shamanistic aggression in relation to host-related arrow-shooting, our Corsican and Amazonian material illustrates that dark shamanistic attacks could incorporate various forms of violence, from blood-sucking to beating with cudgels to tearing apart with bare hands. Could we therefore entertain the possibility that other sabbath-narratives containing seemingly arbitrary and savage killings could – like Isobel's arrow-shooting passages – reflect dark shamanistic practices characterised by ecstatic compulsion and underpinned by fatalistic beliefs concerning death? The occasional narrative overtly welcomes such an explanation. The following, taken from a trial that took place in Hungary in 1756, is redolent of the accounts of the *mazzeri* and *kanaimà* in its depiction of compulsion, killing and retrospective remorse. It is also notable for its direct reference to 'the will of destiny'. Pócs writes

> In 1756, Katalin Szabó from Nagyvázsony talked about her bewitching nocturnal round trips and 'being totally deprived of my senses, I became an exile ... during the night, to the will of destiny. I should have set fire to the houses of four inhabitants: István Már, Cseke, Széderi, and Baranyai.' Squeezing through the smoke hole, she set fire to two of them, but then she felt bitterly sorry. Why had God allowed her to 'carry out such evil deeds?'[54]

Few accounts are as explicitly relevant as Szabó's, but with regard to Scotland at least, it is notable that although most sabbath-narratives do not feature host-related arrow-shooting, a significant minority conform to Isobel's confessions in the sense that they depict groups of individuals who roam around the countryside, sometimes in the form of animals, entering houses and seemingly randomly killing a succession of humans and animals in a chillingly clinical way. The testimony of Margaret Duchill, given at Alloa in 1658, is typical:

> Sche confest ane meiting in the Cuningar of all the sevine with the divell in the likeness of catts, who went to the [...] and destroyed ane kow to Edward Burnes. Ane other meitting one night and they went to Tullibodie and killed ane bairne. Another meitting and went to bow house and killed ane horse and ane kow to William Monteath. Ane other meitting and they went to Clakmannan and killed ane child to Thomas Bruce. Ane other meitting and they went to Caldone's and was the death of two bairnes of his.[55]

Using the interpretative lens constructed here, can we speculate that the arbitrary, death-bringing perambulations of the Alloa witches involved compulsive, dark shamanistic practices? And that just as Isobel may have been compelled, on certain nights of the year, to participate in death-bringing arrow-shooting hunts, so Duchill and her companions may have been swept up and compelled to participate in death-bringing house-to-house processions; fulfilling, in these unwelcome visions and dreams, their dark shamanistic role as messengers and agents of fate? The hypothesis sketched out in this chapter needs further research before we can attempt to answer such questions. Nevertheless, rudimentary as it is, it clearly invites us to pay more attention to the role of dark shamanism in the history of Europe's witches.

Notes

1. Emma Wilby, *The Visions of Isobel Gowdie: Magic, Witchcraft and Dark Shamanism in Seventeenth-Century Scotland* (Brighton, 2010), 39–40. For the original trial document, see NRS, GD125/16/5/1/1.
2. Ibid., 47–8.
3. Robert Kirk, *The Secret Common-Wealth* (Cambridge, 1976), 59–60.
4. Ronald Black (ed.), *The Gaelic Otherworld: John Gregorson Campbell's 'Superstitions of the Highlands and Islands of Scotland' and 'Witchcraft and Second Sight in the Highlands and Islands'* (Edinburgh, 2005), 304–5.
5. Wilby, *Visions*, 92–3.
6. Black (ed.), *Gaelic Otherworld*, 47.
7. Wilby, *Visions*, 165–6, 171–3, 71.
8. Ibid., 215–36.
9. *HP*, iii, 10.
10. John Francis Campbell (ed.), *Popular Tales of the West Highlands*, 2 vols. (Edinburgh, 1860), ii, 71–2.

11. Carlo Ginzburg, *Ecstasies: Deciphering the Witches' Sabbath*, trans. Raymond Rosenthal (Harmondsworth, 1991).

12. In *Visions* I circumvented this problem by replacing the term 'following the goddess' with (more clumsy, but less contentious) 'female-led spirit-groups', 301–3. For a critique of Ginzburg, see Willem de Blécourt, 'The return of the sabbat: mental archaeologies, conjectural histories or political mythologies?', in Jonathan Barry and Owen Davies (eds.), *Palgrave Advances in Witchcraft Historiography* (Basingstoke, 2007), 125–45.

13. Carlo Ginzburg, *The Night Battles: Witchcraft and Agrarian Cults in the Sixteenth and Seventeenth Centuries*, trans. John Tedeschi and Anne Tedeschi (London, 1983).

14. Gustav Henningsen, ' "The Ladies from Outside": an archaic pattern of the witches' sabbath', in Bengt Ankarloo and Gustav Henningsen (eds.), *Early Modern European Witchcraft: Centres and Peripheries* (Oxford, 1990), 191–215.

15. Notable works in this field, in addition to the above, have been Éva Pócs, *Between the Living and the Dead: A Perspective on Witches and Seers in the Early Modern Age*, trans. Szilvia Rédey and Michael Webb (Budapest, 1999), and Wolfgang Behringer, *Shaman of Oberstdorf: Chonrad Stoeckhlin and the Phantoms of the Night*, trans. H. C. Erik Midelfort (Charlottesville, VA, 1998). For more recent discussions of the shamanistic paradigm, see Gábor Klaniczay 'Shamanism and witchcraft', *Magic, Ritual and Witchcraft*, 1 (2006), 214–21, and Gábor Klaniczay and Éva Pócs (eds.), 'Witchcraft mythologies and persecutions', *Demons, Spirits, Witches*, vol. iii (Budapest and New York, 2008), 35–49.

16. Ginzburg, *Ecstasies*, 96–7.

17. Lizanne Henderson and Edward J. Cowan, *Scottish Fairy Belief: A History* (East Linton, 2001), 136.

18. Margo Todd, *The Culture of Protestantism in Early Modern Scotland* (New Haven, Conn., 2002), 219.

19. The quotation refers to the visits of the Swiss *Säligen Lütt*, in Behringer, *Shaman of Oberstdorf*, 69.

20. See Henningsen, 'Ladies', 196. Many examples can also be found in Éva Pócs, *Fairies and Witches at the Boundary of South-Eastern and Central Europe* (Helsinki, 1989).

21. For the *benandanti*, see Ginzburg, *Night Battles*, 1–32. For the *táltos*, see Pócs, *Between the Living and the Dead*, 134–9.

22. Neil L. Whitehead and Robin Wright (eds.), *In Darkness and Secrecy: The Anthropology of Assault Sorcery and Witchcraft in Amazonia* (Durham, NC, 2004), 10.

23. Neil L. Whitehead, *Dark Shamans: Kanaimà and the Poetics of Violent Death* (Durham, NC, 2002), 14–15. The Guyanese believe that, while in spirit form, the *kanaimà* directly attacks, and consumes, the physical body of the victim.

24. Ibid., 97.

25. Johannes Wilbert, 'The order of dark shamans among the Warao', in Whitehead and Wright (eds.), *In Darkness and Secrecy*, 21–50.

26. Whitehead, *Dark Shamans*, 14, 104, 66, 90–1.

27. Ibid., 115, 117.

28. For an example, see Kira Van Deusen, *Singing Story, Healing Drum: Shamans and Storytellers of Turkic Siberia* (Montreal, 2004), 76.

29. Ginzburg, *Night Battles*, 61. See also Behringer, *Shaman of Oberstdorf*, 23.
30. Wilby, *Visions*, 332–3. Compulsion is evident in Whitehead and Wright (eds.), *In Darkness and Secrecy*, 40, 39. For an African example, see Norman Cohn, *Europe's Inner Demons: The Demonization of Christians in Medieval Christendom* (2nd edn., London, 1993), 178.
31. Whitehead, *Dark Shamans*, 114.
32. Black (ed.), *Gaelic Otherworld*, 303–4.
33. Alexander Carmichael, *Carmina Gadelica: Hymns and Incantations*, 2 vols. (2nd edn., Edinburgh, 1928), ii, 358.
34. Ibid., 357.
35. Campbell (ed.), *Popular Tales*, ii, 71–2.
36. *HP*, iii, 18–19.
37. *Extracts from the Presbytery Book of Strathbogie, 1631–1654*, ed. John Stuart (Spalding Club, 1843), p. xii.
38. Wilby, *Visions*, 43, 44.
39. Dorothy Carrington, *The Dream-Hunters of Corsica* (London, 1995), 58, 88, 110.
40. Ibid., 107.
41. I. F. Grant, *Highland Folk Ways* (2nd edn., Edinburgh, 1995), 366.
42. For Agnes Sampson's divinatory prayer, see Normand and Roberts (eds.), *Witchcraft*, 236–7.
43. Wilby, *Visions*, 337–8.
44. Ibid., 48.
45. Carrington, *Dream-Hunters*, 106, 99. This thesis is supported by wider anthropological comparisons. Though not necessarily articulated as such, dark shamanistic practices are fundamentally fatalistic: see Wilby, *Visions*, 342–3.
46. For examples, see Charles Stépanoff, 'Devouring perspectives: on cannibal shamans in Siberia', *Inner Asia*, 11 (2009), 283–307, and Whitehead and Wright (eds.), *In Darkness and Secrecy*, 7.
47. Donald J. Withrington and Ian R. Grant (eds.), *The Statistical Account of Scotland: Banffshire, Moray and Nairnshire, 1791–1799* (2nd edn., Wakefield, 1982), 718.
48. Alexander Nicholson (ed.), *A Collection of Gaelic Proverbs and Familiar Phrases* (Edinburgh, 1881), p. xxii.
49. John Lorne Campbell (ed.), *A Collection of Highland Rites and Customes: Copied by Edward Lhuyd from the Manuscript of James Kirkwood* (Cambridge, 1975), 103.
50. Wilby, *Visions*, 346–61.
51. Whitehead and Wright (eds.), *In Darkness and Secrecy*, 47; Whitehead, *Dark Shamans*, 124.
52. Whitehead, *Dark Shamans*, 50, 53–76.
53. Stuart Clark, *Thinking with Demons: The Idea of Witchcraft in Early Modern Europe* (Oxford, 1997), 509.
54. Pócs, *Between the Living and the Dead*, 96.
55. John E. Simpkins (ed.), 'Examples of Printed Folk-Lore concerning Fife with some notes on Clackmannan & Kinross-shires', *County Folk-Lore*, 7 vols. (London, 1914), vii, 325.

9
Flying Witches in Scotland

Julian Goodare

The belief that witches could fly was a key component of the early modern concept of witchcraft. In Scotland, many witches told stories of flight – even if, like Barbara Parish in Livingston in 1647, they obscured this fact by using another word for it:

> She raid to Burdihouse and was eight dayes their and said that she left a ould seck in her place quhill she come againe and that their was eight of them in company with her that went to Burdiehouse and the thing that she raid on was a runge.[1]

Witches' flight has been little studied in Scotland. This chapter will seek to fill a gap by drawing together a wide range of evidence about popular beliefs concerning flying witches. As well as a wide variety of modes of flight, the survey will also extend to consider other magical modes of travel, such as instant transvection and sailing in sieves. It will also discuss the possible reality behind reports of flight, touching on psychological studies of out-of-body experiences.

I

Folk belief about witches' flight was varied. Flight could be voluntary or involuntary, could employ vehicles such as straws to ride on, or could be undertaken in human or animal form. The chapter will review these and other motifs, and evaluate the varied types of evidence in which the motifs are found. Bearing in mind that flying is absent from many witchcraft trial records, the chapter will also ask how widespread the belief in witches' flight was in Scotland. To anticipate, the answer will be that it was normal to believe that Scottish witches flew – but that it was still a remarkable belief.

One possible reason for the neglect of flight in Scottish witchcraft studies is that Christina Larner, the great pioneer of the subject, dismissed the subject in her remarkable reconstruction of the system of popular belief. She quoted two leading cases involving flight (Isobel Shirie and Isobel Gowdie) and ascribed them to 'dreams, nightmares, and collective fantasies'.[2] She then moved rapidly on without further comment, to interpret the witches' view of their sabbath in realistic terms. Witches' confessions, as Larner read them, showed the sabbath as a straightforward festive occasion of the kind that Scottish peasants got into trouble with the church for having. Larner made clear that none of the confessions described real events straightforwardly, and in that sense they were *all* 'fantasies'; yet when they strayed from the realistic, they became aberrations. Larner was certainly right to identify peasant festivity as an important ingredient in Scottish witches' confessions, but it was not the whole story.

Information about popular belief in witches' flight comes from a variety of sources. The single biggest group is the confessions of suspected witches, which could have been contaminated by elite assumptions and leading questions. However, the accounts of flight contain little of the repetition of standard motifs that one finds in, for instance, accounts of the making of the demonic pact. Not only are accounts of flight less common, they are also more varied. Some of the flight material may have come from leading questions, but not much came straight out of learned demonology. Moreover, some of the confession material can be paralleled in other sources, especially neighbours' testimonies against suspected witches. Some confessions mention flight, not by the confessing witch, but by someone else. These too might have been contaminated by leading questions, but the danger is less, and again, the material seems too varied for it to have been straightforwardly imposed by interrogators.

Many confessing witches, then, seem to have been free to tell their own stories about flight. This does not mean that they were telling the truth (if only because the literal truth, that they really flew, does not warrant extended consideration), nor does it even necessarily mean that they literally believed the stories that they were telling; but it does mean that their confessions derive from popular culture. Many of the beliefs about flight seem in fact to have been shared between the common folk and the elite, but the elite also had demonological preoccupations, especially about whether flight occurred bodily or in spirit. The rarity with which the confessions discussed this issue indicates that they largely showed witches' flight as it was understood in popular culture. It is that culture that this chapter seeks to understand.

How did early modern folk imagine flight? They did not think of powered machines, nor of anything like today's cartoon superheroes. They thought of rising by possessing a quality of lightness and airiness.[3] They thought of birds, they thought (though more rarely) of bees and other insects, and they thought of being carried by the wind. To be sure, they also thought of magic; but even magic could not transcend the boundaries of the imagination. Witches' flight had to be imaginatively credible.

II

How, then, did Scottish witches fly? There is no clear evidence that they flew on broomsticks; nor did they necessarily need a vehicle of any kind. Nevertheless, it may be helpful to begin with the vehicles that a few witches used – several of which are in fact gathered in a single case. Margaret Watson, in Carnwath in 1644, was accused of attending witches' meetings at which there had been 'ane great multitude' of witches present. She confessed that 'Mailie Paittersone read upone ane cat, Jonet Lockie read upone ane cock and thy aunt Margaret Watsone read upone ane thorne trie and thyself read upone ane bottell of strae and the said Jeane Lauchlane upone ane bourtrie.'[4]

The vehicles Watson gives us, therefore, are three plants – a hawthorn tree, an elder tree (bourtree) and a bundle of straw – and two animals – a cat and a cock. The hawthorn and elder were both ill-omened.[5] Watson may have been the only witch to mention flying on them, but the hawthorn, at least, occurs in other witchcraft contexts.[6] As for the straw, this was probably imagined as a vehicle for flight because of its lightness. Watson rode upon a bundle of straw, but the most famous witches to fly on straws were Isobel Gowdie and her companions, in Auldearn in 1662, who mainly flew on single straws. Gowdie imagined these straws as being blown along in the wind, 'ewin as strawes wold flie wpon an hie way'.[7] There were in fact several kinds of straws; Gowdie's first confession mentioned wild-straws and corn-straws. Yet more remarkably, these witches also rode on the bodies of people whom they had shot; their souls went to Heaven, 'bot ther bodies remains w[i]th ws, and will flie as hors to ws als small as strawes'. In Gowdie's second confession she mentioned 'windlestrawes or beenstakis'.[8] A 'windle' was a bundle of straw, which brings us back to Margaret Watson; 'beenstakis' were beanstalks, effectively a third kind of straw. There was also a 'bunwede', a stalk of ragwort, on which Marion Hunter confessed to having ridden in Lanark in 1650.[9]

Gowdie's confessions provide a rare example of a spell for flight: the witches would 'say hors and hattok in the divellis nam', enabling them to ride on straws in whirlwinds.[10] 'Hattock', linguistically, was a diminutive of 'hat', and the phrase seems to have been connected with Norse legends in which a hat was thrown to a mortal to enable them to join a fairy ride. The same phrase in a later Orkney story was 'Up hors, up hedik', while there are also Gaelic stories involving a magic cap for flight.[11] For Gowdie, the spell animated her straw so that she could fly on it; it became a symbolic 'horse'. In the Orkney story, the straw was actually transformed into a horse. As for the hat or cap, Janet Boyman stated in 1572 that she had 'sene twentie tymes the evill blast that is to say the wind with a thing lyke ane hatt in it quhirland about the stray and ay at sic tyme thair is ane evill spreit or ane war thing neir hand by'.[12] The hat may be a significant component of this belief system.

Mention of horses brings us to flight on an animal, of which, as with flight on plants, there was only a modest amount. We have already encountered Margaret Watson's cat and cock. The cat was a common animal in Scottish witchcraft, usually with witches being transformed into cats. A cock was a favoured animal to which to transfer diseases.[13] It was a 'creature full of lust', and the aphrodisiac 'cock ston' was related to elf-shot.[14] The only other animal vehicles are swallows, mentioned by the canon lawyer William Hay in the 1530s in a discussion of the famous Canon *Episcopi*. The women whom he described 'profess that they ride at night on some kind of beasts or swallows'.[15] These swallows, it has recently been argued, were the vehicles for a shamanistic cult involving fairy-like beings, the 'seely wights'.[16]

Perhaps more common than flight on an animal was flight on a transformed human. We have already encountered this with Isobel Gowdie, and it also occurs in another famous case, the last Scottish witch to be executed. Two witches were prosecuted in Sutherland in 1727, a mother and a daughter; the mother was executed while the daughter escaped. The mother was reported to have 'ridden upon her own daughter, transformed into a poney, and shod by the devil', making the daughter lame in hands and feet.[17] This comes from a tradition collected in the early nineteenth century, which added that the daughter's son, still living until recently, had also been lame. Was the whole story invented to explain the son's lameness? It seems unlikely that such a belief could have been freshly invented in the period after 1727, because, as we shall see, similar stories had already been told in the seventeenth century. It is quite likely that 'Janet Horne' was really believed at the time to have transformed and ridden on her daughter; at any rate, the belief should be recognised as one that was current at the time.[18] The story did not explicitly mention flying, but as in other such cases, magical 'riding' was probably understood as involving flight.

The earlier case closely paralleling that of 1727 is that of Isobel Shirie and the other witches of Forfar in 1661. Here, too, not only did the witch transform and ride on another person, but that other person was also a witch. Shirie was herself transformed into a horse and ridden, both by other witches and by the Devil. Agnes Spark confessed that other witches 'did speake of Isabell Shirie and say that shoe was the divills horse, and that the divill did alwayes ryde upon hir, and that she was shoad like ane mare or ane horse'. She added that Shirie 'carried hir away' to a meeting about midnight. Janet Howat, similarly, confessed that Shirie 'carried' her to two meetings. Elspeth Alexander and Janet Stout confessed that Shirie was nicknamed 'The Horse'.[19] The case of Anne Armstrong, from Corbridge, Northumberland, in 1673, was similar and may even have been influenced by Scottish beliefs.[20]

More typical of Continental belief was the idea of the witch transforming, and riding upon, an innocent person. As we have seen, Isobel Gowdie and her companions sometimes rode on the bodies of people whom they had shot with elf-shot, transformed into straws. This appears to be a version of the idea of witches abducting and riding on innocent people, though the idea of killing the people first was unusual. The witch who transforms and rides an innocent person would later be a common figure of Gaelic folklore.[21] This may well lie behind the testimony of Robert Brown, in Balmerino in 1649, who insisted on his deathbed 'that Elspeth Seith and other two did ryde him to deathe'.[22] An intermediate idea was expressed by the accused witch Margaret Duchell, in Alloa in 1658, who confessed 'that ane night the said Elisabeth Blak came to hir at midnight and took hir out of hir awne house to the crofts of Alloway, quhair the Devill came to them, and as shoe said, rede them both'.[23] Duchell was not an innocent person when Black, or the Devil, rode her, but she seems, like the innocent people, to have been coerced into flight.

There was, then, a variety of vehicles for Scottish witches – and this fact may have its own significance. Margaret Watson's cat, cock, hawthorn tree, elder tree and bundle of straw have all been discussed individually, but have more to reveal as a group. One theme in stories of magical transport seems to have been the deliberate incongruity of different modes of transport.[24] Watson could have confessed that the witches had all used the same kind of vehicle (cats, say), but she preferred to list a mixture of animal and plant vehicles. Isobel Gowdie mentioned various different straws, as well as humans transformed into straws. Flight had to be imaginatively credible; what we are looking at here is a story that, in order to be credible, has to be made as weird as possible. Even this weirdness was not random, however, but structured in recognisable ways.

Animal transformations were often linked with flight in a more straightforward way: witches transformed themselves into flying animals. No full study of shape-shifting has yet been carried out in Scotland, but the most common animals for it overall were probably hares and cats. The cases involving flight, however, emphasise bees and birds – usually crows. One, unusually, comes from a neighbour's statement. Megot Laing, in Elgin in 1597, was accused by a man 'callit Raye' of being a witch who 'apperit ... in the lyknes of ane be[e] and yeid in with a yirning and incontinent as he tuk doun the yirning and pat it under ane tub scho returned in her awin schape agane'.[25] Isobel Elliot and Marion Veitch, in Paiston and Humbie in 1678, flew in the shape of bees, carrying the poison used to kill Veitch's grandson in their 'cleuchis, wings and mouth'.[26] They may have been connected with the witch followers of the renegade minister Gideon Penman, in East Lothian in 1678, who confessed 'that sometymes he transformed them in bees, in ravens, in crows, and they flew to such and such remote places'.[27] A witch defended by George Mackenzie of Rosehaugh in this period faced the accusation that it was 'deponed by two penitent Witches, that she and they did flee as Doves to the meeting place of Witches'.[28] The Alloa witches, in the 1650s, sank a boat 'in the lyknes of corbies'.[29] Thomas Lindsay, a young boy connected with the Bargarran case of 1697, confessed that 'if he pleas'd he could fly in the likeness of a crow upon the mast of a ship'.[30]

Taking the form of a bird led naturally to flight, and in such cases flight may have been assumed even when it was not stated explicitly. In the confession of Helen Taylor, in Eyemouth in 1649, she and other witches visited a house in the likeness of various animals. 'Margaret Dobson was in the liknes of ane blak hen, and went in at the chimley head.'[31] The most likely way for a hen to enter a chimney from outside would have been to fly up to it.

Some of the vehicles for flight, especially straws, suggest the idea of being carried in the wind. The wind, especially if it was a whirlwind, could also carry witches without the aid of any vehicle. This motif could sometimes be associated with the idea of fairies carrying people away in whirlwinds.[32] Thus, Christian Nauchtie, in Elgin in 1629, 'confessit scho was three severall tymes away, ilk tyme aucht dayis away, and scho was taine away with a wind'. Others in her company included two dead people, and people with white faces and boss (hollow) backs, who seem to have been fairies.[33] On the other hand, whirlwinds are found in cases with no obvious fairy element. Bessie Flinker, in Liberton in 1661, confessed to having been 'taken up on the hills by a whirl of wind' to a witches' meeting.[34] Her confession was brief and heavily demonic; perhaps the motif was suggested to her by her interrogators, but it probably originated in popular belief.

One case of a witch being carried in the wind, but without explicit mention of a whirlwind, was that of John Fian, one of the North Berwick witches of 1590–1591. He was convicted of allowing himself 'to be carried to North Berwick kirk (he being lying in a closed bed in Prestonpans), as if he had been soughing athwart the earth'. He was also carried out to sea by the Devil, 'skimming over all the sea without land, in a boat'; this does not sound like an ordinary voyage. He also chased a cat in Tranent, 'in the which chase he was carried high above the ground with great swiftness'.[35]

Several cases simply state that the witch flew, without specifying a vehicle or method. A rare case where flight was witnessed (or at least asserted) by a witch's neighbours comes from Canongate kirk session in 1628. Christian Stewart complained that John Stirling and his wife Katherine Pratt had called her a witch. Two witnesses testified that Stirling and Pratt 'callit the said Cristeane ane witche and that they saw hir with hir slefis and mutch fleing abone thair headis cuming from Leyth'.[36] The sleeves and 'mutch' (cap) seem to have been thought magical, perhaps even connected with the 'Horse and Hattock' spell. The kirk session, however, did not believe the accusation. It seems to have been possible, but not common, to expect to see a witch flying.

III

Usually, flight seems to have taken some time, but there are a few cases where it may have been instantaneous. Strictly instantaneous transvection was demonologically unorthodox; demons were believed to be unable to transgress natural laws, and thus could not move objects from one place to another without traversing the intermediate space.[37] However, instantaneous transvection might still occur as a folk belief. Scottish folklore about the medieval alchemist Michael Scot told that, when in Bologna, he fetched his meals magically from the royal kitchens of France and England. The instantaneousness of the operation was a central point of the story – the food was still hot.[38]

Thus the 'Boy of Leith', aged ten when he told his story in 1684, visited the fairies every Thursday night. Sometimes he and his companions were 'carried into France or Holland for a night'.[39] The North Berwick pamphlet *Newes from Scotland* related the story of a pedlar who discovered some witches and 'was in a moment conveyed at midnight from Scotland to Bordeaux in France'; the pamphlet dismissed the story as 'most false', but presumably someone had believed it.[40] Helen Guthrie, in Forfar, confessed in October 1661 that 'she knowes that Elspet Bruice and Marie Rynd and severall other witches went to see the King's coronatione' which had taken place in Westminster on 23 April.[41] A related idea, sometimes known as bilocation, occurs in the case of Elspeth Wood, in Kilmalcolm in 1699. She talked to the minister of Kilmalcolm one Sunday, 'and yet that same day she or some in her shape was seen sitting in Kililan kirk the whole day'.[42]

A story in Lord Duffus's family in 1695 brings together several of these ideas and also connects us with Isobel Gowdie's spell for flight. One of Duffus's ancestors had heard the noise of a whirlwind, and 'voices crying horse and hattock (this is the word which the Fairies ar said to use when they remove from any place)'; he cried 'horse and hattock' also, and was caught up and 'transported through the aire by the Fairies'. He feasted with them, fell asleep, and next day awoke to find himself in the French king's cellar with a silver cup in his hand. Duffus himself thought the story 'fabulous'.[43]

IV

Destinations of flying witches varied. Quite often they flew to the witches' sabbath, though this was usually somewhere local. There are occasional indications of a remote, folkloric sabbath venue like Benevento in Italy or Blåkulla in Scandinavia.[44] The remote sabbath held 'upon a hill in Atholl' in 1597 is one example; flight is not mentioned but is surely the most likely means by which 2,300 witches could have been thought to gather there.[45] Gideon Penman's followers, quoted above, flew to 'remote places'. As we have seen, some witches flew to fairyland, often being 'carried' involuntarily. In addition to the cases discussed by Lizanne Henderson and Edward J. Cowan, the case of Margaret Fulton may be mentioned; she was one of the Bargarran witches of 1697. She was a charmer, and 'her husband had brought her back from the fairies'.[46] Janet Cowie, in Elgin in 1647, said that 'the fairie had taken hir away to Messindiu wher she slept all night'.[47]

Often, however, flying witches' destinations are unspecified. When the witnesses saw Christian Stewart flying above their heads, they presumably did not know where she was going. Some witches used their powers to accomplish a variety of errands, such as Isobel Gowdie's arrow-shooting flights or John Fian chasing his cat. Flying was occasionally associated, not with travel, but with dancing at a witches' meeting. Christian Mitchell, in Aberdeen in 1597, confessed to attending a meeting at which Satan played music and 'ye all dansit a devilische danse, rydand on treis'.[48] These 'treis' (logs) also extend the range of vehicles for flight; they seem similar to the 'runge' ridden by Barbara Parish, quoted at the head of this chapter.

V

A study of witches' flight can usefully be extended to consider other magical modes of transport. Witches could travel over the sea in ways that were analogous to flight; often they seem to have been hovering just above the surface. This motif occurs repeatedly in the North Berwick trials, with alleged attempts to interfere with the North Sea voyages of James VI and his bride. The very first recorded words of the first confession of the first witch, Geillis Duncan, were: 'Gillie confesses that in the midst of the firth they met with the [blank: witches?] of Coppenhown' (Copenhagen). The witches, both of Scotland and of Denmark, seem to have hovered under their own power to this maritime encounter. Duncan also described another sea journey in a boat like a chimney, with the Devil going before them in the form of a rick of hay; the boat 'flew like a swallow'.[49] This is reminiscent of the 'beasts or swallows' that we have seen mentioned by William Hay.

Hovering over water continued in the seventeenth century. Marie Lamont, in Inverkip in 1662, confessed that she and several other witches 'went out to the sea betwixt [Inverkip] and the land of Arran', where they met a ship and tore off its sails.[50] In Forfar, Helen Guthrie and her companions decided to sink a ship 'lying not farr off from Barrie'; she held the cable by which the ship was fastened, while 'the rest with the divill went into the sea upon the said cable as she thought'.[51] Both of these sound like the North Berwick witches. Margaret NicLevin, in Bute in 1662, confessed that the Devil carried her 'under his auxter' (armpit) to a boat that she wanted to sink; a storm arose, but God prevented the boat from sinking. The Devil later dropped NicLevin on a rock near the coast, from which she was rescued by another woman. John Macpherson, one of those in the boat, testified that she had told him at the time that she had saved the boat from the storm.[52]

The motif of crossing water also applied to inland waters. Isobel Young, in East Barns in 1629, was accused of having crossed a millpond in a stormy night, 'throw the watter... be extraordiner transportatioun without hors or uther help bot be the devill to haif sua convoyit hirselff'.[53] Robert Wilson, in Crook of Devon in 1662, crossed the river Devon in a similarly uncanny way, being accused that 'ye said that ye came home over Devon, the water being very great'.[54] Janet Kerr, in Duddingston in 1661, was helped by the Devil to cross the water at Tweedside.[55] Even when flying over land, witches may essentially have been hovering, rather than reaching any great altitude. This was common in reports of Hungarian witches' flight.[56]

The North Berwick witches' most famous maritime adventures, though, involved a vehicle: the sieve, or riddle as it was called. Agnes Sampson confessed that they had often been 'out of Scotland on the sea in their riddles', which 'made no stay but slid speedily away'. Euphemia MacCalzean was associated with a convention of witches who 'passed over the sea in riddles' to a ship which they raided and then sank. The contemporary pamphlet about the affair, *Newes from Scotland*, related that two hundred witches had set sail, each in their own riddle, to participate in the notorious witches' gathering in the church of North Berwick at Hallowe'en 1590.[57]

The motif of the riddle predated North Berwick. The poet Alexander Montgomerie, in the 1580s, claimed that his antagonist, Polwarth, would 'saill the see in a sive'.[58] Not all Montgomerie's material was folkloric, but it is plausible to believe that this was. Further riddles occurred in seventeenth-century popular belief. According to a slander case in 1622, Marjorie Bonnyman called Grissel Urral a witch and said that 'hir mother was a witche and rowit in a riddell'.[59] Margaret Philp told a neighbour that a spirit had said to her, 'Remember thow not that thow and I did sail in the ridle togither in the fleuck pot with severall others.'[60] A 'fleuck' was a flounder, so a 'fleuck pot' was presumably a fish kettle, perhaps an alternative means of magical transport.

VI

References to flight are quite common in records of Scottish witchcraft cases. Probably only a minority of the detailed records say explicitly that a given witch 'flew'; but we should add to these a large number of records in which flight appears in casual and allusive ways. A witness in the case of Isobel Cumming said that she 'redd over the new wall upone her owne belt'. The verb is 'redd' (rode), but the impression seems to be that she was airborne. A second witness had been surprised that Cumming arrived at a distant market before him, despite being 'old and weak'; he did not believe her explanation that she had travelled by boat, and he clearly thought that she had remarkable powers of transvection.[61] Isobel Haldane, in Perth in 1623, was 'taikin furth quhidder be God or the devill scho knawis not' and 'caryit to ane hill syde' where she met the fairies; there is no explicit statement that she was airborne, but it seems unlikely that her unidentified captor carried her on foot.[62] John Stewart, in the Maxwell of Pollok case of 1677, confessed that when three of his fellow-witches visited his house they 'went out at the window, thorow which they entered', although he had opened the door.[63] Elizabeth Maxwell, in Dumfries in 1650, was seen 'ryding upoun a cat'.[64] Cats do not usually fly, but then, people do not usually ride on them either. Reports of unusual and magical 'riding' are likely to imply flight.

There is also the issue of incomplete sources. The commissioners' report to the privy council on the Bargarran case of 1697 gives a seemingly full account of the witches, summarising their confessions. It mentions that James Lindsay 'was carried' to a meeting in Bargarran orchard. But a further source, a note of the crown advocate's speech to the assize, tells us additionally that Lindsay 'appeared to William Semple suddenly, and flew about like a fowl, for an opportunity to strike him'.[65] If we had further sources for some other witches, we might find more such material.

VII

In an influential work employing psychological studies, Edward Bever has recently argued that out-of-body experiences lie behind some reports of witches' flight.[66] This is a developing topic, and firm conclusions would be premature, but my own impression is that Bever's work, and the psychological studies underpinning it, are probably applicable in some way to the Scottish evidence. The questions are, how can they be applied, and to which cases?

Bever and I are historians. Perhaps we should begin by taking stock of what the psychologists are telling us. Bever stresses the autonomy of the out-of-body experience and its distinctness from another much-studied phenomenon, sleep paralysis. However, this is questionable.[67] He relies heavily on the work of Allan Cheyne and Todd Girard, but they see out-of-body experiences as part of a nexus of related phenomena which very much includes sleep paralysis. They also distinguish between 'illusory motor experiences' (IME) and 'out-of-body experiences' (OBE), with the latter, as they see it, involving a sense of separation from one's body or looking down on one's body from outside ('autoscopy'). Flight, as such, could be experienced in either IME or OBE mode. However, Cheyne and Girard see the IME and OBE experiences as linked, and further argue that OBEs themselves should be understood as two linked phenomena – 'out-of-body feelings' and 'out-of-body autoscopy', the former of which can lead to the latter.[68] Meanwhile, Michael Marsh has linked the out-of-body experience with the near-death experience.[69] The categorical and causal relationships between all these phenomena remain matters of debate, but the out-of-body experience is clearly part of a larger picture.

In analysing flying witches, a psychologist would probably want answers to a number of questions. Were the experients asleep or awake when their experience occurred, and if asleep, were they in the rapid eye movement (REM) or non-REM phase of sleep? How long did the experience last? Did the experients float to the top of the room (as is common in modern OBE reports), or did they travel long distances? Did they experience spinning or falling, or autoscopy? Was the experience blissful, or frightening? Had the experients taken any narcotics or intoxicants? Unfortunately, the Scottish witchcraft material can shine only a few flickering beams of light onto such dark and difficult issues. Interrogators of Scottish witches were uninterested in some of these questions, while in others, their interests are likely to have influenced the interrogation process in unhelpful ways. Let us see, nevertheless, what the confessions they obtained can tell us.

The interrogators had little interest in dreams, in the duration of flight, in flight to the top of the room, or in motor factors such as floating, spinning or falling. They may have assumed that demonic flight would be unpleasant, but there is no evidence of questioning about this. They were sometimes interested in whether flight occurred bodily or in spirit, which might have elicited statements about autoscopy; I have not found any, however. They might well have been interested in the demonological topic of ointments causing flight, which would have uncovered information about narcotics or intoxicants; the apparent absence of such material indicates that Scottish witches' flight was rarely, if ever, drug-induced.

Overall, it seems likely that OBEs, as they are currently (but imperfectly) understood by psychologists, lie behind at least a few of the reports by Scottish witches that they themselves flew. However, more work will have to be done before we can say much about individual cases. Moreover, much of the Scottish evidence comes from other sources – reports by neighbours that a witch flew, as with Megot Laing, or reports by a witch that another witch flew, as with Isobel Shirie. Such reports could not credibly be underlain by an OBE.

Flying witches in Scotland thus need to be understood in cultural as well as psychological terms. Margaret Watson may or may not have had an OBE, but it was certainly culture and not psychology that led her to describe flight on a hawthorn tree, an elder tree, a bundle of straw, a cat and a cock. The age-old nature–nurture debate is not going to be resolved in these pages, but the evidence presented in this chapter surely shows that the belief in flying witches was a significant cultural force in early modern Scotland. In the conclusions that follow, some of the reasons for this will be reviewed.

VIII

Flight is an escapist fantasy. Here it should be recognised that Larner, in her stress on peasant festivity as an ingredient of popular witch beliefs, had hit on an important principle. Peasant festivity, being rare, was itself usually an escapist fantasy. Witchcraft, to the ordinary folk of early modern Scotland, scratching a precarious existence in the face of falling living standards and the looming fear of starvation, was linked to magic, and magic offered the power to carry them away to a land of Cockaigne. There was feasting there, of course, and music and dancing. As Larner showed so well, there was freedom from 'want'.[70] Folk could readily imagine all this, so long as they could imagine having magical power. But what better way to imagine escapist magical power than by imagining the power to fly?

This is why flight was generally such a positive motif in Scottish witchcraft. Early modern Scots often feared witchcraft, but they did not imagine that flying witches would swoop down on them out of the skies like helicopter gunships, bringing death and destruction. Fear, and even disapproval, are rarely mentioned in accounts of flight, and flight is rarely associated with malefice. Nor does the Devil play much of a role except as a rare and obvious interrogatorial imposition. The proliferating vehicles for flight convey instead a sense of wonder and exhilaration. Flying witches were doing something extraordinary.

There were also darker aspects to witches' flight. One was the fear of being 'ridden' by a witch – not an ordinary form of malefice, but one that some people feared, especially if they had experienced sleep paralysis. Another aspect, perhaps related, was the way in which some witches believed themselves to have been 'carried', often by the fairies; not all of them welcomed this, especially those for whom sleep paralysis was the likely cause. Finally, there was Isobel Gowdie and her death-dealing flights, which open a window into a cultural tradition that was positive only to the extent that it was fatalistic. Gowdie's flights appear to be unique in themselves, but Emma Wilby has persuasively argued that her case is no aberration. All its components can be paralleled elsewhere; it is only in combination that they appear so remarkable.[71]

Witches' flight, because it was extraordinary, may have contributed to a sense that there were gradations of witchcraft, with some witches having a more impressive range of powers than others. At the upper end of the range there was Gowdie herself, a kind of *über*-witch – confessing not only to flying, but also to shooting arrows, visiting fairyland, having wild sex with the Devil, shape-shifting in various guises, and carrying out elaborate magical rituals both for good and for ill, to all of which her interrogators listened with horrified fascination. At the lower end of the range were witches whose powers were obviously limited. One was Elizabeth Anderson, a girl aged 17 who was drawn into the Bargarran case of 1697. She met three other witches in Bargarran orchard; at the end they 'disappeared in a flight', but she herself 'went home on foot'.[72] Anderson may have been trying to limit her guilt, but it is still significant that she did so in this way.

Elizabeth Anderson, the witch who could not fly, was clearly untypical. The casual way in which flight is alluded to in many Scottish witchcraft cases is an indication that it was considered to be normal. There are numerous briefly-recorded cases that mention only malefice, and even more that mention only the demonic pact, but they do not seem qualitatively different from comparable cases that also mention flight. This suggests that even if there were numerous witches of whom it was not said that they could fly, there were very few of whom it was believed that they could *not* fly. The belief in witches' flight was an autonomous motif, but it was linked with many other important matters that were closely tied in with witchcraft – notably beliefs in the witches' sabbath and in shape-shifting. These too were extraordinary beliefs. The common folk of early modern Scotland believed, not just that some witches flew, but that flying witches were normal witches. Flying witches were extraordinary, but then, witchcraft itself was extraordinary.

Notes

1. Angus Macdonald (ed.), 'A witchcraft case of 1647', *Scots Law Times (News)* (10 April 1937), 77–8. 'Quhill' = until; 'runge' = plank.
2. Christina Larner, *Enemies of God: The Witch-Hunt in Scotland* (London, 1981), 152. The inadequacy of this is also commented on by Emma Wilby, *Cunning Folk and Familiar Spirits: Shamanistic Visionary Traditions in Early Modern British Witchcraft and Magic* (Brighton, 2005), 185–6. The Shirie and Gowdie cases will be discussed below. The Survey of Scottish Witchcraft database also neglected to include a field for witches' flight, though numerous relevant cases can be gathered from the fields Dreams/Visions, Elphane/Fairyland, Ridingdead and Shape-Changing, all in the WDB_Case table.
3. Clive Hart, *The Dream of Flight: Aeronautics from Classical Times to the Renaissance* (London, 1972), 24–5.
4. *RPC*, 2nd ser., viii, 150.
5. Jacqueline Simpson, '"The weird sisters wandering": burlesque witchery in Montgomerie's *Flyting*', *Folklore*, 106 (1995), 9–20, at p. 16.
6. E.g. Pitcairn (ed.), *Trials*, ii, I, 543.
7. Quoted in Emma Wilby, *The Visions of Isobel Gowdie: Magic, Witchcraft and Dark Shamanism in Seventeenth-Century Scotland* (Brighton, 2010), 39. For an older transcript see Pitcairn (ed.), *Trials*, iii, II, 604. For more on this case see also Emma Wilby, '"We mey shoot them dead at our pleasur": Isobel Gowdie, elf arrows and dark shamanism', Chapter 8 in this volume.
8. Wilby, *Visions*, 40, 44; cf. Pitcairn (ed.), *Trials*, iii, II, 604, 608.
9. *Selections from the Registers of the Presbytery of Lanark, 1623–1707*, ed. John Robertson (Abbotsford Club, 1839), 77.
10. Wilby, *Visions*, 39–40 (and pp. 91–4 for discussion); cf. Pitcairn (ed.), *Trials*, iii, II, 604. If spells for flight were rare in Scotland, flying ointments (much discussed in some places on the Continent) seem to have been non-existent in popular belief. In 1685, George Sinclair mentioned them only in relating an English case: *Satans Invisible World Discovered*, ed. Thomas G. Stevenson (Edinburgh, 1871), 188.
11. Alan Bruford, 'Trolls, hillfolk, finns, and Picts: the identity of the good neighbours in Orkney and Shetland', in Peter Narváez (ed.), *The Good People: New Fairylore Essays* (Lexington, Ken., 1991), 116–41, at p. 127; Alan Bruford, 'Scottish Gaelic witch stories: a provisional type list', *Scottish Studies*, 11 (1967), 13–47, at pp. 27–30 (also giving further instances of the phrase 'Horse and Hattock').
12. NRS, indictment of Janet Boyman, 1572, JC26/1/67.
13. J. M. McPherson, *Primitive Beliefs in the North-East of Scotland* (London, 1929), 230–1.
14. Hunter (ed.), *Occult Laboratory*, 215.
15. William Hay, *Lectures on Marriage*, ed. John C. Barry (Stair Society, 1967), 120–1.
16. Julian Goodare, 'The cult of the seely wights in Scotland', *Folklore*, 123 (2012), 198–219.
17. Charles K. Sharpe, *A Historical Account of the Belief in Witchcraft in Scotland* (London, 1884), 199.

18. Edward J. Cowan and Lizanne Henderson, 'The last of the witches? The survival of Scottish witchcraft belief', in Julian Goodare (ed.), *The Scottish Witch-Hunt in Context* (Manchester, 2002), 198–217, at pp. 205–9.

19. Joseph Anderson (ed.), 'The confessions of the Forfar witches (1661)', *PSAS*, 22 (1887–1888), 241–62, at pp. 247, 249–50, 252.

20. C. L'Estrange Ewen, *Witchcraft and Demonianism* (London, 1933), 119, 358–61.

21. Bruford, 'Scottish Gaelic witch stories', 19–21. In these stories the ridden victim usually outwits the witch.

22. Alexander Laing, *Lindores Abbey and its Burgh of Newburgh* (Edinburgh, 1876), 218–19. This looks like a case of sleep paralysis, for which see Margaret Dudley and Julian Goodare, 'Outside in or inside out: sleep paralysis and Scottish witchcraft', Chapter 7 in this volume.

23. BL, Egerton MS 2879, fo. 8v.

24. Similarly, Swedish witches were thought to ride on broomsticks, goats or people (often people in authority such as sheriffs): Bengt Ankarloo, 'Sweden: the mass burnings (1668–76)', in Bengt Ankarloo and Gustav Henningsen (eds.), *Early Modern European Witchcraft: Centres and Peripheries* (Oxford, 1993), 285–318, at p. 314.

25. *Records of Elgin, 1234–1800*, 2 vols., ed. William Cramond (New Spalding Club, 1903–1908), ii, 55. 'Yeid' = went; 'yirning' = whining; 'incontinent' = immediately.

26. SSW. Presumably 'cleuchis' = claws, although the spelling is unusual.

27. Sir John Lauder of Fountainhall, *Historical Notices of Scotish Affairs*, 2 vols., ed. David Laing (Bannatyne Club, 1848), i, 198–9.

28. [Sir George Mackenzie,] *Pleadings in some Remarkable Cases before the Supreme Courts of Scotland, since the year 1661* (Edinburgh, 1673), 185.

29. BL, Egerton MS 2879, fo. 4r. 'Corbies' = crows.

30. *A True Narrative of the Sufferings and Relief of a Young Girle* (Edinburgh, 1698; Wing catalogue no. C7475B), p. xxv.

31. David Webster (ed.), *Collection of Rare and Curious Tracts on Witchcraft and the Second Sight* (Edinburgh, 1820), 108.

32. Lizanne Henderson and Edward J. Cowan, *Scottish Fairy Belief: A History* (East Linton, 2001), 37.

33. Cramond (ed.), *Records of Elgin*, ii, 211.

34. Quoted in Christina Larner, Christopher H. Lee and Hugh V. McLachlan, *A Source-Book of Scottish Witchcraft* (Glasgow, 1977), 258.

35. Normand and Roberts (eds.), *Witchcraft*, 226, 228, 230. For more on North Berwick see Victoria Carr, 'The countess of Angus's escape from the North Berwick witch-hunt', Chapter 2 in this volume.

36. NRS, Canongate kirk session minutes, 1619–29, CH2/122/2, p. 467. Stirling and Pratt confessed their fault: ibid., p. 469.

37. Stuart Clark, *Thinking with Demons: The Idea of Witchcraft in Early Modern Europe* (Oxford, 1997), 165.

38. J. Wood Brown, *An Enquiry into the Life and Legend of Michael Scot* (Edinburgh, 1897), 210–11.

39. Henderson and Cowan, *Scottish Fairy Belief*, 64.

40. Normand and Roberts (eds.), *Witchcraft*, 310.

41. Anderson (ed.), 'Confessions of the Forfar witches', 254.

42. Hugh V. McLachlan (ed.), *The Kirk, Satan and Salem: A History of the Witches of Renfrewshire* (Glasgow, 2006), 342.

43. Hunter (ed.), *Occult Laboratory*, 153.

44. See articles on these in Richard M. Golden (ed.), *Encyclopedia of Witchcraft: The Western Tradition*, 4 vols. (Santa Barbara, Calif., 2006).

45. Julian Goodare, 'The Scottish witchcraft panic of 1597', in Goodare (ed.), *The Scottish Witch-Hunt in Context*, 51–72, at p. 59.

46. *Account of Two Letters* (appended to the *True Narrative*), 7. See also Henderson and Cowan, *Scottish Fairy Belief*, 36–9.

47. *Records of Elgin*, ii, 357.

48. *Spalding Misc.*, i, 165; cf. 167.

49. Normand and Roberts (eds.), *Witchcraft*, 136, 138, 140.

50. Sharpe, *Historical Account*, 133.

51. Anderson (ed.), 'Confessions of the Forfar witches', 254.

52. *HP*, iii, 5, 7. For more on this case see Liv Helene Willumsen, 'Witches in Scotland and northern Norway: two case studies', in Peter Graves and Arne Kruse (eds.), *Images and Imaginations: Perspectives on Britain and Scandinavia* (Edinburgh, 2007), 35–67, at pp. 40–50.

53. *SJC*, i, 97. For more on this case see Lauren Martin, 'The witch, the household and the community: Isobel Young in East Barns, 1590–1629', Chapter 4 in this volume.

54. R. Burns Begg (ed.), 'Notice of trials for witchcraft at Crook of Devon, Kinross-shire, in 1662', *PSAS*, 22 (1887–1888), 211–41, at p. 227.

55. SSW.

56. Éva Pócs, *Between the Living and the Dead: A Perspective on Witches and Seers in the Early Modern Age*, trans. Szilvia Rédey and Michael Webb (Budapest, 1999), 77.

57. Normand and Roberts (eds.), *Witchcraft*, 148, 267–8, 314. Sampson also confessed to having been in an invisible 'boat like a chimney' in which the witches raided, and then sank, a ship: ibid., 138, 149. It has been argued that the riddles could have been real coracles: P. G. Maxwell-Stuart, *Satan's Conspiracy: Magic and Witchcraft in Sixteenth-Century Scotland* (East Linton, 2001), 151. However, no reason is given for describing coracles as riddles. Similarly, Maxwell-Stuart argues that an account of women rowing with oars 'clearly indicates a normal ferrying craft' (ibid.); however, this was the 'boat like a chimney'. The riddles were clearly intended as magical parts of an essentially magical story.

58. Alexander Montgomerie, *Poems*, 2 vols., ed. David J. Parkinson (STS, 2000), i, 152, l. 214.

59. Cramond (ed.), *Records of Elgin*, ii, 172. Another witness had the phrase as 'saillit in a riddell'.

60. William Cramond, *The Church and Churchyard of Rathven* (Banff, 1930), 26–9.

61. Cramond (ed.), *Records of Elgin*, ii, 298–9.

62. *RPC*, 2nd ser., viii, 353.

63. Sinclair, *Satans Invisible World Discovered*, 14 (relation 1).

64. A. E. Truckell (ed.), 'Unpublished witchcraft trials', *Transactions of the Dumfriesshire and Galloway Natural History and Antiquarian Society*, 3rd ser., 51 (1975), 48–58, at p. 50.

65. *True Narrative*, p. xli; *Account of Two Letters*, 7.

66. Edward Bever, *The Realities of Witchcraft and Popular Magic in Early Modern Europe* (Basingstoke, 2008), 118–29.
67. Bever says that 'Cheyne's research suggests that the two are only coincidentally related' (*Realities*, 465, n. 207), citing J. A. Cheyne and T. A. Girard, 'Spatial characteristics of hallucinations associated with sleep paralysis', *Cognitive Neuropsychiatry*, 9 (2004), 281–300. On the contrary, this article treats OBEs as a 'factor' of sleep paralysis and its findings 'provide additional evidence for the internal integrity of, and distinctions between, Intruder and V-M hallucinations' ('vestibular-motor' hallucinations, including OBEs) (p. 294).
68. J. Allan Cheyne and Todd A. Girard, 'The body unbound: vestibular-motor hallucinations and out-of-body experiences', *Cortex*, 45 (2009), 201–15. For a statement that OBEs 'frequently occur' during sleep paralysis, see Devin B. Terhune, 'The incidence and determinants of visual phenomenology during out-of-body experiences', *Cortex*, 45 (2009), 236–42, at p. 240. These articles are part of a 'Special Section on Out-of-Body Experiences' in this journal, pp. 201–58. For more on sleep paralysis and witchcraft see Dudley and Goodare, 'Outside in or inside out'.
69. Michael N. Marsh, *Out-of-Body and Near-Death Experiences: Brain-State Phenomena or Glimpses of Immortality?* (Oxford, 2010).
70. Larner, *Enemies of God*, 148.
71. Wilby, *Visions*, ch. 4.
72. *True Narrative*, p. xl. On another occasion her father 'carried her over the river in a flight', but they continued their journey to Dumbarton on foot.

10

The Urban Geography of Witch-Hunting in Scotland

Alistair Henderson

Geographical variations have always been a difficult aspect of witch-hunting in Scotland to explain. Christina Larner held that witchcraft was essentially a rural phenomenon, reliant upon a 'witch-believing peasantry' whose face-to-face relationships fostered reputations and made neighbours willing to name witches to the authorities.[1] The connection between witchcraft and rural areas has been generally accepted by historians of witch-hunting, in Europe as well as Scotland.[2]

It is perhaps not surprising that towns have not been associated with witch-hunting in Scotland. After all, only a small minority of Scots lived in towns even by the end of the seventeenth century. The Survey of Scottish Witchcraft confirms that a large majority of those accused of witchcraft lived in rural areas. There is no need to challenge Larner in her attribution of witch-hunting to rural society. However, towns were certainly not impervious to accusations; indeed, some towns were highly involved centres of panics. Analysing the urban minority may help us understand the witch-hunt in Scotland. The main approach is statistical, analysing variations in rates of intensity of prosecution. It is also suggested that some cases in towns may have had distinct urban features, relating to more intense local government, burgh politics and economy.

I

This chapter is about 'towns' in the sense of nucleated settlements of people pursuing non-rural occupations. Most such settlements were also 'burghs', in that they possessed institutional status. Larger towns were 'royal burghs' with international trading privileges, while smaller ones could be 'burghs of barony' entitled to trade internally. The chapter will also take account of some urbanised settlements without official burgh status but with a population density comparable to other towns.

Seventeenth-century Scotland was still a rural country by European standards, but it was urbanising faster than most. In the early sixteenth century, only 1.6 per cent of the population lived in towns with over 10,000 inhabitants, but by the 1750s, 9 per cent did so.[3] Most towns were smaller than that, but small towns too were growing in size and number. By 1707, there were 51 burghs of barony that had been established since 1660.[4] Prosecution of witchcraft in these smaller towns, this chapter will argue, may have been connected to their rapid growth and the economic pressures that affected their inhabitants.

We have little systematic information about the population of Scotland before the 1690s. However, evidence of urban populations can be gathered from a tax on valued rents in royal burghs in 1639.[5] This shows that Edinburgh was by far the largest town, and that most urban settlements contained fewer than 2,000 inhabitants. This can be compared with the 1690s hearth tax information to show the growth and decay of particular towns. Urbanisation was limited to the Lowlands and especially to the areas along the Forth, with Edinburgh and West Lothian having the highest density of urban settlement.[6] This region also saw the most severe witch-hunting.

The most obvious connection that could be made between witch-hunting and the towns is the intensity of urban government, compared with that of rural communities.[7] Even the smallest burghs had a council that supervised the inhabitants closely and could take an interest in accusations of witchcraft. Typically the council would comprise twelve or more merchants (sometimes craftsmen could also be councillors) who would oversee economic matters in the town. The council would be headed by a smaller group with executive powers, the 'magistrates', typically a provost and about four bailies. The magistrates held a court that settled minor criminal, as well as civil, matters in the town. It was often the magistrates who sought a commission of justiciary necessary for the trial of a witch. Urban authorities were perhaps no more zealous in prosecuting witches than others, although their concerns – ultimately the economic prosperity of the town – might have influenced their desire to root out ungodly citizens and preserve social order.

Urban authorities also had religious responsibilities. Burgesses who served as councillors often also served as elders and deacons on their kirk session, which was likely to hear initial complaints of witchcraft and to carry out pre-trial investigations.[8] Perhaps the prosecution of witches in towns helped to establish the status of townspeople within the urban hierarchy. Godliness supported their economic and political authority.

Another possible context for urban witchcraft accusations was the economic instability of medium-sized towns during the turmoil of the seventeenth century and what have been identified as 'localised short-term urban crises' during the sixteenth century.[9] Fishing towns on the east coast of Scotland relied heavily on only one trade.[10] If a sizable proportion of the workforce was killed in a disaster, the urban community was ruined. Similarly, coastal trading ports were affected by the loss of Dutch trade in the mid seventeenth century. Larner, who initially raised this question, was unsuccessful in drawing direct connections between such disasters and witch-hunting panics.[11] However, as we shall see, the prevalence of accused witches in small east-coast settlements is significant and could be connected with an awareness of the economic vulnerability which accompanied their rapid rise to the status of burghs.

II

Any statistics for the seventeenth century must be treated with caution, and those for witchcraft are no different. The gaps in surviving evidence, or fleeting references to witch prosecution, mean that no statistics can be complete or reliable. In the statistics below, from the Witchcraft Survey, it is assumed that where an accused witch was recorded as living in a 'burgh' they resided or at least worked in the town itself; if they had been brought into town from a rural area, their parish or settlement would have been recorded instead. In Scotland, in fact, parish boundary and burgh boundary coincided much more often than they did in England, though there were exceptions like Haddington, whose parish was 36 square miles.[12] The accused witches recorded as living in parishes containing burghs (but not specifically in burghs) are not considered 'urban', but rather as individuals potentially connected to the nearby town. In Table 10.1, therefore, two figures are given for numbers of accused witches in most burghs: a core figure for the 'burgh' and an additional figure, in brackets, for the 'parish'. These figures are collated with urban population statistics and towns are grouped by size.[13] These statistics include suspects from 'towns' that were urban parishes of comparable size to burghs but without burgh status.

A number of towns seem to have experienced few, if any, accusations. This is not really surprising, as other research has shown that around 65 per cent of parishes did not produce any suspects.[14] In fact, only 11 per cent of towns contained no suspects at all, because towns were

Table 10.1   Burgh and urban parish suspects by town size[1]

Population (approx. in 1639)	Town*	Number of accused burgh/ {parish}‡	Population	Town	Number of accused burgh/ {parish}
>4,000			1,000–1,500		
	Edinburgh	9 {1}		Tain	2 {9}
	Aberdeen	34 {1}		Dunbar	5 {13}
	Glasgow	12 {0}		Brechin	1 {4}
	Dundee	1 {0}		Culross	23 {10}
	North/South Leith	7 {12}		Dysart	36 {1}
	St Andrews	14 {2}		Arbroath	13 {3}
	Dumfries	9 {0}		Dunfermline	21 {12}
	Perth	8 {2}		Renfrew	0 {1}
	Inverness	3 {0}		*Alloa* (1691)	0 {12}
	Montrose	7 {1}	750–1,000		
	Canongate	3 {5}		Lanark	5 {0}
	Ayr	19 {8}		Peebles	2 {12}
3,000–4,000				North Berwick (1691)	2 {18}
	Stirling	3 {3}		Rutherglen	0 {0}
	Haddington	20 {22}		Anstruther E./W.	0 {1}
	Irvine	4 {20}		Cullen	1 {0}
	Elgin	16 {1}		Jedburgh	12 {2}
	Kirkcaldy	29 {2}		*Kinross*	0 {3}
	Dalkeith (1691)	9 {11}		Kinghorn	3 {0}
2,000–3,000				Crail	24 {1}
	Burntisland	8 {3}		Inverkeithing	38 {5}
	Linlithgow	1 {0}			
	Hamilton (1691)	0 {2}	500–750		
	Kelso (1691)	0 {6}		Forres	0 {0}
	Bo'ness (1691)	7 {26}		*Dingwall*	1 {1}
	Kirkcudbright	0 {0}		Pittenweem	20 {1}
	Dumbarton	13 {0}		*South Queensferry* (1691)	25 {0}
				Selkirk	3 {2}
1,500–2,000				Stranraer	1 {0}
	Banff	0 {0}	<500		
	Cupar	3 {0}		Nairn	2 {0}
	Lauder	9 {8}		Wigtown	0 {0}

Rothesay	2 {1}		Kilrenny	0 {1}
Forfar	8 {0}		Dornoch	1 {0}
Paisley (1691)	2 {11}		Falkland	2 {3}
Greenock (1691)	0 {7}		*Annan*	0 {0}
			Inveraray 1691	1 {0}
			Lochmaben	1 {0}
			New Galloway	0 {0}
			Sanquhar	0 {0}
			Whithorn	0 {0}
			(Wemyss)	2 {8}
			(Fortrose)	0 {3}
			(Newburgh)	8 {0}

---

[1] Data in all tables and charts taken from the Survey of Scottish Witchcraft.

*Towns listed are royal burghs from the 1639 valued rents of burghs, with the following exceptions. Towns listed in *italics* were burghs of barony (non-royal burghs) in 1639 (a few of these later became royal burghs, but this is not indicated). Those with no burgh status by 1691 but that could also be classed as 'towns' at this time are listed in brackets. Some towns appeared only in the later 1691 hearth tax, as indicated.

‡The main figures show numbers of accused witches in the burgh itself. Figures in brackets show additional accused witches from the urban parish, which may include the adjacent rural area.

generally larger and had a more concentrated population than rural parishes. The larger the unit of study, the smaller the proportion that will contain no witches.

The number of accused witches as a proportion of the total population of each town was lower for the larger towns and far higher for the smaller towns. Beginning with towns containing at least 4,000 inhabitants – of which Edinburgh was much the largest – the statistics show that Edinburgh, with its associated burghs of Canongate and Leith, had a typical absolute number of suspects for this group of towns, but this represents only a tiny relative number, because of Edinburgh's size. The number of suspects in Dundee, Inverness, Montrose, Perth and Dumfries was lower. Aberdeen contained the highest number of suspects, although many of these were part of just one panic, in 1597. Most of these towns (Glasgow, Dundee and Aberdeen) may well have had populations of around 10,000 by the 1640s, and Edinburgh was larger still. The number of suspects as a proportion of these towns' populations was very low.

By contrast, there were several smaller towns – with populations of between 500 and 1,500 – that actually contained a larger absolute number of suspects than the large towns. This of course translates into a very much higher proportion per capita. Within towns such as South Queensferry, Dysart, Inverkeithing and Newburgh, the urban population would have been well acquainted with suspected witches.

Figure 10.1 illustrates the proportional impact that witch accusations would have had on urban populations. This brings out the striking difference between the smaller and the medium to larger-sized towns in the number of suspects as a proportion of the overall town populations. For towns of between 500 and 1,500 inhabitants, the experience of witch accusations would have affected more of the town than in the larger towns, with approximately 10 per thousand townspeople being accused over the whole period. If one adds to this the friends, neighbours and family of the accused the wider impact can be appreciated. By contrast, in towns of over 4,000, only around 3 per thousand people were accused.

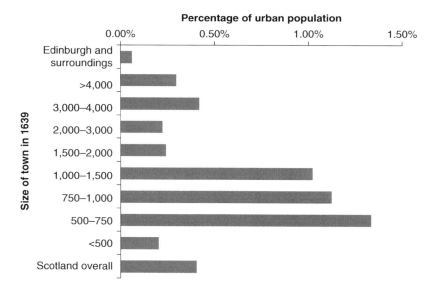

Figure 10.1   Urban suspects by town size, as percentage of town population
(Data are taken from the combined burgh and parish figures in Table 10.1 with approximate town sizes as in 1639. The '>4,000' group includes Edinburgh, but Edinburgh figures are also given separately. Figures for Scotland overall (rural and urban combined) are shown at the foot of the table for comparison.)

III

A regional comparison of urban cases is revealing. The map on p. xiii above shows the locations of Scotland's counties and principal towns. These counties can be aggregated into regions containing varying densities of urban settlement.[15] Not all regions can be discussed here, but a comparison of urban–rural patterns in the three regions of Fife, Tayside and the East Borders takes in many of Scotland's towns and illustrates the important issues.

The Fife region, comprising the counties of Fife and Kinross, contained by far the greatest number of urban cases, with a total of 232. Fife contained fifteen towns, only one of which (St Andrews) had over 4,000 inhabitants, while the majority had fewer than 1,000 each. This was nevertheless a remarkably urbanised region, especially along the Forth coastline. The poet Arthur Johnston (*c.*1579–1641) described how 'Towns are so scattered on all the shore, that one/Might be described and many joined together in the one' in his celebration of their courageous maritime communities.[16] These small towns formed an almost continuously urbanised coastline. Ferry links between Burntisland and Leith must have facilitated the spread of news and ideas between Edinburgh and Fife, and also along the Forth coast. Trading contact with the centre of justice may have influenced the high number of trials in Fife towns.

Considering that the total number of suspects from Fife was 382, the 232 urban suspects represent 61 per cent. The combined urban population of the region can be estimated, using the 1755 census, as about 20,500.[17] Out of a total county population of about 70,400 at that date, the urban proportion was just under 30 per cent. Thus, per capita, roughly twice as many suspected witches in Fife lived in its many small towns as in the countryside.

In the Tayside region (the counties of Forfar and Perth), the largest towns, Dundee, Perth and Montrose, produced only one, eight and seven suspects, respectively. The urban proportion of the Tayside population was 13 per cent. This region had a total of 192 suspects, and the total number of urban suspects was 38. The urban proportion was thus 20 per cent, showing somewhat more witches in the towns of Tayside than in its countryside; but this result should take into account the fact that thirteen of the thirty-eight urban witches came from just one small town, Arbroath. Tayside overall produced the fewest witches, fewer even than the Highland region as a proportion of its population.[18]

Despite an increasing national population, Dundee and Perth had stagnated, and this may help to explain why there were few witches there. Aberdeen, too, along with Dundee, suffered in the covenanting wars of the 1640s.[19] Aberdeen had many witches, but only four cases after 1631. Instead of fuelling fears of witchcraft, it seems more likely that economic decline was tangible and self-explanatory. Economic dislocation has also been suggested as a reason for the lack of hostility to witches in towns of the southern Netherlands.[20]

The East Borders region, comprising the counties of East Lothian, Berwick, Selkirk, Peebles and Roxburgh, contained a large number of suspects (841), with an urban proportion of approximately 20 per cent of the total regional population. The fifty-two urban suspects therefore represented only 6 per cent of the total. But there were several small towns in this region, with populations comparable to those of the Forth fishing towns. Why did Lauder, Peebles, Kelso, Jedburgh and Selkirk produce far fewer suspected witches? These border towns did not contain much of the national population and the population density of the counties was about half of that for the central belt of Scotland.[21] It should be borne in mind that this was the region of most intense witch-hunting in Scotland overall; perhaps what we are seeing is not so much an actual reluctance to prosecute witches in Lauder and Peebles, more an upsurge of rural witch-hunting in this region.

IV

Statistical patterns are useful for a general analysis, but must be complemented by local and individual case-studies in order to better understand how accusations and prosecutions developed within towns. West Lothian provides some valuable examples. The town of Bo'ness experienced a large outbreak of accusations in 1679–1680 in which twenty-one people from the parish were named. Out of these at least eleven can be identified as having lived in the town of Bo'ness, and another three would have had contact with the town through their husbands' occupations. Elizabeth Hutcheson, a shopkeeper married to a merchant in Bo'ness, confessed to being visited by the Devil in her shop until other people entered and he disappeared.[22] The four others whom she named were all married women; two had skipper husbands and one was married to a 'cainer' (an overseer of fishing). They may have been some of her customers. Hutcheson was tried with Elizabeth Scotland, also the wife of a merchant, who named one of the women and several other indwellers. They were obviously not poor people but part of a flourishing fishing community and engaging in business with each other. Their investigations were carried out by local men, many of whom were skippers or maltmen (making or dealing in malt), as well as a minister and the bailie depute. Together they would have formed an intense local authority. Complaints of torture resulted in their release by order of the high court. The large number of men investigating this case and their occupations suggests that they probably all knew the accused women's husbands. Their apparent attempts to force confessions by torture confirm that witchcraft was feared as much in the towns, where a large proportion of the West Lothian accusations are found, as in the fields. A male suspicion may have existed about what women were involved in while their husbands were out at sea. Moreover, the exchange of goods by married women in towns, like those in Bo'ness, is an urban version of 'women's work' – a context for witch-hunting that has already been explored.[23] This evidence supports an argument that cases of urban witch-hunting were not qualitatively dissimilar to rural cases. It also illustrates that in small urban communities the authorities, who were familiar with and possibly had personal motives against the accused witch, had a stronger desire to deal with them quickly and firmly than their counterparts in larger burgh councils.

Table 10.2 shows peak years of accusation in the towns of Fife. In each year of national panic, at least one town produced three or more suspects. One can also notice several years outside these periods when individual towns experienced small panics. Stuart Macdonald has looked carefully at this region, showing that witch-hunting was highly

Table 10.2 Panics in Fife burghs

Panic year(s) [*national panic]	Burgh(s) with three or more suspects [*including parish suspects]
1597*	Kirkcaldy (16); Pittenweem (5)
1621	Inverkeithing (6)
1623	Inverkeithing (12)
1624	Culross (7)
1626	Dysart (4); Kirkcaldy (3)
1630*	Dysart (10)
1634	Culross (4)
1637–1638	Dysart (4)
1643*	Crail (19); Dunfermline (15); Culross* (5); Pittenweem (4)
1644	Dysart (4); Pittenweem (3); St Andrews (3)
1649*	Dysart (11); Inverkeithing (10); Burntisland (4); Dunfermline* (5); Culross (3)
1661–1662*	Newburgh (7); Falkland* (5)
1675	Culross* (5)
1704	Pittenweem* (4)

localised and that it was the presbyteries that took the initiative in prosecuting witches. However, he does not seem to consider the urbanisation of the Forth coastline as a facilitator in the spread of witch-hunting.[24] Most suspects came from the towns which were situated closely together along the coastline rather than inland towns in entirely rural areas.

Most of the Fife cases were concentrated in the southwest corner, around Inverkeithing, Dunfermline and Culross.[25] These towns were all fairly small during the seventeenth century. Proximity to Edinburgh, in Fife at least, was probably not that important, as some other parishes in the same presbytery produced few, if any, suspects when others gave many. In 1643–1644, during the most intense panic to affect Fife, when (unusually) three out of four presbyteries had suspects, it was the coastal towns of Culross, Crail, Pittenweem, Anstruther, Kirkcaldy and Dysart that contained most witches. The presbytery of Cupar, on the other hand, contained comparatively few accused witches.[26] The fact that it also had no significant towns apart from Cupar itself, and did not share any of the Forth coastline, where suspects were rife, might not be coincidental.

The density of settlement on the coast may have been a factor in the spill-over of cases in the panic of 1649. This was mainly confined to the presbytery of Dunfermline, along with suspects from the neighbouring parishes of Dysart, Torryburn and Wemyss.[27] Table 10.2 shows that more urban suspects in the 1649 panic came from Dysart than the burgh of Dunfermline. Meanwhile, Kirkcaldy did not have a single accused witch in that year despite being so close to its witch-ridden neighbour. In fact there were few occasions when neighbouring towns had simultaneous panics. This reflects the extent to which townspeople on the coast of Fife identified suspects strictly within their own communities and how these small towns still possessed their own strong identities.

Recurring panics in Dysart, Culross and Inverkeithing suggest that local memory was important for the identification of witches in subsequent years. As these were mostly coastal towns built to capture trade it would seem likely that there was greater communication between them, allowing the fear of witches to spread, but only in years of national panics, especially 1643 and 1649, when towns further east of the witch-hunting core (Crail, Pittenweem, St Andrews) became involved.

V

For many of the urban witches, little information is recorded about their social status, but where such information survives it can be useful in providing a context to their accusation. An accused witch could complain to the local or higher authorities if they had the right connections. A number of urban suspects were wives or widows of burgesses and bailies, and their status within the town was perhaps a cause of resentment.[28] Louise Yeoman has found such motives for the accusation of high-status suspects.[29] Burgess status would have provided greater security, especially in old age, but could have made targets of the women who were fortunate enough to be married to a burgess.

Two cases from Fife illustrate how married women in this position were defended by their husbands. Margaret Young from Dysart was married to William Morrison, a merchant burgess. He appealed to the privy council in 1644 for his wife's release, describing the witches who had accused her as 'some malicious persons who wer brunt out of spleen and invy'. This implies resentment towards her status. The lack of reliable evidence against Young was confirmed when, despite attempts by the minister to gather complaints against her, she was finally released.[30] The authorities might also have had financial motives for prosecuting married women – they were maybe easier targets than their husbands for rivals or enemies. Similar patterns have been found in a German case-study.[31]

Young's case does not reveal an active 'witch-hunter' of the kind studied by Yeoman, but the case of Janet Finlayson in 1597, from Burntisland, does. It was the bailies who pursued her the hardest. They were finally brought before the privy council for persistently apprehending the suspect for witchcraft, their motive apparently 'being to enriche thamesellfis with the said complenaris guidis and geir'.[32] This is revealing of the vindictiveness behind accusations in a competitive urban setting. Both these cases were during peak years of prosecution when the witch stereotype of an unmarried or widowed woman was likely to have broken down and rivalries encouraged accusations. It is also a reminder of the intensity of urban government in addition to that of the kirk sessions that still had authority within burghs.

There are other cases of accused women married to burgesses, but often little information survives for their cases. The political and property motives in the cases referred to above differ from more typical reasons for suspected witchcraft. For skilled men, towns gave the opportunity for greater social advancement. Women married to successful men (especially in smaller towns) could have become targets because they shared in their husbands' status and wealth. However, they could usually rely on male support to petition the authorities. Of course, there may have been other women accused who had burgess husbands who were not recorded because they did not become involved in the case themselves. Still, there is little doubt that widows were less fortunate. Scottish kinship was agnatic, and when their husbands died, women would become detached from the male kin group, losing their husbands' protection. This hints at more distinctly urban characteristics in those cases where spouse information survives.

VI

One fascinating aspect of the geography of witch-hunting in Scotland is the rarity of cases in Edinburgh itself. This is particularly notable given the dominance of the surrounding Lothian region in providing most suspects overall. One can find a large number in the town of Haddington, a significant number in the towns of West Lothian (although few from the largest, Linlithgow) and a huge number in the towns of Fife. By comparison, very few suspects are recorded as inhabitants of the capital city, which was by far Scotland's largest town in the sixteenth and seventeenth centuries. Only eighteen suspects can be identified as living in the town and its adjacent suburb of Canongate (a separate burgh in its own right), which contained eight of these cases.

A possible yet unproven explanation for the fewness of Edinburgh's witches is that it was the centre of government and the seat of the court of justiciary. The higher number of cases tried in this court resulting in acquittals is probably relevant and a statistical comparison with acquitted suspects from towns would be useful.[33] A more plausible context is the changing occupational structure of the town from the mid seventeenth century, from being based on foreign trade to central administration, including professionals such as lawyers and physicians. A greater involvement of educated townspeople and legal professionals in trials may have been a restraining influence.[34] The size and occupational diversity of larger burgh councils such as Edinburgh's could have reduced the interest the authorities had in individual cases. By comparison smaller burgh councils and kirk sessions, whose members were part of closer communities, may have had a more united interest to protect their wealth and trade against potentially catastrophic acts of witchcraft.

Although Edinburgh had a rising professional sector (about 8 per cent of the population in 1639), a large proportion of the 'unfree' (non-burgess) inhabitants of the town could be classed as 'poor'; approximately one-third of families in 1694 were on or below the poverty line.[35] If we accept that most witchcraft suspects in Scotland were of low social status, it is surprising that more witches were not prosecuted in Edinburgh. This might have less to do with the social status of the suspect than with the social structure of the society around them, the social difference which existed between neighbours or clients and the formally educated civic elite leading the trials.

What of the possibility of urban connections with the surrounding countryside, where healers more commonly resided? The North Berwick panic of 1590–1592 shows how a witch-hunt could begin with local accusations in rural Haddingtonshire and then involve higher-status Edinburgh suspects, Barbara Napier and Euphemia MacCalzean.[36] On the whole, though, witch-hunting connections between Edinburgh and its hinterland are difficult to find. An analysis of burgh and urban parish cases by year provides an overview of this relationship.[37] The results show very little or no correlation between cases in the rural county of Edinburgh and the capital itself during periods of 'national panic'. For instance, during the 1661–1662 panic there were no cases in Edinburgh or Leith despite numerous suspects being accused in neighbouring Dalkeith presbytery and Liberton parish.[38] Local research into witch-hunting in Dalkeith supports these findings.[39] Despite trading links between Dalkeith and Musselburgh (both burghs of regality), the geographical range of accusations did not extend beyond single or immediately neighbouring parishes. Disputes that developed into witchcraft accusations tended to involve relations between family and friends that had turned sour, suspects spotted in suspicious places or money issues.[40] Some of these would have been more likely in the smaller parish communities of Dalkeith than in the densely inhabited closes of Edinburgh. Proximity to the centre of justice does not appear to have acted as a restraining influence on local witch-hunting either; the justiciary court was sent out to Dalkeith to try some suspects in 1661 but found every witch guilty even after confessions were retracted.[41]

It might be helpful to compare the Edinburgh area with a similar pattern found in Geneva by William Monter.[42] He showed that Geneva had strong connections with its witch-hunting neighbour, the duchy of Savoy, and that immigrants from the duchy appeared in Genevan witch trials. The republic of Geneva had around 12,000 urban inhabitants but only around 2,000 peasants in the surrounding rural *mandements*. The proportion of the county population of Edinburgh living in the capital itself during the seventeenth century would have been closer to a half, with comparably more in the surrounding rural settlements. In Geneva, the rural enclaves produced roughly half of the trials for witchcraft despite containing under a seventh of the Republic's overall population.[43] In the county of Edinburgh, a total of ten cases could be found in the burgh itself and its various urban parishes that extended into the countryside. A further twenty-seven suspects came from the adjacent burgh and parish of Canongate (eight) and nearby urban parishes of North and South Leith (nineteen). Combined with the Edinburgh suspects this translates as 12 per cent of the total number of cases in the county (374). The remainder came from Dalkeith and other rural parishes, including settlements like Gilmerton which were comparable with the Genevan *mandements*. With 45 per cent of the population, but responsible for 88 per cent of the cases, the rural and suburban hinterland of Edinburgh produced twice as many cases per person as the towns themselves.[44]

To a great extent, the localised nature of panics in the suburbs around Edinburgh (even in nearby Leith) explains the lack of simultaneous accusations in the capital. However, it fails to explain why there were so few Edinburgh cases overall. Monter showed that in Geneva there was a leniency towards witchcraft suspects, with only a small proportion being executed.[45] Statistical similarities aside, specific comparisons with Geneva are difficult to find. Also, during Geneva's religious and political disturbances between 1625 and 1650, prosecutions virtually disappeared. In the middle of the Covenanting wars, Edinburgh and Leith together had eight cases between 1643 and 1645 – something of an upsurge, although one would expect more of an effort by the reformers of the Scottish godly state to extirpate witchcraft from the home of government. Most of these cases preceded the outbreak of plague that killed between a quarter and a third of the population of Edinburgh from 1644 to 1649. In contrast to Geneva, where plague-spreading conspiracies led to panics, outbreaks of the disease in Edinburgh may have reduced the desire to hunt witches.[46]

How distinctively 'urban' were Edinburgh's witchcraft cases? In other burghs such as Lanark and Peebles, livestock was frequently moving in the town.[47] The rural context of most accusations of witchcraft (in particular acts of malefice directed against livestock) is usually given as a reason for the relative lack of urban suspects; this explanation may not entirely hold for smaller burghs. However, it may go some way to explaining the pattern in Edinburgh itself.

Where malefice did occur in Edinburgh it was often directed against humans, for example in the detailed case of Agnes Finnie, from Potterrow on the edge of Edinburgh, accused in 1645 of using witchcraft to harm and even kill her neighbours. Ten of the twenty charges against Finnie related to her occupation as a shopkeeper: dissatisfied customers, refusals of credit, and demands for small debts in connection with her moneylending. The sudden misfortune of a craft deacon was also attributed to her abilities, in which 'his woraldlie estait and his hail meanes vanisched away fra him', following an argument with Finnie over the punishment of her son-in-law for an offence.[48] Further evidence of cases with urban characteristics would support the theory that witchcraft in towns contained distinctively urban features.

There is also strong evidence for witch-related folk belief in Edinburgh. The case of Janet Barker from 1643, also a shopkeeper in Edinburgh, reveals both demonic and folk elements of popular belief. As well as the detailed description of her relationship with the Devil and his promise to make her the best-dressed servant in town, her confession included a healing ritual of placing a black card under someone's door.[49] It is therefore incorrect to ascribe witchcraft to peasant conservatism, when middling members of the urban population had similar beliefs. As an 'indweller', Barker would probably have been brought up in the town;[50] yet her folk beliefs play just an important role as those contained in the evidence of many rural witches.

To what extent Barker's beliefs, and the folk traditions in other urban cases, can be regarded as distinct urban traditions is deserving of further research. The growth of Edinburgh at this time was due partly to the influx of servants and other people from the countryside;[51] this would probably have facilitated exchanges of beliefs, and it is surprising that social advancement in the town did not result in more cases. Bernd Roeck has suggested that rural witchcraft beliefs could have been imported in German cities, a theory that might explain why cities still experienced accusations despite their appearance of being centres of rational behaviour and philosophy.[52]

The last sight of many more witches was of Edinburgh as they went to the stake. If they were brought in for trial in the court of justiciary and found guilty, they were usually executed on Castle Hill. Over sixty witches were put on trial and executed in Edinburgh, and the carrying out of the sentence was a spectacle for its inhabitants.[53] Instead of fuelling the desire to prosecute witches, perhaps the greater frequency of public burnings in the capital actually reminded its inhabitants of the continued threat of witchcraft; they saw that executions had not brought it to an end and that proceeding against a witch was not necessarily a practical solution. Or perhaps people's need for witch-hunting was satisfied if they saw witchcraft being punished, even if the guilty suspects came from elsewhere.

People in early modern Edinburgh certainly believed in witchcraft. The few cases from the burgh itself show that urban and rural belief was basically homogeneous. Research into some relatively late cases of witchcraft in London also supports this idea and is similar to other findings in Venice and Denmark. In large towns and cities, charges tended to concern harm to people, even though some urban areas like Southwark also had access to agricultural land.[54] Urbanisation did not necessarily mean an end to previously rural belief systems, as often there was a continuity of the same social networks of kin from countryside to town.[55] There could be parallels between rapid urbanisation in the seventeenth century and the disintegration of previously stable social networks in the nineteenth century due to immigration and urbanisation. Certainly the existence of stable social networks was important for reputations to develop. These might have been disrupted by outbreaks of plague, particularly in the 1640s. Generally speaking, towns still maintained close communities despite rapid population increases; as Edinburgh was growing on a greater scale, however, social networks would have been under more strain.

Just as the rapid growth of small towns appears to have provided a suitable context for witch-hunting, so in some cases their stagnation and decline might have been a factor in the last trials. From the mid seventeenth century Edinburgh and Glasgow were becoming the two dominant cities whereas previously the urban population had been more evenly distributed among the other regional centres. However, small towns like Pittenweem experienced decline from the mid seventeenth century and there was a panic there in the early eighteenth century. The late cases (1701 onwards) studied by Alexandra Hill reveal a high proportion of urban witchcraft suspects, mostly in small towns – Anstruther Easter, Kirkcudbright (two cases), Edinburgh, Pittenweem (eight cases), Bo'ness, Inverness (two cases), Dumfries and Thurso (five cases).[56]

VII

The nature of urbanisation in Scotland is an important context in which to understand the accusation and prosecution of witches. Statistics show that the proportion of 'urban' suspects varied with the size of the town. There was a strikingly high proportion – three times the national average – of suspects from small towns of between 500 and 1,500 inhabitants. The prevalence of suspects from towns in the most urbanised counties, such as Lothian and Fife, compared with those in more rural counties with dispersed urban settlements is also important. Around Edinburgh (but not in it), and in Strathclyde and Fife, there were high proportions of urban suspects.

Towns tended to have an intense experience of witch-hunting because in addition to their own witches, many rural witches were tried and executed in towns. Townspeople themselves were subject to greater authority. The concentration of suspects in the burghs of Fife is striking, as is the lack of direct witch-hunting connections between them. In generating accusations, networks between neighbours and family were probably just as important in these towns as in the countryside, but the government and burgess patriarchy of the burgh was essential for the identification and interrogation of suspects. The rarity of witch-hunting in Edinburgh is striking; explanations based on its unique occupational structure, sheer population size and proliferation of surrounding witch-hunting settlements seem most plausible.

The phenomenon of distinctively urban witchcraft needs more attention. Business rivalries, neighbourhood disputes and a male suspicion of women married to higher-status husbands in the town characterise some cases. Town dwellers could still have agricultural occupations in Scotland, and it is difficult to say that completely separate 'urban' and 'rural' types of witchcraft existed. For burgesses and indwellers, the burgh was a close community which relied upon neighbourly goodwill just like rural settlements. Moreover, even the smallest burghs on the Forth had economic interests of which merchants and craftsmen, and their spouses, were fully aware. Pressures to get on with family and neighbours were as apparent in small towns as in the countryside. In towns, as in the countryside, such relations could break down and lead to witchcraft accusations, though the content of some disputes was distinctively urban. Without Scotland's urban structure it seems unlikely that so many witches would have been accused.

Notes

1. Christina Larner, *Enemies of God: The Witch-hunt in Scotland* (London, 1981), 193.
2. Robin Briggs, *Witches and Neighbours: The Social and Cultural Context of European Witchcraft* (2nd edn., Oxford, 2002), 265.
3. Ian D. Whyte, *Scotland's Society and Economy in Transition, c.1500–c.1760* (Basingstoke, 1997), 115.
4. Michael Lynch, 'Urbanisation and urban networks in seventeenth century Scotland: some further thoughts', *Scottish Economic and Social History*, 12 (1992), 24–41, at p. 34.
5. Michael Lynch, 'Continuity and change in urban society, 1500–1700', in R. A. Houston and I. D. Whyte (eds.), *Scottish Society, 1500–1800* (Cambridge, 1989), 85–117, at pp. 101–4.
6. Michael Flinn (ed.), *Scottish Population History* (Cambridge, 1977), 188–90.

7. Julian Goodare, *The Government of Scotland, 1560–1625* (Oxford, 2004), 190–1.
8. Michael Lynch, 'Introduction: Scottish towns, 1500–1700', in Michael Lynch (ed.), *The Early Modern Town in Scotland* (London, 1987), 1–35, at p. 16.
9. Lynch, 'Introduction', 8.
10. David H. Sacks and Michael Lynch, 'Ports, 1540–1700', in Peter Clark (ed.), *The Cambridge Urban History of Britain, vol. ii, 1540–1840* (Cambridge, 2000), 377–424, at p. 420.
11. She argued that in Pittenweem, 'witchcraft accusations began to rise' after the burgh 'lost over 100 adult males' at the battle of Kilsyth in 1645, leaving fishing boats to rot at their moorings: Larner, *Enemies of God*, 82. However, this appears to be an error. The Survey of Scottish Witchcraft shows seven Pittenweem cases from the panic of 1643–1644 and then no more until the local panic there of 1704. Larner also misdated the battle to 1649.
12. Lynch, 'Urbanisation and urban networks', 28.
13. Where only the county or presbytery of residence is recorded, these suspects are excluded from the 'urban' total as they may have lived in rural parishes. The results therefore give a minimum number of cases from towns.
14. Lauren Martin, 'Scottish witchcraft panics re-examined', in Julian Goodare, Lauren Martin and Joyce Miller (eds.), *Witchcraft and Belief in Early Modern Scotland* (Basingstoke, 2008), 119–43, at pp. 133–4.
15. The following regions are among the ten used by Martin, 'Scottish witchcraft panics re-examined', 124.
16. http://www.nls.uk/maps/early/blaeu/page.cfm?id=951
17. Estimates for town sizes were based on the 1691 hearth tax returns. This had to be used in combination with data from the 1755 census.
18. Martin, 'Scottish witchcraft panics re-examined', 125.
19. Ian D. Whyte, *Scotland Before the Industrial Revolution: An Economic and Social History, c.1050-c.1750* (London, 1995), 176.
20. Briggs, *Witches and Neighbours*, 265.
21. Whyte, *Scotland's Society and Economy*, 115.
22. SSW; this is probably correct in linking her shop with her husband's merchandise (see below).
23. Lauren Martin, 'The Devil and the domestic: witchcraft, quarrels and women's work in Scotland', in Julian Goodare (ed.), *The Scottish Witch-hunt in Context* (Manchester, 2002), 73–89, esp. pp. 86–7.
24. Stuart Macdonald, *The Witches of Fife: Witch-Hunting in a Scottish Shire, 1560–1710* (East Linton, 2002), 36–7 and *passim*.
25. Macdonald, *Witches of Fife*, 38.
26. Ibid., 39, 46.
27. Ibid., 83.
28. In the SSW database a total of twenty-four such cases can be found.
29. Louise Yeoman, 'Hunting the rich witch in Scotland: high status witchcraft suspects and their persecutors, 1590–1650', in Goodare (ed.), *Scottish Witch-Hunt in Context*, 106–21.
30. Macdonald, *Witches of Fife*, 82; *RPC*, 2nd ser., viii, 28; SSW.
31. Bob Scribner, 'Witchcraft and judgement in Reformation Germany', *History Today*, 40, no. 4 (April 1990), 12–19.
32. Macdonald, *Witches of Fife*, 73–5.

33. Julian Goodare, 'Witch-hunting and the Scottish state', in Goodare (ed.), *The Scottish Witch-Hunt in Context*, 122–45, at pp. 131–2.
34. Bernd Roeck, 'Witchcraft in early modern Germany: urban witch trials', *Magic, Ritual, and Witchcraft*, 4 (2009), 82–9, at p. 87. Roeck also points out that 'the metropolises of early modern Europe – Paris, London, Madrid, Rome, Naples, Stockholm, Antwerp, and Amsterdam – represent blank spots on the map of the witch panic' (p. 83).
35. Whyte, *Scotland Before the Industrial Revolution*, 202.
36. Normand and Roberts (eds.), *Witchcraft*, 54.
37. Such a table is too large to be included in this paper.
38. The most recent case found in Edinburgh was in 1659. However, the burgh of Canongate had three cases during the 1661–1662 panic. For detailed analysis, see Alistair Henderson, 'The Urban Geography of Witchhunting in Scotland' (MA Dissertation, University of Edinburgh, 2008).
39. Anna L. Cordey, 'Witch-Hunting in the Presbytery of Dalkeith, 1649 to 1662' (University of Edinburgh MSc thesis, 2003), 1–2, 17–18. Cf. Anna Cordey, 'Reputation and witch-hunting in seventeenth-century Dalkeith', Chapter 6 in this volume.
40. Cordey, 'Witch-Hunting', 28–30.
41. Ibid., 66–7.
42. E. William Monter, 'Witchcraft in Geneva, 1537–1662', *Journal of Modern History*, 43 (1971), 179–204.
43. Monter, 'Witchcraft in Geneva', 201–3.
44. These figures include 50 or so cases where the exact place of residence is unknown (only the county or presbytery are recorded as 'Edinburgh'), but even taking this into account the disproportionate number of rural cases is still clear and corresponds with the results for Geneva. For a broader discussion, reaching similar conclusions to those drawn here, see Brian P. Levack, *The Witch-Hunt in Early Modern Europe* (3rd edn., Harlow, 2006), 137–40.
45. Monter, 'Witchcraft in Geneva', 186–7.
46. Ibid., 183–4.
47. Whyte, *Scotland Before the Industrial Revolution*, 186.
48. *SJC*, iii, 627–75.
49. Brian P. Levack (ed.), *The Witchcraft Sourcebook* (London, 2004), 210–12.
50. Whyte, *Scotland Before the Industrial Revolution*, 202. Whyte refers to Aberdeen, but Edinburgh would have been similar.
51. Whyte, *Scotland Before the Industrial Revolution*, 179.
52. Roeck, 'Urban witch trials', 85–6.
53. For more on this, see Laura Paterson, 'Executing Scottish witches', Chapter 11 in this volume.
54. Owen Davies, 'Urbanization and the decline of witchcraft: an examination of London', *Journal of Social History*, 30 (1997), 597–617, at pp. 597, 599.
55. Davies, 'Urbanization', 599–600, 603–4.
56. Alexandra Hill, 'Decline and survival in Scottish witch-hunting, 1701–1727', Chapter 12 in this volume.

11
Executing Scottish Witches
Laura Paterson

The sayde Doctor Fian was soone after araigned, condemned, and adjudged by the law to die, and then to bee burned according to the lawe of that lande, provided in that behalfe. Whereupon hee was put into a carte, and beeing first strangled, hee was immediatly put into a great fire, being readie provided for that purpose, and there burned in the Castle hill of Edenbrough on a Saterdaie in the ende of Januarie last past, 1591.[1]

What became of Scottish witches after their death sentence was proclaimed? How, where, when and by whom were witches executed, and what can this tell us about the attitudes of early modern Scottish society towards the crime of witchcraft? By studying the surviving accounts of the expenses sustained in trying and executing Scottish witches, a good deal of information can be brought together about this. The process was both laborious and expensive, yet the hunting and destruction of witches was still considered to be a worthwhile pursuit and was carried on into the eighteenth century.

I

The execution process may be best understood if it is placed in context. This chapter thus begins with a brief account of the earlier stages in which witches were processed. Expenses could include the initial costs of the imprisonment of the suspected witch, including food and drink to sustain her, as well as the cost of the process for extracting a confession. In March 1596, the council of Aberdeen granted £20 to Gilbert Bairnis for 'the expenses maid be him in sustenatioun of the witches preceding that date'.[2] A dispute between the parish of Balmerino and the magistrates of Cupar saw the magistrates refuse to house a suspected witch in the town prison, suspecting that the parish would not pay for the witch's incarceration. The magistrates' alternative offer, imprisonment in the thieves' hole, was refused by the parish as it was not considered a secure place where the suspect could be watched. As Stuart Macdonald argues, secure imprisonment was important for obtaining a confession.[3]

Over and above these basic imprisonment costs there would often be expenses incurred during the extraction of a confession from the suspect. In a number of cases the expenses for men to watch the witch are recorded. In 1649, this process cost the estate of Burntcastle £45, which paid two men to watch the suspected witch Margaret Dunhame for the space of thirty days.[4] This implies that in at least some cases, if not the majority, the process of watching or waking was being employed to induce suspects to confess.[5] The expense account for Margaret Dunhame also records the payment of £6 to John Kincaid, the infamous witch-pricker, for 'brodding' the witch.[6] A professional witch-pricker would insert needles into a suspect's body in an attempt to find the witch's mark.

Such a confession was normally required, before a commission would be granted, by the privy council, to try the witch.[7] After a confession was extracted, a member of the community would travel to Edinburgh to petition the privy council for a commission, which would allow the local magistrates to try the witch within their local parish. This was often the single largest item of expenditure and in some cases these expenses could soar to astronomical heights. This is clearly shown in the case of an unknown estate that hoped to gain a commission to try thirteen witches. This cost £310 9*s*. 4*d*. when the local laird travelled to Edinburgh to petition the king's advocate.[8]

If and when a commission was granted, a trial would be held. For those witches who were tried locally, the granting of this commission may as well have been a death sentence. The people of the witch's community had already decided that the witch in question was an extremely dangerous individual and a threat to Christian society. One study, taking the peak period of Scottish witchcraft trials as 1620–1674, has found that local trials then had an execution rate of 87 per cent.[9]

II

Once the sentence was passed, preparations began immediately for the execution. One of the most pressing concerns must have been to find someone who was willing to execute the witch. The large towns, including Edinburgh and Aberdeen, appear to have had professional executioners; the Aberdeen accounts consistently refer to the executioner as Jon Justice (possibly a pseudonym).[10] However, in many of the smaller towns and parishes there was no one willing to carry out the gruesome task.

The occupation of executioner was unpopular in the early modern period. The executioner was paid to torment, maim and kill people for money. If the executioner's infamy is considered in terms of a code of honour system, it becomes more enlightening. This theory may be particularly applicable in Scotland, where, during the early seventeenth century, James VI was still struggling to tackle the problem of blood feuds, which saw elite Scottish families attempting to restore their honour through fights and feuds. Pieter Spierenburg relates this argument to that of medieval society's view of the knight, as opposed to the mercenary: 'the valiant knight was a hero, but the mercenary never acquired his status'.[11] The executioner was hated because he was using physical violence against a person unconnected with himself and receiving payment for this act, which was considered dishonourable. The infamy with which the executioner was treated usually extended to his wife and children. The position of executioner was thus a difficult one to fill and in many cases the role of executioner was hereditary. There is at least one Scottish example of this, in 1629, where the son of the executioner was paid 12*s.* to act as the dempster at the executions of three witches in Peebles.[12] The dempster was a traditional official who pronounced the sentence and who was sometimes expected to double as the executioner.[13]

Executioners could be shared. William Coke and Alison Dick were due to be executed in Kirkcaldy in 1633; a man was sent to Culross to collect an executioner from there.[14] Attitudes towards the executioner might help to explain the accommodation afforded to him. For the execution of a witch in Kirkcudbright in 1698, William Kirk was paid 4*s.* per day for twenty days in which he was accommodated in the prison.[15] Perhaps there was no one in the locality willing to take the executioner into their home or inn. There were other instances, throughout Europe, where the executioner's infamy was considered 'contagious', damaging the reputation of any who associated with him.[16] In some communities the touch of the executioner, or even objects which he had touched, could be contagious.

If the executioner could cope with the bloody work, and with the infamy that came with it, then his position could be lucrative. The executioner whose task it was to end the lives of three unfortunate witches in Peebles was paid £10 in 1633. He and his son were accommodated by Johnne Frank, who received £3 12s. for his troubles.[17] In many cases, the executioner would also receive expenses. William Kirk was granted 1s. on 20 August 1698 to purchase drink and 'ane leg of mutton', and also various grants following this to ensure that he had a reasonable stay.[18] It was clearly important to ensure the satisfaction of the executioner.

III

The cost of the prosecution and execution of a convicted witch could seriously mount up. Costs amounted to £92 14s. in 1649 with the case of Margaret Dunhame, payable by the estate of Burntcastle. The factor who took the account of the expenses, Alexander Louddon, deducted £27 which Dunhame had of her own, which was claimed by the estate.[19] The seizure of a witch's goods appears to have been common – if she or he had any worth seizing. In 1644, after the conviction of Catherine Logie, the bailies of South Queensferry were instructed to enter her home and seize upon what could be found. These possessions were used to cover the expense of her execution.[20] Paula Hughes's study of trial commissions granted by the committee of estates in the panic of 1649–1650 shows that one in five of the commissions ordered an inventory of the witch's goods to be taken, which may give some idea of the proportion of witches who were thought to have property worth confiscating.[21]

In some cases, the 'escheat' of a convicted witch (the right to collect their moveable property, nominally forfeited to the crown) could be gifted to relatives or friends. However, the local authorities might contest such a gift. In 1675, the magistrates and burgh council of Culross complained that despite the 'great panes and expense this place has been at in prosequieting the four witches to deathe', there were diverse people receiving the gift of the witches' escheat. They commissioned John Kennoway, the burgh clerk, to petition the exchequer to grant the escheat to the burgh or, failing this, he was to ask that whoever obtained the escheat should pay the costs of the execution: 'whosoever get the gift they may be ordered to take it with the burdene of the said accompt'. In 1677, the magistrates and council were still attempting to recover the cost of the execution from those who had received the escheat.[22] It is clear then that most localities would expect, or at least hope, to receive the goods of the witch once they were convicted of witchcraft.

More efforts seem to have been made to recover the property of witches who were actually known to have property. This can be seen in a case in Dumfries in 1659, when Helen Muirhead was singled out from among nine witches who were ordered to be taken to the 'ordinar place of execution for the burgh of Dumfries' and executed. Their moveable goods were to be escheated. However, the particular instructions for Muirhead's moveable goods were that they were to be 'intromitted with by the Sheriff of Nithsdaile, to seize upon and herrie the samin for the king's use'.[23] Muirhead has been estimated by the Survey of Scottish Witchcraft to have been in her early fifties; she had recently been widowed. The accusation appears to have arisen over a dispute with her brother-in-law over her terce – her right to a liferent interest in her deceased husband's land. It seems that Muirhead's moveable property was considered worth confiscating. As she was a widow, the property was also hers alone, while a married woman's moveable property was under the control of her husband.

If the escheat of the convicted witch was unavailable, or failed to cover the total cost of the prosecution and execution, then the recovery of these expenses had to be sought elsewhere. The authorities would often order the relatives of the convicted witch to pay for the execution. In South Queensferry in 1644, the session decreed that James Lowrie should be responsible for the expenses of burning his wife. He was also ordered to pay for the burning of the beggar witch Marion Stein, as well as making up the deficit of the expenses for the burning of the witch Catherine Logie, if her moveable goods did not cover the cost of her execution.[24] There are a number of other examples of husbands being forced to pay for their wives' executions, and in one case in 1643 John Dawson was forced to pay for the burning of his mother.[25]

In many cases, the expenses could not be reclaimed in this way, and the executions drained the finances of the local community. In Kirkcaldy in 1633, the expenses of executing William Coke and Alison Dick were split almost evenly between the burgh (£17 1s.) and the kirk session (£17 10s.).[26] The presbytery of Dalkeith appealed to the privy council in 1628 to allow them to confiscate the escheat of the best-off witches to pay for their many other prosecutions. These had been such a drain on their community that they had been forced to 'take money out of the boxe of the poore of their presbyterie'.[27]

There were thus very few financial beneficiaries from witch-hunting in Scotland. Those who appear to have benefited most were the witch-prickers and the executioners.[28] They were rarely established members of the community and cannot have instigated a witch-hunt for financial gain. The fact that Scottish society was willing to invest time and resources into the process of prosecuting witches is an important aspect of Scottish witch-hunting.

IV

Attitudes towards the crime of witchcraft were also displayed through the choice of execution site. Sites chosen for executions of criminals were rich in symbolism, which could relate to not only the crime committed by the individual, but also that individual's status within their community. In some areas there seems to have been a deliberate correlation between the choice of execution site and the crime committed. A study of these correlations may be most effectively shown through the execution sites chosen in the city of Edinburgh – a place where particularly large numbers were executed, because many witches from elsewhere were sent for trial to the central justiciary court there.

The most prominent Edinburgh execution sites were Castle Hill and the Gallowlee between Edinburgh and Leith (what is now Pilrig). There were also a few early examples where the witch was sentenced to be executed north of the Brig O' Leith (what is now North Leith). In Edinburgh it is evident that particular sites were reserved for particular crimes, but the authorities also considered the right of a particular social class to receive their execution in a particular area.

The Mercat Cross, adjacent to St Giles Cathedral and the Tolbooth, was used for various other criminals, but is only known to have been used in four witchcraft cases – three beheadings and one hanging. The beheadings were of three members of the aristocratic Erskine family (Robert Erskine and two of his sisters), while the hanging was of Jean Weir.[29] All of these cases, as we shall see, involved other crimes as well as witchcraft. Beheading was considered to be honourable, and was usually only granted to the upper echelons of society. Esther Cohen has argued that execution within the town instead of the peripheries was less shameful for the criminal, which might suggest that the condemned was considered to be someone of importance.[30]

The Gallowlee, on the boundary between the jurisdictions of Edinburgh and Leith, was the second most prominent site after Castle Hill.[31] The two miles between Edinburgh and its port of Leith were not urbanised, but the road between them was well used by merchants and traders. This site could therefore attract crowds from both Edinburgh and Leith. The fact that the gallows also occupied a site beyond the bounds of both Edinburgh and Leith also supports Cohen's emphasis on the peripheries of the town. Similarly, in Aberdeen, witches were taken into the hills outside the town for execution.[32]

The most common place for Edinburgh's witchcraft executions was Castle Hill. This had earlier been the single most common place for the execution (also by burning) of Protestant heretics between 1528 and 1558.[33] As with the Gallowlee and other sites, Castle Hill was beyond the boundaries of the town – an area of open space separating the Castle itself from the built-up area around the head of the High Street and Lawnmarket. Prisoners would often be housed in the Tolbooth, next to St Giles Cathedral in the High Street. The prisoners were then 'dragged at the horse's tail', tied to a hurdle, to their place of execution. The symbolism suggests that the criminal had committed a crime so heinous that their feet were not fit to walk on the earth. The central location of the Tolbooth and the short distance to Castle Hill meant that many of the people from the market place could follow the procession along the High Street, to witness the execution; there would also be room for crowds in the Castle Hill space. The Castle, perched on its volcanic crag, dominated the whole of the Edinburgh area. The smoke from the pyre would have been seen from almost all public areas in the town and for miles beyond.

The authorities' choice of location for the execution was only one aspect of staging a successful spectacle. The choice of particular days and times also feature in the records, which refer to the execution of witches. In some cases a specific day was assigned for executions to take place. In Dumfries, witches were always executed on the Wednesday following the trial.[34] Some cases record a specific time of day for the executions to take place – usually between two and four in the afternoon.[35] One of the ways in which the execution of Euphemia MacCalzean in 1591 was unusual was that it was 'about aucht hours at nycht'.[36] By having specific days and times, which would be known to the local people, the authorities ensured that a crowd would turn out for the spectacle. Indeed, it is obvious that crowds did turn out to see the execution of witches, sometimes in large numbers. The financial account of the execution of Margaret Bane in Aberdeen in 1597 records the cost of someone carrying four spars to the site of the execution, which would be used to 'withstand the preas of the pepill'.[37] This shows that the authorities anticipated a crowd. Two of the four spars were broken, which suggests that the crowd was either so large that its press against the spars was too much for them to bear, or that there was some commotion where the crowd intentionally pushed against the barrier.

The condemned victim may have been allowed to make a last speech. There is hardly any information about this (it would not have been recorded in our main sources, the financial accounts), but there are one or two indications. Two of the North Berwick witches, Geillis Duncan and Bessie Thomson, were able to make long statements at the

Castle Hill of Edinburgh 'after they had been delivered free' (presumably they had arrived bound to a hurdle) on 4 December 1591. Duncan and Thomson declared that their confessions implicating Barbara Napier and Euphemia MacCalzean had been false. These retractions were orchestrated by Napier's and MacCalzean's supporters, who included several bailies and other important people, so this was not a routine occasion.[38] There is some information for a more typical witch, Margaret Barclay, executed at Irvine in 1618. Under torture she had suffered agonies of indecision, alternately affirming her confession and then retracting it. At the place of execution she told the minister that her confession of her own guilt had been true, but that her accusation of witchcraft against Isobel Crawford had been false. 'And sua utterit thir wordis – God's blessing and myne be among you all, and pray for me; and hir braith chokit be the executioner, hir handis being up to the heavins, uttering thir wordis – Lord ressave my saull in his mercie.'[39] Later in 1658 Colonel Sawrey reported on the execution of the convicted witch Janett Saers. The minister, who would usually be present at executions of convicted criminals, would have urged Janett Saers to confess to her crimes to which she replied, 'Sir, I am shortly to appear before the Judge of all the earth, and a lye may damne my soule to hell. I am cleare of witchcraft, for which I am presently to suffer.'[40] This was the last opportunity for witches to confess their true guilt or innocence with only the destination of their immortal souls to consider. Perhaps they believed that if they went to their deaths having confessed to their true beliefs, God would forgive them and save them from eternal damnation.

It is, therefore, clear that the Scottish authorities took care in their choice of site, day and time of execution. The location of the site of the execution was critical to the message that the authorities wished to portray. The sites would be specially chosen to ensure that the burning could be seen from afar, especially by the local community, to reinforce the authority of the magistrates. They wished to create a spectacle not only for those living locally, but also for any visitors who might be passing. It seems that Scottish society wished to make a statement about its determination to rid itself of those who committed sinful acts. These spectacles of justice display an attempt, by the authorities, to make visible the public order and restore the balance of society.

V

In Scotland, by far the most common method for executing a witch was strangling and burning. The vast majority of cases where the method of execution has been recorded show this. Some of the few cases where a different method was used can be explained by examining the individual cases more closely. A rare case in which the victim was hanged occurred in 1670. This was Jean Weir, the sister of the prominent Edinburgh citizen Major Thomas Weir, who was also executed. Despite part of the accusations against Jean involving witchcraft, the main focus of her crime was her incestuous relationship with her brother, which probably explains why she did not suffer the traditional death for witchcraft.[41] Another case in which the crime was not simply 'witchcraft' was that of Donald McIlmichael, executed in Inveraray in 1677. He was explicitly prosecuted under the 1563 witchcraft act, but the crime of which he was convicted was that of 'theft and of consulting with evill spirits sundry times' – and he was hanged.[42]

A similar pattern emerges in the few cases of beheading. Robert Erskine and his sisters Annas and Issobell Erskine have already been mentioned; they were found guilty of consulting with witches, poisoning and treasonable murder.[43] For their crimes they were beheaded at Edinburgh's Mercat Cross in 1614. The accusation that the Erskines had consulted witches, a crime incorporated in Scotland's witchcraft act, seemed to take a less prominent place in their crimes; therefore they were not subjected to the traditional witch's death.[44]

According to the Witchcraft Survey, around 12 per cent of Scottish witches were sentenced to burn alive. However, in these cases the Survey has taken those sentences that order the witch to be burnt literally, and it is probably an overestimate. Certainly there were a small number of cases where the convicted witch was burnt alive – possibly if a witch had committed a particularly serious and wicked offence. One infamous example is the case of Euphemia MacCalzean, one of the North Berwick witches of 1591, in whose case the king took a personal interest. There is also an account of witches being burnt alive in Brechin in 1608, by an unknown court (perhaps the regality court), in a manner that the privy council regarded as illegal:

> they were brunt quick [i.e. alive] eftir sic ane crewell manner, that sum of thame deit [i.e. died] in despair, renunceand and blaspheme-and and utheris, half brunt brak out of the fyre, and was cast quick in it again, quhill they were brunt to the deid.[45]

The most common method of execution, the sentence given out in 85 per cent of the 141 known cases where a sentence was recorded, was that of strangling and burning. A typical sentence of this type was as follows:

To be tane be the lockman, hir hands bund, and be caried to the head of the Lon [loan, i.e. lane], the place of execution, and ther knit to ane staik, wiried to the death, and brunt in asses.[46]

These sentences, which stipulate that the witch should be 'wiried' (strangled) at the stake, imply that the method of strangulation should be garrotting. By this method the victim is tied to the garrotte or strangling-pole with their back against it while the executioner tightens a cord, wrapped around their neck, with a stick. However, the financial accounts of a few executions indicate that the method of strangulation was hanging. In Peebles in 1628, and Dumfries in 1650, the expense accounts for the execution of witches include the cost of erection of a gibbet.[47] This implies that these witches would first be hanged before their bodies were burnt, in which case a stake would perhaps not be needed. Such a process is clear for Helen Stewart in Shetland, who was burnt 'when she had hung some little time on the Gibbet'.[48] References to 'hanging' could mean strangulation at a stake, though, as in 1612 with the order by the Haddington sheriff court 'that the said Bessie Hendersoun salbe tane and careit to the sandis of Hadingtoun and there bound to ane staik quhill and hangit to the deit and there efter to be brunt in aschis'.[49] Once the strangulation (by whichever method) was completed, the pyre would be lit.

VI

This brings us to the actual burning of the witch's body. The materials for building the pyre varied somewhat, but peat and coal were common base materials. In Aberdeen peat was the material of choice, presumably because this was available locally while coal was not. The materials used were usually recorded in 'loads'; the size of these loads is not clear and perhaps varied, but a 'load' was probably several hundred pounds.[50] Ten loads of coal were used to burn Johne Fian in Edinburgh in 1590, whereas only five loads of coal and three loads of peat were needed to burn three witches in Peebles in 1628.[51] The materials could be quite costly: when Aberdeen burnt Helen Gray and Agnes Webster in 1597, twenty-two loads of peat were required at a cost of £2 15s.[52]

Coal and peat were heavy and long-burning fuels, hard to light. Additional easily combustible materials were used to encourage the fire in its initial stages – most commonly heather and broom, presumably dried. In some of the accounts, particularly those from Aberdeen in 1597, there are also references to tar barrels and iron barrels. The tar, and in some cases resin, would be used within the pyre, and perhaps would also be spread over the completed pyre, to help the fire burn efficiently. Iron barrels were cheap barrels for dry goods, made of wood and with iron straps. These were most likely used to create a stable base for the pyre, ensuring that the piles of other materials did not collapse. The iron could have been salvaged afterwards for reuse.[53] The pyre built around a wooden stake would have had to be secure enough for both the witch and the executioner to climb up and balance upon it while the witch was strangled against the stake, and to ensure that it would support the weight of the witch during the burning process.

The local community must usually have been involved in the building of pyres. In a slander case brought by Grissel Urrall in Elgin in 1622, we encounter a woman who was keen to join the task force for this purpose: 'Janet Gordoun deponit that Jeane Bonyman, spous to Alexander Lesly, said scho houpit in God to cary peitis to the bak of the Ladie hill to burne hir [Urrall] as hir mother suld hawe bein brunt.'[54] Women, as well as men, were used to heavy lifting and carting. If the witch had been unpopular during her lifetime, the work of assembling the pyre could have been a welcome task engendering a spirit of community togetherness.

At the centre of the pyre would be set the stake. This would be crafted by a carpenter before being transported to the site of the execution. Tentative calculations suggest that this stake would be in the region of five metres in length. This is based on the need for the stake to be secured underground to stabilise it, and to leave sufficient height to construct the pyre around it and secure the witch on top. The stake is likely to have been secured underground at an approximately one metre depth, and the first two metres of the stake above ground would have been hidden by the raw materials of the pyre. Finally the top part of the stake would be approximately two metres in order to give the necessary support for the witch to be first strangled against and then to support the weight of the body during the burning process. If the stake was not secured sufficiently underground then it might begin to lean sideways taking the witch with it away from the flames. Perhaps this is what happened in the Brechin case, mentioned above, when the witches who were being burnt alive managed to break out of the fire. The fairly high cost of the stake, including the raw material (timber was scarce in much of Scotland), the working of it into a stake and the setting of it into the ground in order to stabilise it, reflects its importance in the execution process. Throughout the witchcraft executions of 1597 this process cost Aberdeen 13s. 4d. for each stake. In most of these cases, one stake appears to have been used for burning several witches; for example,

Christian Mitchell, Bessie Thom and Isobel Baron appear to have been tied to the same stake.[55] Woodcuts of the martyrdoms of English heretics often show the same practice.

VII

Once lit, the pyre would reach high temperatures. The maximum temperature achievable with wood is around 1,000°C, while the coal and peat would reach higher temperatures of around 1,300°C.[56] However, it is unlikely that these maximum temperatures would have been achieved in practice. Experimental pyres, constructed largely of wood, reached a maximum temperature of around 800–900°C within half an hour of being lit.[57] However, in a pyre much of the heat is lost to the atmosphere and, unlike in a modern crematorium, the heat is focused only on one side of the body. It is almost impossible to keep a uniform temperature across the pyre, so the peripheries are cooler than the centre. Wind strength and directional changes would affect the temperature of the pyre. Strong winds would make it burn faster, but not necessarily more efficiently; it would be more likely to cause the burn to be uneven, which might result in the collapse of the pyre. Rain, depending on the weight, would also cause the cessation of the pyre or at least a reduction in the temperature.

The experimental pyres did not contain peat or coal, and, although these materials are capable of reaching higher temperatures, they are also likely to take longer to achieve any real heat. Most Scottish pyres were made up primarily of peat. It was important that the fire was tended in all weather conditions to ensure that it reached its optimum temperature and remained at this level for as long as possible. It would take a minimum of half an hour for a pyre built of wood to reach the temperature of a cremator, but it is likely to have taken longer than this for the peat and coal to reach this temperature. It has been estimated that the pyre would take around two hours to burn down; however, after this time it is expected that remains of the body would rest on the bed of hot ash.[58] If the pyre was burnt overnight, the majority of the soft tissue and bone material would be destroyed.

VIII

It is nevertheless likely that there would have been some bodily remains left in the ashes. In most cases there would be bone fragments, and the ashes formed during the destruction of the rest of the body would be left mixed with the ashes of the pyre itself. What became of these remains is not clear, but it is unlikely that they would be left where the wind could blow them through the town. It has been suggested that the 'Witches' Lake', a bay of the sea, in St Andrews was used to dispose of executed witches' ashes.[59] In other cases the witches' ashes may simply have been raked over and buried at the foot of the gallows. Sir Walter Scott wrote in 1830 that 'The alterations and trenching which lately took place for the purpose of improving the Castlehill of Edinburgh displayed the ashes of the numbers who had perished in this manner.'[60]

What is clear, however, is that the witches would not be given a decent Christian burial within a churchyard. Throughout the period in question Scotland was an intensely religious country, especially following the Reformation in 1560. The Reformation saw Scotland adopt Protestant Calvinism and reject its Catholic heritage. It is clear that Scotland took its religion very seriously; this even involved revolting against Charles I during the period which has become known as the Scottish Revolution. In a Protestant Calvinist country, such as Scotland, a witch was considered to be the inverse of someone who embraced Christ. In the eyes of many leading churchmen witchcraft was not considered in terms of the social menace, but in terms of the sin against God. Thus, witchcraft was considered to have a dominant position within the hierarchy of sin.[61]

It would appear that this intensely religious aspect of witchcraft had a direct effect on the way witchcraft cases were dealt with. If a person was understood to be a witch they would be considered a threat to the community in which they lived. Although the church itself was forbidden to have the blood on its hands by executing the witch, it could influence the method of punishment. Strangling and burning should be seen as having deeply religious symbolism. It was rare for other criminals to be burnt in Scotland; apart from witches, there were only the Protestant heretics before the Reformation and a handful of women who committed husband-murder. Witchcraft was evidently a crime which was considered beyond purely civil punishment. While the body of a murderer or common thief would often be kept on public display, which would add to the infamy of the individual, the total eradication of the body was an even greater disgrace.

This tradition of separating public display of bodies from the total eradication of bodies can be traced throughout history. As early as the first century Tacitus noted in his *Germania* two peculiarities in the German punitive system. He noted that different penalties were reserved for crimes that should be publicised by hanging, including traitors and deserters, and shameful crimes, which saw the culprit buried out of sight under a hurdle in a swamp. It has been argued that the deed of punishment belonged to a 'common European substratum of custom, which was quite deliberately kept unaltered' in order to ensure the understanding between the authorities and the spectators at the execution.[62] The actions of authorities in early modern Scotland certainly prove that they intended to send a strong message about crime and its punishment in a way that would have been clearly understood by the public. In order to publicise the punishment they had received for their crimes the bodies of many executed criminals hung on the gibbet for days before being buried at the foot of the gallows. The witches' crimes, however, were first publicised by the performance associated with the strangling and burning their bodies in a highly visible location, but the result of this punishment was the complete eradication of the witches' bodies. Perhaps burning the body of the convicted witch was a specific practice associated with purging the community of sin.

A Christian burial was considered extremely important, not least in the eyes of the populace. It is likely that many held literal interpretations of the resurrection. This literal belief that the physical body would be raised up on the Day of Judgement made the burial of dead bodies vitally important to pre-industrial Christian society. There was also a popular belief that if a body was buried incorrectly then the soul might 'walk'.[63] Early modern people may have had less of a sense of distinction between the body and the mind. Those who were dying in this period appeared to have as much concern over the fate of their body as the destination of the soul. Those sufficiently well informed in theology were not expecting to prevent the resurrection of the body in the final 'generall jugement', since even the damned were to be resurrected. The Confession of Faith of 1560 stated that 'the sey sall gif hir deid, the eird [i.e. earth] thay that thairin be inclosit, yea the eternal our God sall streiche out his hand on the dust', whereupon the damned would be 'tormentit for ever, asweill in thair awin bodyis, as in thair saulis'.[64] But how widely this was known is an open question.

The importance of Christian burial, which took place within the churchyard and with traditional religious rites, can be seen in society's treatment of the unfortunate members of their communities. Paupers who could not afford to pay for their own burial would usually be granted a Christian burial, paid for by the parish. In some of these cases the pauper might be permitted the use of a communal coffin, which at least granted him the dignity of being carried to his grave in the proper manner.[65] Even criminals, although they were tried under a legal system which could prescribe death for crimes as petty as picking pockets, were not usually denied a Christian burial. Only a crime such as treason would see the denial of this right. In this case, the criminal would often be buried at the foot of the gallows, usually after having their body parts displayed at various points around the city.[66]

Other members of society who were denied a Christian burial included those who had committed suicide. Suicides' bodies were normally buried outside the churchyard, and were sometimes subjected to additional punishments (official, popular or both) such as being dragged to their burial place or being exposed on a gibbet before burial – though stakes were not driven through their bodies, unlike in some parts of England.[67] Stillborn babies were also denied Christian burial. These were considered to be barely human, and certainly not Christian, as they had not been baptised. As a result the midwife who delivered the baby was to dispose of it in a secret place where no one would ever find it.[68]

It appears then, in most cases, that individuals who had been baptised received a Christian burial, and only in a few noticeable cases was the body disposed of in some other manner. This demonstrates the importance of the Christian burial to early modern society. It also reflects upon the actions and situations of those individuals who were not considered worthy of a Christian burial. In the majority of these cases the individuals had, through direct or indirect means, been considered to have offended God. However, despite their actions, and the community's unwillingness to allow their bodies to contaminate those of the good Christians who were buried in the churchyard, the bodies were not completely destroyed.

The fate of Scottish witches, however, was first to be strangled to death and then to have their dead bodies burnt. The body of the witch was being punished after her physical death, which would support the theory that the early modern society of Scotland still considered the body to be responsible for the actions of the individual. The society wished to punish the witch beyond death by making bodily resurrection impossible. It is also likely that the witch's body was considered to be contaminated by evil, like that of an individual who had committed suicide.

This process of punishing the body of a deceased person for crimes they committed during life is clearly apparent in witchcraft cases. Janet Smellie, who was accused of witchcraft in 1649, committed suicide in prison. The magistrates, 'with the advyse of Mr William Adair, minister, ordained that the corpse of Jonet Smelie, a witch who had died in the Tolbuith, salbe drawin upoune ane slaid to the gallowis foot and brunt in asches'.[69] The dead body of a witch could still be considered to be tainted with their sins and could contaminate the community if not destroyed. The witch's actions of renouncing her baptism and accepting the Devil as her master clearly made her not only unworthy of a Christian burial, but also so evil that her whole existence must be totally eradicated. Perhaps, this attitude towards witches, and the crimes they committed, can explain the steely determination of early modern Scots to seek out and destroy witches in their communities, regardless of the cost.

IX

This determination led to an estimated 2,500 executions being carried out between the imposition of the witchcraft act in 1563 and its repeal in 1736.[70] Although the cost of prosecution was an unwelcome burden upon the community, and the prospect of recovering the expenses was often unlikely, the local communities of Scotland were still driven to hunt witches. Contrary to any suggestions that witch-hunting was carried out by individuals who desired to profit from the process, the opposite seems to have been at work in Scotland. Scottish society's determination to purge itself of witches outweighed the financial burden of the witch-hunts.

Having convicted an individual for witchcraft, the authorities wished to stage a spectacle, perhaps to display the godliness of their community, by executing the witch in a highly visible location. This religious aspect of the crime of witchcraft, in Scotland, is particularly clear from the methods of execution. Usually a convicted witch would be sentenced to strangle and burn. The burning of the witch's body represented an attempt to punish the witch not only in life, but also in death. The witch's body was totally eradicated and as such would be denied a Christian burial. Early modern Scottish society believed that the crime of witchcraft was so evil that it had to be completely destroyed, along with the witch's body.

Notes

1. *Newes from Scotland* (London: William Wright, n.d. [*c.* 1591]), sig. D2v.–D3r.; cf. Normand and Roberts (eds.), *Witchcraft*, 323.
2. *Spalding Misc.*, v, 66.
3. Stuart Macdonald, *The Witches of Fife: Witch-hunting in a Scottish Shire, 1560–1710* (East Linton, 2002), 136.

4. Hugo Arnot, *A Collection and Abridgement of Celebrated Criminal Trials in Scotland, 1536–1784* (Edinburgh, 1785), 434.
5. Stuart Macdonald, 'Torture and the Scottish witch-hunt: a re-examination', *Scottish Tradition*, 27 (2002), 95–114, at p. 102.
6. Arnot, *Criminal Trials*, 434.
7. Christina Larner, *Enemies of God: The Witch-Hunt in Scotland* (London, 1981), 107.
8. *RPC*, 3rd ser., vi, 628–9.
9. Liv Helene Willumsen, 'Seventeenth-Century Witchcraft Trials in Scotland and Northern Norway' (University of Edinburgh PhD thesis, 2008), 65–6.
10. On at least one occasion in 1616, Perth's executioner was appointed by the kirk session, reporting to the burgh council: *The Perth Kirk Session Books, 1577–1590* (SHS, 2012), 15.
11. Pieter Spierenburg, *The Spectacle of Suffering: Executions and the Evolution of Repression from a Preindustrial Metropolis to the European Experience* (Cambridge, 1984), 28.
12. *Charters and Documents Relating to the Burgh of Peebles, with Extracts from the Records of the Burgh, 1165–1710*, ed. William Chambers (Scottish Burgh Records Society, 1872), 416.
13. *Sheriff Court Book of Fife, 1515–1522*, ed. William C. Dickinson (SHS, 1928), p. lxix.
14. David Webster (ed.), *Collection of Rare and Curious Tracts on Witchcraft and the Second Sight* (Edinburgh, 1820), 123–4.
15. John Maxwell Wood, *Witchcraft and Superstitious Record in the South-Western District of Scotland* (Dumfries, 1911), 78–9.
16. Spierenburg, *Spectacle of Suffering*, 18–19.
17. *Peebles Charters*, 416.
18. Wood, *Witchcraft and Superstitious Record*, 78–9.
19. Arnot, *Criminal Trials*, 434.
20. Alexander Morison, *Historical Notes on the Ancient and Royal Burgh of Queensferry* (Bathgate, 1927), 78.
21. Paula Hughes, 'The 1649–50 Scottish Witch-Hunt, with Particular Reference to the Synod of Lothian and Tweeddale' (University of Strathclyde PhD thesis, 2008), 76.
22. David Beveridge, *Culross and Tulliallan; or, Perthshire on Forth, Its History and Antiquities, Etc.*, 2 vols. (Edinburgh, 1885), i, 350. John Kennoway was probably related to James Kennoway, a previous burgh clerk of Culross, another keen witch-hunter with an interest in a witch's property: Louise Yeoman, 'Hunting the rich witch in Scotland: high-status witchcraft suspects and their persecutors, 1590–1650', in Julian Goodare (ed.), *The Scottish Witch-Hunt in Context* (Manchester, 2002), 106–21, at pp. 115–18.
23. William M'Dowall, *History of the Burgh of Dumfries: With Notices of Nithsdale, Annandale, and the Western Border* (3rd edn., Dumfries, 1906), 407.
24. Morison, *Royal Burgh of Queensferry*, 78.
25. David Cook, *Annals of Pittenweem, 1526–1793* (Anstruther, 1867), 49–50.
26. *Peebles Charters*, 416.
27. *RPC*, 2nd ser., ii, 469–70.
28. On prickers, see W. N. Neill, 'The professional pricker and his test for witchcraft', *SHR*, 19 (1922), 205–13.

29. SSW.
30. Esther Cohen, *The Crossroads of Justice: Law and Culture in Late Medieval France* (Leiden, 1993), 189.
31. This site was used for executing Thomas Aikenhead in 1697 and is discussed by Michael F. Graham, *The Blasphemies of Thomas Aikenhead: Boundaries of Belief on the Eve of the Enlightenment* (Edinburgh, 2008), 2–3.
32. SSW.
33. Jane E. A. Dawson, 'The Scottish Reformation and the theatre of martyrdom', in Diana Wood (ed.), *Martyrs and Martyrologies* (Woodbridge: Studies in Church History vol. 30, 1993), 259–70, at p. 260.
34. SSW.
35. Ibid.
36. Sir William Fraser, *Memorials of the Earls of Haddington*, 2 vols. (Edinburgh, 1889), i, 81. This was on 25 June, so it would still have been daylight.
37. *Spalding Misc.*, v, 66.
38. Normand and Roberts (eds.), *Witchcraft*, 197–9.
39. *Trial, Confession, and Execution of Isobel Inch, John Stewart, Margaret Barclay & Isobel Crawford, for Witchcraft, at Irvine, anno 1618* (Ardrossan and Saltcoats, n.d. [1855]), 14.
40. C. H. Firth (ed.), *Scotland and the Protectorate* (SHS, 1899), 382.
41. SSW.
42. *HP*, iii, 36–8.
43. SSW.
44. Part of the 1563 act had said that it was a crime to consult witches, but this was never implemented: Julian Goodare, 'The Scottish witchcraft act', *Church History*, 74 (2005), 39–67, at pp. 56–8.
45. *RPC*, xiv, 605.
46. *RPC*, 2nd ser., viii, 355–60.
47. *Peebles Charters*, 416; A. E. Truckell, 'Unpublished witchcraft trials', *Transactions of the Dumfriesshire and Galloway Natural History and Antiquarian Society*, 3rd ser., 51 (1975), 48–58, at p. 57.
48. George Sinclair, *Satans Invisible World Discovered*, ed. Thomas G. Stevenson (Edinburgh, 1871), 14 (relation 1).
49. NRS, Haddington sheriff court, extract decree books, 1611–14, SC40/7/13, fo. 92v. I am grateful to Dr Harriet Cornell for this reference.
50. R. D. Connor and A. D. C. Simpson, *Weights and Measures in Scotland: A European Perspective* (East Linton, 2004), 128, 130.
51. *Extracts from the Records of the Burgh of Edinburgh,* Marguerite Wood (ed.), *A.D. 1589–1603 [Etc.]* (Edinburgh, 1927), 333–4; *Peebles Charters*, 416.
52. *Spalding Misc.*, v, 68.
53. I am grateful for advice on ironwork from Dr Aaron Allen.
54. *Records of Elgin, 1234–1800*, 2 vols., ed. William Cramond (New Spalding Club, 1903–8), ii, 172.
55. *Spalding Misc.*, v, 66–7.
56. Christopher W. Schmidt and Steve A. Symes, *The Analysis of Burned Human Remains* (London, 2008), 4.
57. Ibid., 165.
58. Ibid., 167.
59. Larner, *Enemies of God*, 110.

60. Sir Walter Scott, *Letters on Demonology and Witchcraft* (London, 1884: first published 1830), 254.
61. Larner, *Enemies of God*, 165–8.
62. Cohen, *Crossroads of Justice*, 191–2.
63. Clare Gittings, *Death, Burial and the Individual in Early Modern England* (London, 1984), 60.
64. *APS*, ii, 534, c. 1 (RPS, A1560/8/3).
65. Gittings, *Death, Burial and the Individual*, 62.
66. Ibid., 69–70.
67. R. A. Houston, *Punishing the Dead? Suicide, Lordship and Community in Britain, 1500–1830* (Oxford, 2010), 211–22, 229–45.
68. Gittings, *Death, Burial and the Individual*, 83.
69. John H. Pagan, *Annals of Ayr in the Olden Time, 1560–1692* (Ayr, 1897), 109.
70. Willumsen, 'Seventeenth-Century Witchcraft Trials', 66.

12
Decline and Survival in Scottish Witch-Hunting, 1701–1727

Alexandra Hill

The decline of witch-hunting was a complex phenomenon. Indeed, it has been called 'the most baffling aspect of this difficult subject'.[1] The intricate nature of the gradual demise and eventual end of witch-hunting in Scotland proves to be no exception to this. Christina Larner, in her seminal work, articulated the then-orthodox view that the decline of witch-hunting correlated to the decline of belief of the educated elites after the Scientific Revolution, though in another passage she seemed to argue for judicial, rather than philosophical, scepticism.[2] Brian Levack, who has examined the decline of Scottish witch-hunting at greater length, has argued strongly that it was dictated by judicial scepticism and that new intellectual views were not influential.[3] This argument has become something of an orthodoxy, though the relevance of the Scientific Revolution has recently been argued by Michael Wasser.[4]

While such interpretations offer useful starting points, they reveal the absence of a comprehensive and detailed study of the late cases in Scotland. Lizanne Henderson has paved the way with her detailed investigation into the survival of witch belief and accusations in the southwest, while Stuart Macdonald's study of Fife sheds light on late cases there.[5] The dramatic possession cases of 1697–1700 in Renfrewshire and 1704 in Fife have attracted welcome attention.[6] The purpose of this investigation, therefore, is to build upon these studies and attempt to conduct a comprehensive analysis of the accusations that surfaced in the final decades of Scottish witch-hunting.

I

The decline of witch-hunting in Scotland is generally thought to have begun after the 1661–1662 panic, after which, apart from brief panics in 1678 and the late 1690s, accusations descended into a series of small-scale and individual cases.[7] Yet, there can be little doubt that conditions existed for witch-hunting to continue to fruit in the eighteenth century. Even after the so-called Glorious Revolution of 1689, when presbyterian orthodoxy was re-established, religious tensions were far from eased. As P. G. Maxwell-Stuart observes, the early eighteenth century witnessed 'a variety of –isms which rose to bestrew the religious landscape, like mushrooms in the night'.[8] Witchcraft became one of a number of crimes targeted in a climate of moral cleansing in the aftermath of the episcopalian era.

Scotland also witnessed an unprecedented stream of literature defending the supernatural world in these years. George Sinclair combated the threat of fashionable atheism by relating tales of witchcraft and apparitions in *Satan's Invisible World Discovered* (1685). The ministers Robert Kirk and John Fraser were similarly motivated, writing on the legitimacy of the fairy world and the phenomenon of second sight.[9] The intellectual framework existed for witchcraft accusations to seed and bud well into the eighteenth century.

For the purposes of this investigation, the accusations that surfaced between 1701 and 1727 have been classified according to group size in order to explore the pattern of decline.[10] See Figure 12.1 for a breakdown

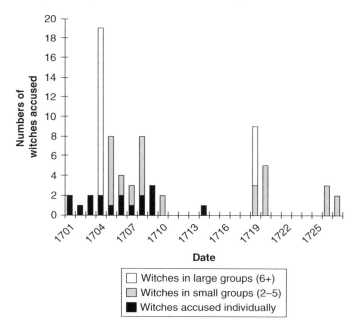

Figure 12.1   Witches by group size, 1701–1727

of these cases by date and group size. Some relevant cases from the period 1697–1700 are also discussed in order to place these other cases in context. Firstly, witches accused individually are discussed. It is perhaps not surprising that individual accusations continued to appear throughout the period, gradually becoming less frequent over time. The second part of this investigation explores small group cases, where between two and five witches were accused together. Such group cases continued well into the eighteenth century, as often as individual cases and even beyond them. The last recorded accusation, in Dornoch in 1727, involved two women. Lastly, larger group cases involving six or more witches are considered. One of these cases occurred as late as 1719. The decline of witch-hunting followed an erratic path, rather than a linear one. Even in its last gasps it remained a multiple affair.

II

Individual witchcraft cases in the early eighteenth century were similar to their earlier counterparts in a number of ways. Neighbourhood tensions resulting in acts of malefice remained a common cause of accusations. Some instances involving refusal of charity adhere precisely to the 'Thomas-Macfarlane' model, in which accusations of witchcraft stemmed from the feeling of guilt a wealthier member of society had after they had refused charity to a beggar.[11] In 1701, Elizabeth Dick, from Anstruther Easter, was summoned to the kirk session for turning grain in the local mill from white to red after she had been refused charity.[12] Janet McRobert, in Kirkcudbright in 1701, was arraigned for supposedly causing Robert Crighton's wife's breast to 'swell to a great height' after she had been given only a small quantity of chaff for her cow. McRobert had quite a reputation, with floating candles, piercing screeches and a spinning wheel going 'without the help of any person' possessing her house.[13] Two years later, in 1703, another Dumfriesshire witch, Janet McMurray from Twynholm, sought revenge on those who refused her charity, killing horses, inflicting 'great pain' and making milk 'useless'.[14] In 1704 in Bo'ness, Anna Wood was accused of witchcraft by Robert Nimmo after he had refused to give her a commission to travel to Holland aboard one of his ships. He claimed that whilst walking home one evening 'he met with six cats', one of which, whom he knew to be Wood, 'did bid kill him'.[15]

The practice of charming continued to give rise to witchcraft accusations. Even during the height of witch-hunting, most cases of charming had remained separate from cases of witchcraft, but from time to time, a few charmers crossed the line and were converted into witches, either by appearing to commit serious malefice or by appearing to make a pact with the Devil.[16] Mary Stewart was summoned before the Kilbride kirk session in 1705, accused of witchcraft 'in regard that she frequently used charms for the healing of diseases'. She was punished merely as a charmer.[17] Katherine Taylor, from Stromness in Orkney in 1708, was clearly a sorceress of repute, although a crippled beggar woman. She visited the house of Katherine Brown in Southside in order to cure Brown's bedridden husband, William Stensgar. Several witnesses claimed that before sunrise the next morning, Brown had emptied a 'large stoup' containing the water in which her husband had been washed 'in a common slap [i.e. drain]'. One witness claimed that in passing by, he 'was overtaken by bodily indisposition' and became afflicted with Stensgar's illness.[18]

Thus, most individual witch accusations in the latter decades of the Scottish witch-hunt very much reflected earlier accusations, with the continued prominence of charming and vengeful malefice. A demonic element continued, although it was perhaps less prominent than it had been during panic years. In 1701, one girl alleged that whilst in Janet McRobert's house 'the devil appeared to her in the likeness of a man, and did bid deliver herself over to him, from the crown of her head to the sole of her foot'.[19] As Edward J. Cowan and Lizanne Henderson point out, 'the Devil had, by this time, been replicating precisely these demands, in exactly the same language, and eliciting identical responses from his intended victims, for over a century'.[20]

The case of Bessie Wanton, in Cupar in 1699, gives an insight into the prominence of the Devil in these late years. James Tarbot, an 18-year-old boy, claimed that Bessie was tormenting him; she had predicted his imminent death and appeared to him on a number of occasions, sometimes in his bed, pricking him with pins and nipping him. According to his mother's testimony, James had fallen into fits rendering him deaf and dumb for eighteen days and able to see invisible sights. James claimed that he had seen a man in Bessie's house who had pressed him to 'go away with him' and had 'promised him bonnie things'.[21]

Certain features of this case, such as financial gain in exchange for compact with the Devil, are reminiscent of those of an earlier era. Yet this was quite like a possession case – a phenomenon that now acquired a new prominence in Scottish witchcraft.[22] It occurred in the same year as the 1699–1700 possession cases of Margaret Laird and Margaret Murdoch in Paisley, and in the aftermath of the famous Christian Shaw case in Renfrewshire. James Tarbot's symptoms seem to have followed the script of the Renfrewshire cases, though they should be distinguished from demonic possession to the extent that it was the witch herself who was carrying out the tormenting (while demonic possession involved a demon entering into the possessed person). However, Tarbot's accusations against Bessie Wanton were not given the same credibility as those in Renfrewshire. The presbytery 'found nothing made appear that could fix guilt upon her'. Tarbot was repeatedly asked by the sceptical presbytery if he was sleeping or dreaming, or if what he was relating 'were not his fancies'. The fact that Tarbot's allegations were dismissed, when the case of Christian Shaw only two years previously had created such a stir, suggests that local elites and zealous ministers were fundamental in fomenting any large-scale panic.

Another individual case with some new features was that of Robert Bainzie. His case of 'charming or withchcraft [*sic*]' was heard by the kirk session of Oyne in 1703. At 'flitting' (moving out of his house), he carried out a magical ritual including killing his dog and burying a cat beneath his hearth. Although this was not recorded explicitly as being an act of malefice, it could well have been intended to harm the next tenant. What is interesting, though, is that even though the session thought of his act as 'witchcraft', they equated this with 'charming' and do not seem to have been interested in a criminal prosecution. Bainzie was merely 'rebuked'.[23]

Jean Brown, in Penninghame in 1706, was one of the remarkable visionaries of Scottish witchcraft.[24] She came to the attention of the kirk session when she arrived in the parish 'under ane ill fame of devilish practices', and soon affirmed that she 'converses ordinarily with spirits' who 'ly with her carnally as men and women do when they beget children'.[25] The presbytery elicited some even more remarkable details. The spirits were the Father, Son and Holy Ghost, to whom she was married; they had shown her a vision of the day of judgement, when the heavens were as thunder and fire. A trial commission was requested, but Brown escaped from prison and disappears from the records.[26]

Brown was unique in several ways and was not part of a group. However, the session investigated her case concurrently with that of two charmers, Mary McNairn and John McNairn, illustrating the extent of moral and behavioural cleansing in Penninghame in 1705–1706. The fact that men such as Thomas McGill were rebuked and forced to repent publicly for drinking and cursing suggests that witchcraft was just one of the many crimes against God in the eyes of the presbyterian ministers.[27]

Some other individual cases, about which less is known, can be mentioned more briefly: Janet Dowlach (Kirkmichael, 1704);[28]

Alexander Deuart (Dumfries, 1707);[29] Christian Wilkieson (Greenlaw, 1708), declared fugitive for witchcraft and charming;[30] Margaret Clark (Cranston, 1709), to be tried before a circuit court;[31] Isobel Anderson (Dunnet, 1714), 'relapse in fornication … and under great presumptions of witchcraft', who was apparently banished with the aid of the sheriff;[32] and Margaret Watson (Walls, Shetland, 1725), investigated for a second time.[33]

Thus, with the exception of Bessie Wanton and Robert Bainzie, there remained a formulaic pattern to these witchcraft accusations in the late seventeenth and early eighteenth century. The main difference was that the central authorities, and in some instances the local authorities, appear to have been adopting a more moderate stance. The rise of non-capital penalties, especially banishment, is one example. Janet McRobert was banished to Ireland;[34] Elspeth Rule, from Dumfries in 1709, the last witch to be tried before the court of justiciary in Edinburgh, was condemned to be branded on the cheek with a hot iron; according to local lore, smoke was seen issuing out of her mouth.[35]

This case also illustrates another point: those who were punished, perhaps especially those who were condemned to death, seem to have obtained an almost legendary status, perhaps because they were less common than before. Again according to local lore, Margaret Myles refused to say the Lord's Prayer on her way to execution in Edinburgh in 1702.[36] The circumstances surrounding Meg Lawson's indictment in 1700 were 'handed down by tradition', so that even her grandchildren continued to suffer from her reputation.[37] A snuff mill belonging to Margaret Laing, one of the Bargarran witches of 1697, became an antiquarian relic and ended up in the National Museum of Scotland.[38]

The case of Helen Kirkpatrick, in Kirkbride in 1706, provides a contrast, illustrating some changing attitudes. Peter Rae, the parish minister, issued a petition against Helen claiming that she had 'grievously abused, slandered and defamed him' by calling him a 'soul-murderer'. In retaliation, Helen issued a petition against him, asserting that he had called her a witch and 'bled her forehead with a lance'. After much contemplation, both parties were called before the congregation on the next Sabbath and rebuked, with Mr Rae declaring that he was 'very sorry to have offended any of the meanest of Christ's members'.[39] Had such a case occurred a century before, it is less likely that Mr Rae would have been punished, and Helen's claims against him might not have received such credit.

Thus, there remained some traditional patterns to individual witchcraft accusations in the eighteenth century. In some areas, however, those accused were met by newly tolerant attitudes among local elites. Witches were less likely to find themselves on trial, and those who were tried were less likely to be condemned to the flames. Of the eighteen witches accused individually in these years, only one (Margaret Myles) is known to have been executed. Nevertheless, nine are known to have suffered non-capital punishment; witchcraft very much remained a punishable crime.

III

Remarkably, small group cases involving two to five witches budded almost as often as individual cases in the years 1701–1727. These group accusations shared many of the characteristics of those accused individually. However, on closer inspection, it is clear that those caught up in a multiple indictment were linked by family ties, by association or by being victims of an individual's zeal.

The parish of Caerlaverock, in Dumfriesshire, produced one small group of witches in 1705 – a group which may have been linked to others through the zeal of one or more ministers. The most obvious minister was Robert Paton, the former minister of Caerlaverock who in 1695 had been transferred to nearby Dumfries. He had been involved in earlier Caerlaverock cases in 1692 and 1697–1699. John Somerville, minister of Caerlaverock, Robert Blair, minister of Holywood, and John Reid, minister of Lochrutton, were all involved with two of the four cases. There were as many as nine ministers involved with the main case.[40] It was a case of demonic possession, and the ministers 'prayed with the familie molested, and after discoursed with all the persons suspected to be the instruments of their disturbance, except Bessie Heslope, whom they could not find'. Heslope was the only person named; the total number of suspects is unknown but was evidently at least four. The original idea was to get 'the Magistrat' (presumably the sheriff-depute) to arrest the suspects, but this did not happen – perhaps he refused? The ministers reported that 'they find several very odd presumptions of witchcraft, yet they can see nothing to fix the same upon any of the persons suspected'. They sent an 'information' to the queen's advocate, but a reply came back that 'no criminal process can be raised', whereupon the presbytery 'thought fit to let it fall and leave the matter to Providence'.[41]

The Caerlaverock group may have been linked to another case counted here as an individual case: that of Janet Hairstains, a vagrant who had been in periodic trouble for suspected witchcraft for some time. In 1709 she was reported as a witch in the parish of Kirkbean, separated from Caerlaverock by the estuary of the Nith, and had also been reported in the neighbouring parish of Torthorwald. Paton, Blair and Reid were all involved in Hairstains' case.[42] Hairstains may not have been involved directly in the Caerlaverock possession case, but she was connected to it by the same ministers' fanaticism.

An explanation for this apparent concern of these Dumfriesshire ministers may be found in a letter of 1704 from the commission of the general assembly to the presbytery of Wigtown, lamenting the 'distressed state of diverse of the reformed church' and the need for ministers to address in their sermons 'the pernicious heresies, idolaters and superstitions of the Romish Church'.[43] Clearly there was a wider climate of presbyterian panic in the southwest, and it was not merely witchcraft that was the object of moral cleansing. On the same day as Bessie Heslope's case was being investigated, Richard Harries came before the presbytery for his 'drunkenness and scandalous behaviour'. A month later, Janet Harper was fined after she had been in 'company of loose and debauched men'.[44]

However, the central authorities did not share the anxieties of these ministers. The king's advocate had written in 1699 that the case of Janet Wharrie, one of the earlier Caerlaverock witches who had been incarcerated for two years for performing various acts of malefice, was 'not so momentous as to require a commission'.[45] Janet Hairstains was treated more and more leniently. In 1700 she was banished for the use of charming, only to return three weeks later![46] In her eventual trial before the circuit court in 1709 she was acquitted.[47] Thus, it is clear that although large-scale witch-hunting still surfaced in these late years, the central authorities – and even some of the local authorities – were beginning to treat them with less severity.

Throughout the period of Scottish witch-hunting, it was common for a witchcraft suspicion to stem from family ties. The case of George and Lachlan Rattray, in Inverness in 1706, was an example of this. They were 'alleged guilty of the horrid crimes of mischievous charms, by witchcraft and malefice, sorcery or necromancy'. The privy council issued a commission to try the offenders locally, but the judges did not allow an execution to take place without a warrant from the council.[48] Such strict guidelines suggest that the privy council was reluctant to let the fate of these two men lie entirely with the Inverness authorities. Only a decade before, the privy council had issued a commission to the Inverness authorities to try two women, named McRorie and McQuicken, which lacked these guidelines and gave them authority to execute them if found guilty.[49] As it turned out, despite the precautions, the Rattrays were still ordained to the flames, but their case was the last execution authorised by the privy council. After the abolition of the Scottish privy council in 1708 (the year after the union of the Scottish and English parliaments), its role in authorising witchcraft trials was taken over by the queen's advocate.

Sadly, little documentation survives of the Rattrays' case. However, the example of the Ratter family, in Shetland in 1708, sheds light on how a family could be caught up in a joint accusation. The Ratters, two sisters and a brother, were seen as being 'great deluders and abusers of the people', their neighbours being 'greatly terrified with their horrid cursing and imprecations'. The family were unpopular in Calvister and were deemed responsible for a number of deaths and misfortunes, often after they had received insufficient alms. In one instance, Elizabeth Ratter threatened Hugh Thompson with crop failure, saying that last year he had refused her a plate of corn and had consequently suffered a poor harvest, whilst his neighbour, who had been generous towards her, had had a better harvest. Her sister Katherine was apparently held responsible for several deaths. She was heard cursing Christopher Thompson 'several tymes' before his untimely death.

The accusations against Andrew Ratter were more extensive than those against his sisters, which is perhaps a reflection of some beliefs surrounding male witches. Male witches were sometimes believed to possess greater powers than their female counterparts and to be on more equal terms with the Devil. George Burroughs was seen as being 'the ring leader of them all' in Salem in 1692.[50] Andrew was reported to have 'leaned on his staff' when performing a certain act of malefice. A staff, or something similar, has been argued to be a symbol of authority for some male witches; Alexander Hamilton in 1630 was said to have been given a 'battoun of fir' by the Devil.[51] Like his sisters, Andrew was accused of harming livestock and hindering their production, causing illness and even killing a child.[52]

It was not merely through family ties, but also as accomplices more generally, that witches were accused together. A fourth suspect, Margaret Watson, was investigated with the Ratters.[53] Another northern group, in Risegill, Caithness, consisted of two suspects: Henry Christian and Ann Sutherland. They were sent for trial at a circuit court in 1710.[54]

What began as an individual case in Kirkcudbright soon began to turn into a serial accusation. There is little documentation, but Janet McKeoner was recorded in November 1707 as having been 'burnt for witchcraft at Kirkcudbright lately'.[55] This was recorded by the Penninghame kirk session in their investigation of William Drew for witchcraft; he had allegedly been named as a witch by McKeoner. However, Drew's case was dropped.[56]

In 1720, an unknown number of witches, at least five in total, were accused of tormenting Patrick Sandilands, the 12–13-year-old third son of Lord Torphichen. It was reported that he 'fell down in trances, from which no horse whipping could rouse him'. Whilst in such fits he supposedly pronounced prophecies, made urine the colour of ink and was lifted up into the air by invisible hands. Eventually Lord Torphichen gave credit to his son's claims and had the tormentors seized, while the minister of the parish proclaimed a fast. Yet, despite showing similar symptoms to the earlier possession cases in 1697–1700 and 1704, the case was nipped in the bud. Patrick was 'sent off' to join the fleet and little more was heard of the affair.[57]

There were several contemporary interpretations of this case. The eccentric William Mitchell, the 'Mad Tinklerian Doctor', used it to prove the existence of witchcraft.[58] Robert Wodrow, minister of Eastwood, seems to have been more sceptical: 'but what to make upon the whole I know not'.[59] These differing accounts perhaps reflect the varying degrees of doubt concerning witchcraft in this period. The fact that Patrick's claims were not given the same credibility as other earlier cases suggests that such cases, whilst providing a means to demonstrate the reality of demonic power for some, were no longer considered convincing evidence to others.

In the parish of Spott, East Lothian, in October 1705, there is a brief reference to 'Many witches burnt on the top of Spott loan'.[60] Following the convention of the Survey of Scottish Witchcraft, this group of 'many' can be counted as containing at least three witches.

Two small groups of witches, also with their precise numbers obscure, were mentioned later in Ross-shire. The minister of Tarbat, David Ross, reported to the presbytery in November 1719 'a great noise in that parish of witches and witchcraft'. An investigatory committee was established, a report was to be made to the 'procurator and agent for the church', and in February 1720 Ross was 'to send south the next week the abstract of the process anent those alleadged guilty of witchcraft'. The case then disappears from the presbytery records.[61] Also in Ross-shire, with no place noted but under the date May 1726, Wodrow noted 'odd accounts of witchcraft there of late, some of them prosecute'.[62] This was certainly a small group, and possibly a large one. The results of the prosecutions are unknown, but Wodrow's wording is ominous.

This was not long before Scotland's final known witchcraft prosecution, itself another small group case in the far north: two women in

Dornoch, Sutherland, a mother and daughter. The mother was executed, while the daughter escaped. The name 'Janet Horne' was assigned to the mother in the early twentieth century, though with dubious authenticity. Even the date is unclear, several references assigning it to 1722, but the date of 1727 was preferred by Cowan and Henderson, who studied the case in as much detail as the fragmentary records allowed.[63]

Therefore, it appears that multiple indictments continued to blossom in the eighteenth century; the decline of witch-hunting was not as sharp as is sometimes assumed. Yet, unlike their earlier counterparts, there appears to be evidence of increased judicial scepticism that prevented these cases from mushrooming out of control. In only four of the eleven groups do we have evidence that one or more of the witches in these small groups was executed.

IV

Turning to the cases of large groups of witches, there were three instances after 1701 when groups of six or more witches were accused together in these final decades. This period followed a burst of witch-hunting in the late 1690s, especially the famous Christian Shaw case of 1697, which fused into the possession of two other young girls, Margaret Murdoch and Margaret Laird. These cases have been discussed elsewhere; here it is important to note the witch-hunting zeal of the local elites, clerical and non-clerical. There were at least twenty-seven ministers involved in the cases of Shaw, Murdoch and Laird, including James Brisbane and Neil Gillies, whilst laymen such as Sir Francis Grant of Cullen and Sir John Maxwell of Pollok also played an active role.[64] However, only seven of the twenty-five witches named in the commission to the privy council in 1697 were executed, and all of the 1699–1700 witches were released without trial. Whilst all the fundamental ingredients for a large-scale hunt were in the mix, systematic doubts emerged from the central authorities. Michael Wasser argues that 1697–1700 marks the 'last major witch-hunt' in Scotland.[65]

However, the events of 1697–1700 did not mark the end of serial witch-hunting in the localities. Despite central scepticism, local fervour remained and gave birth to some large-scale accusations in the eighteenth century.

The scale of witch-hunting in the late 1690s should be emphasised, with 107 recorded cases altogether in the period 1697–1700.[66] One less-studied serial accusation, occurring in the same years as the Renfrewshire cases, should perhaps be mentioned here: a series of accusations that surfaced in Easter Ross. The surviving records show two groups, one of three and one of twelve, but the cases were evidently connected since they occurred in the same locality at the same time. Three women, deemed responsible for a number of misfortunes, were the subjects of precognitions taken at Fortrose in October 1699. Following an altercation with Mary Nicinnarich, Alexander Maclay fell ill, recovering only after drinking a glass of her milk. Margaret Provost's reputation was such that a local laird took matters into his own hands and 'pulled down the house about her ears'. The laird's gardener, who had assisted in the demolition, subsequently 'swelled as big as two men' and 'got such a voracious stomach that he would eat as much as six'.[67] Meanwhile twelve other people were 'alleged guilty of the diabolical crimes and charms of witchcraft'. A commission of local lairds was appointed by the privy council to put them to trial by an assize, but then to report back with recommendations. Margaret Monro and Agnes Wrath confessed, and were convicted with eight others in the local court. The other two, John Glass and Mary Keill, had nothing found proven against them, but were still sentenced to be fined and banished. All this shows local belief in the criminality of these witches and extrajudicial action by the authorities. However, the privy council took a more moderate attitude. Those who had been convicted were ordered to receive an arbitrary but non-capital punishment, while Glass and Keill were ordered to be freed from Fortrose jail.[68]

Turning to the large groups after 1700, the first was the 1704 possession case of Patrick Morton in Pittenweem. This reinforces the idea that local fervour was crucial. The barbarous lynching of Janet Cornfoot unequivocally establishes the extent of popular belief. Brian Levack suggests that the war against France provided a suitable climate for witchcraft accusations: soldiers quartered in the town undermined godly discipline, raping women and encouraging villagers to drink during Sunday sermons.[69] It comes as no surprise that the presbyterian minister, Patrick Cowper, was at the forefront of the accusations. The author of a pamphlet against the affair asserted that the minister orchestrated it and 'exercised more civil authority than any of the Baillies'. He claimed that Cowper read an account of the Christian Shaw case to Morton and encouraged him to implicate Beatrix Laing.[70] Another pamphlet alleged that Cowper was so determined to force a confession from these women that he beat Janet Cornfoot with his staff and turned a blind eye to her brutal murder.[71] Eight in total were named: Isobel Adam, Thomas Brown, Janet Cornfoot, Janet Horseburgh, Margaret Jack, Beatrix Laing, Nicolas Lawson and Lilias Wallace. Yet all were released (except Brown who died in prison), with Cornfoot's lynching occurring when she returned to the town. Laing and Lawson were prosecuted again in 1708–1709 (counted here as a small group), but again were released.[72] The central authorities were not convinced by the zeal of local elites. In the recriminations afterwards, one of the bailies, William Bell, was forced to apologise in 1710 for maltreating Janet Horseburgh. Brian Levack writes that this 'may have dealt a final blow to intense witch-hunting in Scotland, as there were no attempts to prosecute entire groups of witches, only individuals, after that date'.[73] Yet we have already seen that there were some small groups after 1710 – and we shall see shortly that there was also one more large group.

Meanwhile, in the neighbouring parish of Torryburn, local elites were aiding witchcraft activity. The events of 1703–1704 unfolded following a rumour that Jean Bizet had been 'molested by Satan' and had arisen from her sleep shouting, 'by God he is going to take me! O Lilly (Adie) with her blew doublet! O Mary, Mary Wilson! Christ keep me!' Following these allegations, Jean Neilson claimed that she too was 'dreadfully tormented' by Lilias Adie. After her arrest, Adie confessed to being in a compact with the Devil and named Agnes Currie and Elspeth Williamson as witches she had recognised at meetings with the Devil. Thus the chain of denunciation had been set in motion; seven were named in 1704 (Adie, Currie and Williamson, plus Bessie Callendar, Mary Carmichael, Janet White and Mary Wilson), plus two who had been executed recently (Grissel Anderson and Euphemia Stirt, apparently in 1703), making a total of nine. The Devil played a prominent part in these confessions, being described by Adie as having a cloven foot and appearing as 'a shadow', and by Williamson as having a silent step on the stubble. Adie's account of her renouncing her baptism correlates exactly to those that had been related for over a century.[74] After the two executions of 1703, and Adie's death in prison, nothing appears to have come of the accusation of 1704. There is no evidence of the central authorities becoming involved; perhaps the case was simply dropped. Nevertheless, the meticulously stereotypical nature of the confessions, and the apparent encouragement to name accomplices, suggest that there were members of the local elite at the heart of the investigation.

Even as late as 1718, large-scale witch-hunting continued to bud. According to Robert Dundas, the king's advocate, there were 'very extraordinary, if not fabulous' discoveries of witchcraft in Caithness. In December 1718, William Montgomery petitioned the sheriff-depute of Caithness that his house had become infested with cats, and one evening he had used his sword to fend off the intruders, killing two of them. He claimed that 'not one drop of blood' came from the injured cats, and no bodies could be found in the morning. The sheriff-depute was not stirred until February 1719, when it was reported that Margaret Nin-Gilbert's leg had fallen off. In a letter to Robert Wodrow, James Frazer reported that Margaret Olson, a tenant of his uncle, had been removed from her lodging on account of 'the wickedness of her behaviour' and replaced by Montgomery. Olson then solicited Nin-Gilbert to 'do mischief' in revenge.[75] In June 1719, the synod of Caithness and Orkney noted a recent 'noise of witchcraft and socerie' in the presbytery of Caithness. The diligence of the presbytery and sheriff was approved, and further action encouraged.[76]

As in the cases previously discussed, it is clear that the local elites played a crucial role. The sheriff-depute appears to have intended to take the case into his own hands and was only checked when the king's advocate intervened and reproached him for not having referred the case to the 'proper method and court'.[77] The minister of Thurso, William Innes, likewise played a vital role. Under his examination Nin-Gilbert confessed to being in league with the Devil, claiming that he appeared to her 'in the likeness of a great black horse ... a black cloud, and sometimes like a black man'. She further admitted to having been 'bodily present' in Montgomery's house in the form of a 'feltered [i.e. shaggy] cat' and was encouraged to name her accomplices. Olson was even pricked for the witch's mark – a practice that had been forbidden by the privy council in 1678.[78] This case contained all the ingredients of a panic; had the king's advocate not intervened, the six women would probably have suffered an unpleasant fate.

It thus becomes clear that local elites were most important in the surfacing and maturing of multiple accusations. In almost all of these cases there is evidence of local elites, more often than not zealous ministers, determined to force a confession and to obtain names of accomplices. It is of particular interest that three of these cases featured possession. According to Brian Levack, the emergence of possession cases in 1690s was part of the 'late seventeenth-century Calvinist religious culture'.[79] In a time of philosophical scepticism, possession offered proof of the existence of evil spirits. It could be argued that Levack's theory could be applied to the non-possession cases in this group as well. The tale related in Thurso and the emphasis on the role of the Devil in Torryburn both suggest that local elites were reaching for sensationalist extremes in order to prove the existence of the supernatural world. Meanwhile, one cannot overlook the fact that the central authorities took an increasingly moderate stance. As Levack points out, possession cases were a double-edged sword. On the one hand they stoked belief, whilst on the other they encouraged scepticism.[80]

V

Overall, the early eighteenth century witnessed a distinct increase of systematic doubts about witchcraft. Central authorities adopted an increasingly moderate attitude to prosecutions. Commissions for trials were often refused and, even if a commission was granted, it was issued with greater caution and supervision than before. Those witches who were put on trial were more likely to be given a non-capital punishment, or even acquitted, rather than being condemned to the flames. The increasing incidence of non-capital punishment was a significant development of the period; for most of the period of Scottish witch-hunting, there had been a single crime – witchcraft – with a single punishment – death. Now, both central and local courts were giving themselves a wider range of options, reducing the seriousness of the death toll.

Nevertheless, belief endured and allegations of witchcraft continued to be made. Even with the emergence of the new philosophies that were attacking belief in the supernatural world, presbyterian fervour and anti-Sadducism seem to have provided the intellectual framework for witch-hunting to survive. At the grass roots level, magic remained very much an integral part of everyday life, and even among educated elites there was a 'mixed bag of beliefs'.[81] As Michael Wasser remarks, 'what was occurring was not a contest between true believers and complete sceptics, but between people with different degrees of doubt, who chose to emphasise different things'.[82] There was, certainly, a falling-off of individual cases after 1709, with only one further individual case (in 1714); but between 1710 and 1727, at least twenty-one witches were accused in groups. Thus, driven by the resilient beliefs of local elites, witch-hunting continued to seed and bud in these decades with the same flavour as it had done in earlier years, and subsequently declined less sharply than is generally assumed. In some localities at least, it was quite remarkably a story of survival.

Notes

1. Keith Thomas, *Religion and the Decline of Magic* (Harmondsworth, 1971), 570.
2. Christina Larner, *Enemies of God: The Witch-Hunt in Scotland* (London, 1981), 78–9, 189–91.

3. Brian P. Levack, 'The decline and end of Scottish witch-hunting', in his *Witch-Hunting in Scotland: Law, Politics and Religion* (London, 2008), 131–44.
4. Michael Wasser, 'The mechanical world view and the decline of witch-beliefs in Scotland', in Julian Goodare, Lauren Martin and Joyce Miller (eds.), *Witchcraft and Belief in Early Modern Scotland* (Basingstoke, 2008), 206–26, at pp. 208–10.
5. Lizanne Henderson, 'The survival of witchcraft prosecutions and witch belief in south-west Scotland', *SHR*, 85 (2006), 52–74; Stuart Macdonald, *The Witches of Fife: Witch-Hunting in a Scottish Shire, 1560–1710* (East Linton, 2002). See also Edward J. Cowan and Lizanne Henderson, 'The last of the witches? The survival of Scottish witch belief', in Julian Goodare (ed.), *The Scottish Witch-Hunt in Context* (Manchester, 2002), 198–217.
6. Hugh McLachlan and Kim Swales, 'The bewitchment of Christian Shaw: a reassessment of the famous Paisley witchcraft case of 1697', in Yvonne G. Brown and Rona Ferguson (eds.), *Twisted Sisters: Women, Crime and Deviance in Scotland since 1400* (East Linton, 2002), 54–83; Michael Wasser, 'The western witch-hunt of 1697–1700: the last major witch-hunt in Scotland', in Goodare (ed.), *The Scottish Witch-Hunt in Context*, 146–65; Brian P. Levack, 'Demonic possession and witch-hunting in Scotland' and 'Witch-hunting and witch-murder in early eighteenth-century Scotland', in his *Witch-Hunting in Scotland*, 115–30, 145–61.
7. Levack, 'Decline and end'.
8. P. G. Maxwell-Stuart, 'Witchcraft and magic in eighteenth-century Scotland', in Owen Davies and Willem de Blécourt (eds.), *Beyond the Witch Trials: Witchcraft and Magic in Enlightenment Europe* (Manchester, 2004), 81–99, at p. 92.
9. Hunter (ed.), *Occult Laboratory*, 77–117, 187–204. For some other works, see Christina Larner, 'Two late Scottish witchcraft tracts: *Witch-Craft Proven* and *The Tryal of Witchcraft*', in Sydney Anglo (ed.), *The Damned Art: Essays in the Literature of Witchcraft* (London, 1977), 227–45, and Hugh McLachlan (ed.), *The Kirk, Satan and Salem: A History of the Witches of Renfrewshire* (Glasgow, 2006).
10. There are several groups of unknown size, where sources refer to 'several' or 'many' witches. Following the practice of the Survey of Scottish Witchcraft, such groups are counted as comprising three witches. The figures are for *cases*, not individual people; three individuals had more than one case. Cases are defined as formal accusations of witchcraft that might have led (and in some cases did lead) to trial and execution.
11. Thomas, *Religion and the Decline of Magic*, 652–69; Alan Macfarlane, *Witchcraft in Tudor and Stuart England* (London, 1970), chs. 15–16.
12. Macdonald, *Witches of Fife*, 144.
13. Extract from the Minute Book of the Kirk Session of Kirkcudbright (6 February–10 April 1701), in J. M. Wood, *Witchcraft in South West Scotland* (Dumfries, 1911), 82–7. Cf. Henderson, 'Survival of witchcraft prosecutions', 61.
14. Extract from the Session Book of Twynholm (18 April–9 May 1703), in Wood, *Witchcraft*, 87–91.

15. Thomas J. Salmon, *Borrowstounness and District: Being Historical Sketches of Kinneil, Carriden, and Bo'ness,* c.1550–1850 (London, 1913), 119–21.
16. On charming, see Joyce Miller, 'Devices and directions: folk healing aspects of witchcraft practice in seventeenth-century Scotland', in Goodare (ed.), *The Scottish Witch-Hunt in Context,* 90–105, and Owen Davies, 'A comparative perspective on Scottish cunning-folk and charmers', in Goodare, Martin and Miller (eds.), *Witchraft and Belief,* 185–205.
17. Extract from the Session Records of Kilbride (3 June 1705), in J. M. Balfour and W. M. Mackenzie (eds.), *The Book of Arran,* 2 vols. (Glasgow, 1910–14), ii, 294–5.
18. Extract from a Process contained in a Session Register (July 1708–5 September 1708), in G. Low, *The Islands of Orkney as Traversed in Summer 1774* (Kirkwall, 1834), 201–3.
19. Extract from the Minute Book of the Kirk Session of Kirkcudbright (6 February–10 April 1701), in Wood, *Witchcraft,* 83.
20. Cowan and Henderson, 'The last of the witches?', 204.
21. NRS, Cupar presbytery records, CH2/82/2, pp. 344–7.
22. Levack, 'Demonic possession'.
23. James Logan, 'Ecclesiastical collections for Aberdeenshire', *Archaeologia Scotica: Transactions of the Society of Antiquaries of Scotland,* 3 (1831), 4–19, at p. 13.
24. For another case involving a well-known visionary, see Emma Wilby, '"We mey shoot them dead at our pleasur": Isobel Gowdie, elf arrows and dark shamanism', Chapter 8 in this volume.
25. *The Session Book of Penninghame, 1696–1724,* ed. Henry Paton (Edinburgh, 1933), 164.
26. SSW; Henderson, 'Survival of witchcraft prosecutions', 62–3.
27. *Session Book of Penninghame,* 161–9.
28. John Hunter, *The Diocese and Presbytery of Dunkeld, 1660–1689,* 2 vols. (London, n.d. [1918]), ii, 60.
29. Christina Larner, Christopher H. Lee and Hugh V. McLachlan, *A Source-Book of Scottish Witchcraft* (Glasgow, 1977), no. 3009.
30. SSW.
31. Ibid.
32. Alfred W. Johnston and Amy Johnston (eds.), *Old-Lore Miscellany of Orkney, Shetland, Caithness and Sutherland,* vol. iii (Coventry: Viking Club, 1910), 48.
33. SSW. The first investigation, discussed below, was as part of a group with the Ratter family.
34. Extract from the Minute Book of the Kirk Session of Kirkcudbright (10 April 1701), in Wood, *Witchcraft,* 87.
35. Cowan and Henderson, 'The last of the witches', 205.
36. Quoted in Chambers, *Domestic Annals,* iii, 217.
37. Thomas Craig-Brown, *The History of Selkirkshire,* 2 vols. (Edinburgh, 1886), ii, 100–1.
38. Hugh Cheape, '"Charms against witchcraft": magic and mischief in museum collections', in Goodare, Martin and Miller (eds.), *Witchcraft and Belief,* 227–48, at p. 244.

232 *Decline and Survival in Scottish Witch-Hunting*

232 *Decline and Survival in Scottish Witch-Hunting*

39. NRS, Penpont presbytery records, CH2/298/1, pp. 287–301.
40. SSW; Hew Scott (ed.), *Fasti Ecclesiae Scoticanae*, 7 vols. (2nd edn., Edinburgh, 1915-), ii, 259.
41. NRS, Dumfries presbytery records, 1701–10, CH2/1284/4, pp. 174, 181, 183, 195.
42. SSW; Henderson, 'Survival of witchcraft prosecutions', 66.
43. Quoted in Henderson, 'Survival of witchcraft prosecutions', 61–2.
44. NRS, Dumfries presbytery records, 1701–10, CH2/1284/4, pp. 181, 185.
45. Henderson, 'Survival of witchcraft prosecutions', 64.
46. Ibid., 66.
47. SSW.
48. Chambers, *Domestic Annals*, iii, 302.
49. Ibid., 136.
50. Paul Boyer and Stephen Nissenbaum (eds.), *Salem-Village Witchcraft* (Belmont, Calif., 1972), chs. 5, 14.
51. Julian Goodare, 'Women and the witch-hunt in Scotland', *Social History*, 23 (1998), 288–308, at p. 305; cf. Julian Goodare, 'Men and the witch-hunt in Scotland', in Alison Rowlands (ed.), *Witchcraft and Masculinities in Early Modern Europe* (Basingstoke, 2009), 148–70.
52. NRS, Shetland presbytery records, CH2/1071/1, pp. 152–8. I am grateful to Mrs Diane Baptie for permission to quote from her transcript of this document and to Professor Liv Helene Willumsen for obtaining a copy of it for me. The Ratters' fate is unknown.
53. SSW.
54. Ibid.
55. *Session Book of Penninghame*, 205.
56. Henderson, 'Survival of witchcraft prosecutions', 71.
57. Charles K. Sharpe, *A Historical Account of the Belief in Witchcraft in Scotland* (London, 1884), 194–5.
58. Ibid., 196–7.
59. Robert Wodrow, *Analecta: Materials for a History of Remarkable Providences*, 4 vols., ed. Mathew Leishman (Maitland Club, 1842–1843), ii, 339.
60. *Statistical Account of Scotland, 1791–99*, vol. v, p. 454 (Spott, County of Haddington), online at http://stat-acc-scot.edina.ac.uk/link/1791–99/Haddington/Spott/5/454/.
61. NRS, Tain presbytery records, 1718–23, CH2/384/4, pp. 59, 61, 63, 68.
62. Wodrow, *Analecta*, iii, 302.
63. Cowan and Henderson, 'The last of the witches?', 205–9.
64. Wasser, 'Western witch-hunt', 153.
65. Ibid., 146–7, 154.
66. SSW.
67. Extract from miscellaneous papers of the Boyds of Trochrigg, quoted in Larner, Lee and McLachlan, *Source-Book*, 275–7.
68. Chambers, *Domestic Annals*, iii, 216–17; Larner, Lee and McLachlan, *Source-Book*, 280.
69. Levack, 'Witch-hunting and witch-murder', 148.
70. 'An Answer of a Letter from a Gentleman in Fife', in David Webster (ed.), *A Collection of Rare and Curious Tracts on Witchcraft and the Second Sight* (Edinburgh, 1820), 72.

71. 'An Account of an Horrid and Barbarous Murder', in Webster (ed.), *Collection*, 73.
72. Levack, 'Witch-hunting and witch-murder', 159–60.
73. Ibid., 159.
74. Minutes and Proceedings of the Kirk-Session of Torryburn (30 June-3 September 1704), in Webster (ed.), *Collection*, 127–43; Macdonald, *Witches of Fife*, 112–13. For statistical purposes all nine are assigned to the same group dated 1704, although two of the cases were slightly earlier.
75. Sharpe, *Historical Account*, 180–90. For more on witches' transformation into cats, see Robert Darnton, *The Great Cat Massacre* (London, 1984), 91–4.
76. Alfred W. Johnston and Amy Johnston (eds.), *Old-Lore Miscellany of Orkney, Shetland, Caithness and Sutherland*, vol. ii (London: Viking Club, 1909), 172.
77. Sharpe, *Historical Account*, 184–6.
78. Ibid., 188–90.
79. Levack, 'Witch-hunting and witch-murder', 146.
80. Levack, 'Demonic possession', 129.
81. Roy Porter, 'Witchcraft and magic in Enlightenment, Romantic and liberal thought', in Marijke Gijswijt-Hofstra, Brian P. Levack and Roy Porter, *Witchcraft and Magic in Europe: The Eighteenth and Nineteenth Centuries* (London, 1999), 191–282, at p. 237.
82. Wasser, 'Western witch-hunt', 161.

Bibliography of Scottish Witchcraft

Julian Goodare

Introduction

This is a bibliography of works on Scottish witchcraft and witch-hunting, primarily in the early modern period. The aim has been to produce a list that historians working on these topics today will find useful. It includes, not only works on Scottish witchcraft *per se*, but also works on closely-related topics that witchcraft scholars cannot ignore – two examples being torture and fairy belief. It omits works of purely historiographical interest and popular works that have no claim to originality. It also omits works concerned with the period after about 1800, unless they also shed light on beliefs and practices of earlier times. Finally, it omits works published before 1800; for these see the bibliographical article by John Ferguson, listed below.

Whether a work is about 'Scotland' may sometimes be debated. A few works have been included because they are substantively about Scotland even though their title does not say so. Also included are works that discuss Scotland and another country (usually England) in a comparative context. On the other hand, works that use some Scottish material in the context of developing a more general case have been excluded.

The bibliography is divided into four sections:

1. Lists of witchcraft cases
2. Published primary sources
3. Published secondary works
4. Unpublished theses

In general, works are listed under the surname of the author. However, a given author's works may be found in various places in the bibliography, partly because of the division into sections and partly because of the following conventions.

Debates in journals are grouped together, listed under the surname of the author of the first article.

Collections of essays have been treated in three different ways:

1. If the book contains a small number of relevant chapters, then these are listed individually under the name(s) of the author(s) of the chapter(s); the book itself is not listed separately.
2. If all or even most of the book's chapters are relevant, then the book receives a single entry under the name(s) of the editor(s) of the book, followed by a list of all the individual chapters. This occasionally results in some chapters being listed that would not otherwise have qualified for inclusion.
3. If the book is a collection of reprints, then this is noted and all the Scottish material that it contains is listed, including full publication details of the

original works. This, too, occasionally results in some works being listed that would not otherwise have qualified for inclusion. Any reprinted works that *are* considered relevant also receive their own entry with the original publication details.

1. Lists of witchcraft cases

G. F. Black, 'A calendar of cases of witchcraft in Scotland, 1510–1727', *Bulletin of the New York Public Library*, 41 (1937), 811–47, 917–36, and 42 (1938), 34–74; also published as G. F. Black, *A Calendar of Cases of Witchcraft in Scotland, 1510–1727* (New York, 1938)

Julian Goodare, Lauren Martin, Joyce Miller and Louise Yeoman, 'The Survey of Scottish Witchcraft, 1563–1736' (www.shc.ed.ac.uk/Research/witches/, archived January 2003, updated October 2003)

Christina Larner, Christopher H. Lee and Hugh V. McLachlan, *A Source-Book of Scottish Witchcraft* (Glasgow, 1977)

Stuart Macdonald, 'The Scottish Witch Hunt Data Base' (CD-Rom, privately published, 2001)

2. Published primary sources

Joseph Anderson (ed.), 'The confessions of the Forfar witches (1661)', *Proceedings of the Society of Antiquaries of Scotland*, 22 (1887–1888), 241–62

R. Burns Begg (ed.), 'Notice of trials for witchcraft at Crook of Devon, Kinross-shire, in 1662', *Proceedings of the Society of Antiquaries of Scotland*, 22 (1887–1888), 211–41

G. F. Black (ed.), 'Confessions of Alloa witches', *Scottish Antiquary*, 9 (1895), 49–52

G. F. Black (ed.), 'Some unpublished Scottish witchcraft trials', *Bulletin of the New York Public Library*, 45 (1941), 335–42, 413–22, 671–84, 763–80; also published as G. F. Black (ed.), *Some Unpublished Scottish Witchcraft Trials* (New York, 1941)

G. F. Black and Northcote W. Thomas (eds.), *Examples of Printed Folklore Concerning the Orkney & Shetland Islands* (Folk-Lore Society: County Folk-Lore, vol. iii: Printed Extracts, no. 5: London, 1903), 'Superstitious beliefs and practices: witchcraft: trials', pp. 55–139

John Christie (ed.), *Witchcraft in Kenmore, 1730–57: Extracts from the Kirk Session Records of the Parish* (Aberfeldy, 1893)

Michael Hunter (ed.), *The Occult Laboratory: Magic, Science and Second Sight in Late Seventeenth-Century Scotland* (Woodbridge, 2001)

James Hutchisone, 'A sermon on witchcraft in 1697', ed. George Neilson, *Scottish Historical Review*, 7 (1910), 390–9

King James VI, *Minor Prose Works*, ed. James Craigie (Edinburgh: Scottish Text Society, 1982) – includes his *Daemonologie* (1597)

King James VI & I, *Selected Writings*, eds. Neil Rhodes, Jennifer Richards and Joseph Marshall (Aldershot, 2003) – includes his *Daemonologie* (1597)

David Laing (ed.), 'An original letter to the laird of Wishaw (now presented to the Museum), relating to the proceedings against James Aikenhead "the

Atheist," and the trial of witches in Paisley in 1696', *Proceedings of the Society of Antiquaries of Scotland*, 11 (1874–1876), 438–45

Angus Macdonald (ed.), 'A witchcraft case of 1647', *Scots Law Times (News)* (10 April 1937), 77–8

Hugh McLachlan (ed.), *The Kirk, Satan and Salem: A History of the Witches of Renfrewshire* (Glasgow, 2006)

J. R. N. Macphail (ed.), 'Papers relating to witchcraft, 1662–1677', in *Highland Papers*, 4 vols. (Edinburgh: Scottish History Society, 1914–1934), iii, 2–38

M. A. Murray (ed.), 'Two trials for witchcraft', *Proceedings of the Society of Antiquaries of Scotland*, 56 (1921–1922), 46–60

Lawrence Normand and Gareth Roberts (eds.), *Witchcraft in Early Modern Scotland: James VI's Demonology and the North Berwick Witches* (Exeter, 2000)

David M. Robertson (ed.), *Goodnight My Servants All: The Sourcebook of East Lothian Witchcraft* (Glasgow, 2007)

George Sinclair, *Satans Invisible World Discovered*, ed. Thomas G. Stevenson (Edinburgh, 1871)

John Stuart (ed.), 'Trials for witchcraft, 1596–1598', *Miscellany of the Spalding Club*, i (1841), 82–193

Trial, Confession, and Execution of Isobel Inch, John Stewart, Margaret Barclay & Isobel Crawford, for Witchcraft, at Irvine, anno 1618 (Ardrossan and Saltcoats, n.d. [c.1855])

A. E. Truckell (ed.), 'Unpublished witchcraft trials', *Transactions of the Dumfriesshire and Galloway Natural History and Antiquarian Society*, 3rd ser., 51 (1975), 48–58, and 52 (1976), 95–108

Michael B. Wasser and Louise A. Yeoman (eds.), 'The trial of Geillis Johnstone for witchcraft, 1614', *Scottish History Society Miscellany*, xiii (2004), 83–145

David Webster (ed.), *Collection of Rare and Curious Tracts on Witchcraft and the Second Sight* (Edinburgh, 1820)

Louise A. Yeoman (ed.), 'Witchcraft commissions from the register of commissions of the privy council of Scotland, 1630–1642', *Scottish History Society Miscellany*, xiii (2004), 223–65

3. Published secondary works

Isabel Adam, *Witch Hunt: The Great Scottish Witchcraft Trials of 1697* (London, 1978)

Priscilla Bawcutt, 'Elrich fantasyis in Dunbar and other poets', in J. D. McClure and M. R. G. Spiller (eds.), *Bryght Lanternis: Essays on the Language and Literature of Medieval and Renaissance Scotland* (Aberdeen, 1989), 162–78

Priscilla Bawcutt, ' "Holy words for healing": some early Scottish charms and their ancient religious roots', in Luuk Houwen (ed.), *Literature and Religion in Late Medieval and Early Modern Scotland* (Leuven, 2012), 127–44

G. F. Black, 'Scottish charms and amulets', *Proceedings of the Society of Antiquaries of Scotland*, 27 (1892–1893), 433–526

Roy Booth, 'Standing within the prospect of belief: *Macbeth*, King James, and witchcraft', in John Newton and Jo Bath (eds.), *Witchcraft and the Act of 1604* (Leiden, 2008), 47–67

John Brims, 'The Ross-shire witchcraft case of 1822', *Review of Scottish Culture*, 5 (1989), 87–91

J. W. Brodie-Innes, *Scottish Witchcraft Trials* (London, 1891)

Alan Bruford, 'Scottish Gaelic witch stories: a provisional type list', *Scottish Studies*, 11 (1967), 13–47

Alan J. Bruford, 'Workers, weepers and witches: the status of the female singer in Gaelic society', *Scottish Gaelic Studies*, 17 (1996), 61–70

Hugh Cheape, 'Lead hearts and runes of protection', *Review of Scottish Culture*, 18 (2006), 149–55

Stuart Clark, 'King James' *Daemonologie*: witchcraft and kingship', in Sydney Anglo (ed.), *The Damned Art: Essays in the Literature of Witchcraft* (London, 1977), 156–81

Edward J. Cowan, 'The darker vision of the Scottish Renaissance: the Devil and Francis Stewart', in Ian B. Cowan and Duncan Shaw (eds.), *The Renaissance and Reformation in Scotland* (Edinburgh, 1983), 125–40

J. G. Dalyell, *The Darker Superstitions of Scotland* (Edinburgh, 1834)

Thomas Davidson, *Rowan Tree and Red Thread* (Edinburgh, 1949)

Kirsty Duncan, 'Was ergotism responsible for the Scottish witch hunts?', *Area*, 25 (1993), 30–6; Ian D. Whyte, 'Ergotism and witchcraft in Scotland', *Area*, 26 (1994), 89–90, and rejoinder by Duncan, 90–2; W. F. Boyd, 'Four and twenty blackbirds: more on ergotism, rye and witchcraft in Scotland', *Area*, 27 (1995), 77

Rhodes Dunlap, 'King James and some witches: the date and text of the *Daemonologie*', *Philological Quarterly*, 54 (1975), 40–6

John Ferguson, 'Bibliographical notes on the witchcraft literature of Scotland', *Proceedings of the Edinburgh Bibliographical Society*, 3 (1895), 37–124

R. Menzies Fergusson, 'The witches of Alloa', *Scottish Historical Review*, 4 (1907), 40–8

Daniel Fischlin, '"Counterfeiting God": James VI (I) and the politics of *Daemonologie* (1597)', *Journal of Narrative Technique*, 26 (1996), 1–27; also published in Graham Caie *et al.* (eds.), *The European Sun: Proceedings of the Seventh International Conference on Medieval and Renaissance Scottish Language and Literature* (East Linton, 2001), 452–74

Keely Fisher, 'Eldritch comic verse in older Scots', in Sally Mapstone (ed.), *Older Scots Literature* (Edinburgh, 2005), 292–313

Mary Floyd-Wilson, 'English epicures and Scottish witches', *Shakespeare Quarterly*, 57 (2006), 131–61

William Gillies, 'The Land of the Little People in medieval Gaelic literary tradition', in Alasdair A. MacDonald and Kees Dekker (eds.), *Rhetoric, Royalty, and Reality: Essays on the Literary Culture of Medieval and Early Modern Scotland* (Leuven, 2005), 51–68

Julian Goodare, 'Women and the witch-hunt in Scotland', *Social History*, 23 (1998), 288–308

Julian Goodare, 'The Aberdeenshire witchcraft panic of 1597', *Northern Scotland*, 21 (2001), 1–21

Julian Goodare, 'The framework for Scottish witch-hunting in the 1590s', *Scottish Historical Review*, 81 (2002), 240–50

Julian Goodare (ed.), *The Scottish Witch-Hunt in Context* (Manchester, 2002). Contents:
* Ronald Hutton, 'The global context of the Scottish witch-hunt', pp. 16–32
* Stuart Macdonald, 'In search of the Devil in Fife witchcraft cases, 1560–1705', pp. 33–50
* Julian Goodare, 'The Scottish witchcraft panic of 1597', pp. 51–72
* Lauren Martin, 'The Devil and the domestic: witchcraft, quarrels and women's work in Scotland', pp. 73–89
* Joyce Miller, 'Devices and directions: folk healing aspects of witchcraft practice in seventeenth-century Scotland', pp. 90–105
* Louise Yeoman, 'Hunting the rich witch in Scotland: high-status witchcraft suspects and their persecutors, 1590–1650', pp. 106–21
* Julian Goodare, 'Witch-hunting and the Scottish state', pp. 122–45
* Michael Wasser, 'The western witch-hunt of 1697–1700: the last major witch-hunt in Scotland', pp. 146–65
* Brian P. Levack, 'The decline and end of Scottish witch-hunting', pp. 166–81
* James Sharpe, 'Witch-hunting, witchcraft and witch historiography: England and Scotland compared', pp. 182–97
* Edward J. Cowan and Lizanne Henderson, 'The last of the witches? The survival of Scottish witch belief', pp. 198–217

Julian Goodare, 'John Knox on demonology and witchcraft', *Archiv für Reformationsgeschichte*, 96 (2005), 221–45

Julian Goodare, 'The Scottish witchcraft act', *Church History*, 74 (2005), 39–67

Julian Goodare, 'Men and the witch-hunt in Scotland', in Alison Rowlands (ed.), *Witchcraft and Masculinities in Early Modern Europe* (Basingstoke, 2009), 148–70

Julian Goodare, 'The cult of the seely wights in Scotland', *Folklore*, 123 (2012), 198–219

Julian Goodare, 'Witchcraft in Scotland', in Brian P. Levack (ed.), *The Oxford Handbook of Witchcraft in Early Modern Europe and Colonial America* (Oxford, 2013), 300–17

Julian Goodare, Lauren Martin and Joyce Miller (eds.), *Witchcraft and Belief in Early Modern Scotland* (Basingstoke, 2008). Contents:
* Julian Goodare, 'Scottish witchcraft in its European context', pp. 26–50
* Lauren Martin and Joyce Miller, 'Some findings from the Survey of Scottish Witchcraft', pp. 51–70
* Edward J. Cowan, 'Witch persecution and popular belief in Lowland Scotland: the Devil's decade', pp. 71–94
* Lizanne Henderson, 'Witch hunting and witch belief in the *Gàidhealtachd*', pp. 95–118
* Lauren Martin, 'Scottish witchcraft panics re-examined', pp. 119–43
* Joyce Miller, 'Men in black: appearances of the Devil in early modern Scottish witchcraft discourse', pp. 144–65
* Brian P. Levack, 'Demonic possession in early modern Scotland', pp. 166–84
* Owen Davies, 'A comparative perspective on Scottish cunning-folk and charmers', pp. 185–205

- Michael Wasser, 'The mechanical world-view and the decline of witch-beliefs in Scotland', pp. 206–26
- Hugh Cheape, '"Charms against witchcraft": magic and mischief in museum collections', pp. 227–48

Alaric Hall, 'Getting shot of elves: healing, witchcraft and fairies in the Scottish witchcraft trials', *Folklore*, 116 (2005), 19–36

Alaric Hall, 'Folk-healing, fairies and witchcraft: the trial of Stein Maltman, Stirling 1628', *Studia Celtica Fennica*, 3 (2006), 10–25

Alaric Hall, 'The etymology and meanings of *eldritch*', *Scottish Language*, 26 (2007), 16–22

Alison Hanham, ' "The Scottish Hecate": a wild witch chase', *Scottish Studies*, 13 (1969), 59–65

R. L. Harris, 'Janet Douglas and the witches of Pollock: the background of scepticism in Scotland in the 1670s', in S. R. McKenna (ed.), *Selected Essays on Scottish Language and Literature: A Festschrift in Honor of Allan H. MacLaine* (Lewiston, NY, 1992), 97–124

Lizanne Henderson, 'The road to Elfland: fairy belief and the Child Ballads', in Edward J. Cowan (ed.), *The Ballad in Scottish History* (East Linton, 2000), 54–72

Lizanne Henderson, 'The survival of witchcraft prosecutions and witch belief in south west Scotland', *Scottish Historical Review*, 85 (2006), 54–76

Lizanne Henderson, 'Charmers, spells and holy wells: the repackaging of belief', *Review of Scottish Culture*, 19 (2007), 10–26

Lizanne Henderson (ed.), *Fantastical Imaginations: The Supernatural in Scottish History and Culture* (East Linton, 2009). Contents:

- Edward J. Cowan, 'The discovery of the future: prophecy and second sight in Scottish history', pp. 1–28
- Louise Yeoman, 'Away with the fairies', pp. 29–46
- George M. Brunsden, 'Seventeenth- and eighteenth-century astrology and the Scottish popular almanac', pp. 47–69
- Hugh Cheape, 'From natural to supernatural: the material culture of charms and amulets', pp. 70–90
- Colin Kidd, 'The Scottish Enlightenment and the supernatural', pp. 91–109
- Douglas Gifford, ' "Nathaniel Gow's toddy": the supernatural in Lowland Scottish literature from Burns and Scott to the present day', 110–140
- Lizanne Henderson, 'Witch, fairy and folktale narratives in the trial of Bessie Dunlop', pp. 141–66
- Margaret Bennett, 'Stories of the supernatural: from local memorate to Scottish legend', pp. 167–84
- John MacInnes, 'The Church and traditional belief in Gaelic society', pp. 185–95
- Juliette Wood, 'Lewis Spence: remembering the Celts', pp. 196–211
- Valentina Bold, 'The Wicker Man: virgin sacrifice in Dumfries and Galloway', pp. 212–20

Lizanne Henderson, ' "Detestable slaves of the Devil": changing ideas about witchcraft in sixteenth-century Scotland', in Edward J. Cowan and Lizanne Henderson (eds.), *A History of Everyday Life in Medieval Scotland, 1000 to 1600* (Edinburgh, 2011), 226–53

Lizanne Henderson, 'The witches of Bute', in Anna Ritchie (ed.), *Historic Bute: Land and People* (Edinburgh, 2012), 151–61

Lizanne Henderson and Edward J. Cowan, *Scottish Fairy Belief: A History* (East Linton, 2001)

Michael Hunter, 'The discovery of second sight in late 17th-century Scotland', *History Today*, 51:6 (June 2001), 48–53

Ronald Hutton, 'Witch-hunting in Celtic societies', *Past and Present*, 212 (August 2011), 43–71

Clare Jackson, 'Judicial torture, the liberties of the subject, and Anglo-Scottish relations, 1660–1690', in T. C. Smout (ed.), *Anglo-Scottish Relations from 1603 to 1900* (Oxford, 2005), 75–101

Laura Kolb, 'Playing with demons: interrogating the supernatural in Jacobean drama', *Forum for Modern Language Studies*, 43 (2007), 337–50

Christina Larner, 'English and Scotch witches', *New Edinburgh Review*, 11 (February 1971), 25–9

Christina Larner, 'James VI and I and witchcraft', in Alan G. R. Smith (ed.), *The Reign of James VI and I* (London, 1973), 74–90

Christina Larner, 'Two late Scottish witchcraft tracts: *Witch-Craft Proven* and *The Tryal of Witchcraft*', in Sydney Anglo (ed.), *The Damned Art: Essays in the Literature of Witchcraft* (London, 1977), 227–45

Christina Larner, ' "*Crimen exceptum*"? The crime of witchcraft in Europe', in V. A. C. Gatrell, Bruce Lenman and Geoffrey Parker (eds.), *Crime and the Law: The Social History of Crime in Europe since 1500* (London, 1980), 49–75

Christina Larner, *Enemies of God: The Witch-Hunt in Scotland* (London, 1981)

Christina Larner, 'Witch-beliefs and witch-hunting in England and Scotland', *History Today*, 31:2 (February 1981), 32–6

Christina Larner, *The Thinking Peasant: Popular and Educated Belief in Pre-Industrial Culture (Gifford Lectures in Natural Theology, 1982)* (Glasgow, 1982)

Christina Larner, *Witchcraft and Religion: The Politics of Popular Belief* (Oxford, 1984). Contents:
- 'James VI and I and witchcraft', pp. 3–22
- 'The crime of witchcraft in Scotland', pp. 23–33
- ' "*Crimen exceptum*"? The crime of witchcraft in Europe', pp. 35–67
- 'Witch beliefs and accusations in England and Scotland', pp. 69–78
- 'Witchcraft past and present: (i) Is all witchcraft really witchcraft? (ii) Was witch-hunting woman-hunting? (iii) When is a witch-hunt a witch-hunt?', pp. 79–91
- 'Relativism and ethnocentrism: popular and educated beliefs in pre-industrial culture (The Gifford Lectures in Natural Theology, 1982)', pp. 95–165

Christina Larner, 'Healing in pre-industrial Britain', in Mike Saks (ed.), *Alternative Medicine in Britain* (Oxford, 1992), 25–34

Jacqueline E. M. Latham, '*The Tempest* and King James' *Daemonologie*', *Shakespeare Studies*, 28 (1975), 117–23

Brian P. Levack, 'The great Scottish witch-hunt of 1661–1662', *Journal of British Studies*, 20 (1980), 90–108

Brian P. Levack (ed.), *Witchcraft in Scotland* (New York, 1992). Reprints. Contents:
- F. Legge, 'Witchcraft in Scotland', *Scottish Review*, 18 (1891), 257–88
- Christina Larner, 'The crime of witchcraft in Scotland', in her *Witchcraft and Religion: The Politics of Popular Belief* (Oxford, 1984), 23–33

- John Ferguson, 'Bibliographical notes on the witchcraft literature of Scotland', *Proceedings of the Edinburgh Bibliographical Society*, 3 (1895), 37–124
- G. F. Black, 'A calendar of cases of witchcraft in Scotland, 1510–1727', *Bulletin of the New York Public Library*, 41 (1937), 811–47, 917–36; 42 (1938), 34–74
- Edward J. Cowan, 'The darker vision of the Scottish Renaissance: the Devil and Francis Stewart', in Ian B. Cowan and Duncan Shaw (eds.), *The Renaissance and Reformation in Scotland* (Edinburgh, 1983), 125–40
- Christina Larner, 'Witch-beliefs and witch-hunting in England and Scotland', *History Today*, 31:2 (February 1981), 32–6
- Brian P. Levack, 'The great Scottish witch-hunt of 1661–1662', *Journal of British Studies*, 20 (1980), 90–108
- W. N. Neill, 'The professional pricker and his test for witchcraft', *Scottish Historical Review*, 19 (1922), 205–13
- M. A. Murray, 'The "Devil" of North Berwick', *Scottish Historical Review*, 15 (1918), 310–21
- William Roughead, 'The witches of North Berwick', in his *The Riddle of the Ruthvens and Other Studies* (Edinburgh, 1936), 144–66
- Helen Stafford, 'Notes on Scottish witchcraft cases, 1590–91', in Norton Downs (ed.), *Essays in Honor of Conyers Read* (Chicago, Ill., 1953), 96–118, 278–84
- A. E. Truckell (ed.), 'Unpublished witchcraft trials', *Transactions of the Dumfriesshire and Galloway Natural History and Antiquarian Society*, 3rd ser., 51 (1975), 48–58, and 52 (1976), 95–108
- James Hutchisone, 'A sermon on witchcraft in 1697', ed. George Neilson, *Scottish Historical Review*, 7 (1910), 390–9

Brian P. Levack (ed.), *New Perspectives on Witchcraft, Magic and Demonology*, vol. iii: *Witchcraft in the British Isles and New England* (London, 2001). Reprints. Contents include:
- P. G. Maxwell-Stuart, 'The fear of the king is death: James VI and the witches of East Lothian', in W. G. Naphy and Penny Roberts (eds.), *Fear in Early Modern Society* (Manchester, 1997), 209–25
- S. W. McDonald, A. Thom and A. Thom, 'The Bargarran witch trial: a psychiatric reassessment', *Scottish Medical Journal*, 41 (1996), 152–8

Brian P. Levack, 'Judicial torture in Scotland during the age of Mackenzie', *Stair Society Miscellany*, iv (2002), 185–98

Brian P. Levack, 'State-building and witch-hunting in early modern Scotland', in Johannes Dillinger, Jürgen M. Schmidt and Dieter R. Bauer (eds.), *Hexenprozess und Staatsbildung: Witch-Trials and State-Building* (Bielefeld, 2008), 77–95

Brian P. Levack, *Witch-Hunting in Scotland: Law, Politics and Religion* (London, 2008). Contents:
- 'Witch-hunting in Scotland and England', pp. 1–14
- 'Witchcraft and the law in early modern Scotland', pp. 15–33
- 'King James VI and witchcraft', pp. 34–54
- 'Witch-hunting in revolutionary Britain', pp. 55–80
- 'The great Scottish witch-hunt of 1661–2', pp. 81–97
- 'Absolutism, state-building, and witchcraft', pp. 98–114
- 'Demonic possession and witch-hunting in Scotland', pp. 115–30

- 'The decline and end of Scottish witch-hunting', pp. 131–44
- 'Witch-hunting and witch-murder in early eighteenth-century Scotland', pp. 145–61

Emily Lyle, *Fairies and Folk: Approaches to the Scottish Ballad Tradition* (Trier, 2007)

J. A. MacCulloch, 'The mingling of fairy and witch beliefs in sixteenth and seventeenth century Scotland', *Folk-Lore*, 32 (1921), 227–44

Stuart Macdonald, *The Witches of Fife: Witch-Hunting in a Scottish Shire, 1560–1710* (East Linton, 2002)

Stuart Macdonald, 'Torture and the Scottish witch-hunt: a re-examination', *Scottish Tradition*, 27 (2002), 95–114

Stuart Macdonald, '*Enemies of God* revisited: recent publications on Scottish witch-hunting', *Scottish Economic and Social History*, 23 (2003), 65–84

S. W. McDonald, 'The Devil's mark and the witch-prickers of Scotland', *Journal of the Royal Society of Medicine*, 90 (1997), 507–11

S. W. McDonald, 'The witch doctors of Scotland', *Scottish Medical Journal*, 43 (1998), 119–22

S. W. McDonald, A. Thom and A. Thom, 'The Bargarran witch trial: a psychiatric reassessment', *Scottish Medical Journal*, 41 (1996), 152–8

William Mackay, 'The Strathglass witches of 1662', *Transactions of the Gaelic Society of Inverness*, 9 (1879–80), 113–21

Hugh V. McLachlan, 'Witchcraft belief and social reality', *Philosophical Journal*, 14 (1977), 99–110

Hugh V. McLachlan, 'The Bargarran witchcraft scare of the 1690s', *History Scotland*, 7:5 (May 2007), 14–19

Hugh V. McLachlan and J. K. Swales, 'Witchcraft and anti-feminism', *Scottish Journal of Sociology*, 4 (1980), 141–66

Hugh McLachlan and Kim Swales, 'The bewitchment of Christian Shaw: a reassessment of the famous Paisley witchcraft case of 1697', in Yvonne G. Brown and Rona Ferguson (eds.), *Twisted Sisters: Women, Crime and Deviance in Scotland since 1400* (East Linton, 2002), 54–83

J. M. McPherson, *Primitive Beliefs in the North-East of Scotland* (London, 1929)

M. A. Manzaloui, 'St. Bonaventure and the witches in "Macbeth" ', *Innes Review*, 14 (1963), 72–4

Lauren Martin, 'Witchcraft and family: what can witchcraft documents tell us about early modern Scottish family life?', *Scottish Tradition*, 27 (2002), 7–22

W. Matheson, 'The historical Coinneach Odhar and some prophecies attributed to him', *Transactions of the Gaelic Society of Inverness*, 46 (1969–1970), 66–88

P. G. Maxwell-Stuart, 'The fear of the king is death: James VI and the witches of East Lothian', in W. G. Naphy and Penny Roberts (eds.), *Fear in Early Modern Society* (Manchester, 1997), 209–25

P. G. Maxwell-Stuart, 'Witchcraft and the kirk in Aberdeenshire, 1596–97', *Northern Scotland*, 18 (1998), 1–14

P. G. Maxwell-Stuart, *Satan's Conspiracy: Magic and Witchcraft in Sixteenth-Century Scotland* (East Linton, 2001)

P. G. Maxwell-Stuart, 'Witchcraft and magic in eighteenth-century Scotland', in Owen Davies and Willem de Blécourt (eds.), *Beyond the Witch Trials: Witchcraft and Magic in Enlightenment Europe* (Manchester, 2004), 81–99

P. G. Maxwell-Stuart, *Abundance Of Witches: The Great Scottish Witch-Hunt* (Stroud, 2005); reprinted as *The Great Scottish Witch-Hunt* (Stroud, 2007)

P. G. Maxwell-Stuart, 'King James's experience of witches, and the 1604 English Witchcraft Act', in John Newton and Jo Bath (eds.), *Witchcraft and the Act of 1604* (Leiden, 2008), 31–46

Joyce Miller, *Magic and Witchcraft in Scotland* (Musselburgh, 2004)

Scott Moir, 'The crucible: witchcraft and the experience of family in early modern Scotland', in Elizabeth Ewan and Janay Nugent (eds.), *Finding the Family in Medieval and Early Modern Scotland* (Aldershot, 2008), 49–59

Chris Neale, *The 17th Century Witch Craze in West Fife: A Guide to the Printed Sources* (Dunfermline District Libraries, 1980)

W. N. Neill, 'The professional pricker and his test for witchcraft', *Scottish Historical Review*, 19 (1922), 205–13

W. N. Neill, 'The last execution for witchcraft in Scotland, 1722', *Scottish Historical Review*, 20 (1923), 218–21

Lawrence Normand, 'Modernising Scottish witchcraft texts', *EnterText*, 3 (2003), 227–37

D. J. Parkinson, ' "The Legend of the Bishop of St Androis Lyfe" and the survival of Scottish poetry', *Early Modern Literary Studies*, 9:1 (May 2003), electronic journal

Coleman O. Parsons, *Witchcraft and Demonology in Scott's Fiction* (Edinburgh, 1964)

Diane Purkiss, 'Sounds of silence: fairies and incest in Scottish witchcraft stories', in Stuart Clark (ed.), *Languages of Witchcraft: Narrative, Ideology and Meaning in Early Modern Culture* (London, 2001), 81–98

Diane Purkiss, 'Losing babies, losing stories: attending to women's confessions in Scottish witch-trials', in Margaret Mikesell and Adele Seeff (eds.), *Culture and Change: Attending to Early Modern Women* (Newark, Del., 2003), 143–58

Anthony Ross, 'Incubi in the Isles in the thirteenth century', *Innes Review*, 13 (1962), 108–9

Sir Walter Scott, *Letters on Demonology and Witchcraft* (London, 1884; first published 1830)

Charles K. Sharpe, *A Historical Account of the Belief in Witchcraft in Scotland* (London, 1884; first published 1818)

Jacqueline Simpson, ' "The weird sisters wandering": burlesque witchery in Montgomerie's *Flyting*', *Folklore*, 106 (1995), 9–20

Alex Sutherland, *The Brahan Seer: The Making of a Legend* (Bern, 2009)

Margo Todd, 'Fairies, Egyptians and elders: multiple cosmologies in post-Reformation Scotland', in Bridget Heal and Ole Peter Grell (eds.), *The Impact of the European Reformation: Princes, Clergy and People* (Aldershot, 2008), 189–208

Michael Wasser, 'The privy council and the witches: the curtailment of witchcraft prosecutions in Scotland, 1597–1628', *Scottish Historical Review*, 82 (2003), 20–46

Emma Wilby, 'The witch's familiar and the fairy in early modern England and Scotland', *Folklore*, 111 (2000), 283–305

Emma Wilby, *Cunning Folk and Familiar Spirits: Shamanistic Visionary Traditions in Early Modern British Witchcraft and Magic* (Brighton, 2005)

Emma Wilby, *The Visions of Isobel Gowdie: Magic, Witchcraft and Dark Shamanism in Seventeenth-Century Scotland* (Brighton, 2010)

Liv Helene Willumsen, 'Witches in Scotland and northern Norway: two case studies', in Peter Graves and Arne Kruse (eds.), *Images and Imaginations: Perspectives on Britain and Scandinavia* (Edinburgh, 2007), 35–67

Liv Helene Willumsen, 'A narratological approach to witchcraft trial: a Scottish case', *Journal of Early Modern History*, 15 (2011), 531–60

Liv Helene Willumsen, 'Seventeenth-century witchcraft trials in Scotland and northern Norway: comparative aspects', *History Research*, 1:1 (December 2011), 61–74

Liv Helene Willumsen, *Witches of the North: Scotland and Finnmark* (Leiden, 2013)

Juliette Wood, 'A Celtic sorcerer's apprentice: the magician figure in Scottish tradition', in Roderick J. Lyall and Felicity Riddy (eds.), *Proceedings of the Third International Conference on Scottish Language and Literature* (Glasgow, 1983), 127–42

Jenny Wormald, 'The witches, the Devil and the king', in Terry Brotherstone and David Ditchburn (eds.), *Freedom and Authority: Scotland, c.1050–c.1650* (East Linton, 2000), 165–80

Louise A. Yeoman, 'The Devil as doctor: witchcraft, Wodrow, and the wider world', *Scottish Archives*, 1 (1995), 93–105

John R. Young, 'The Scottish parliament and witch-hunting in Scotland under the covenanters', *Parliaments, Estates and Representation*, 26 (2006), 53–65

4. Unpublished theses

Michelle Brock, 'The Fiend in the Fog: A History of Satan in Early Modern Scotland' (University of Texas at Austin PhD thesis, 2012)

Anna L. Cordey, 'Witch-Hunting in the Presbytery of Dalkeith, 1649 to 1662' (University of Edinburgh MSc by Research thesis, 2003)

John Gilmore, 'Witchcraft and the Church in Scotland subsequent to the Reformation' (University of Glasgow PhD thesis, 1948)

Lizanne Henderson, 'Supernatural Traditions and Folk Beliefs in an Age of Transition: Witchcraft and Charming in Scotland, c.1670–1740' (University of Strathclyde PhD thesis, 2004)

Paula Hughes, 'The 1649–50 Scottish Witch-Hunt, with Particular Reference to the Synod of Lothian and Tweeddale' (University of Strathclyde PhD thesis, 2008)

Paul M. Kidd, 'King James VI and the Demonic Conspiracy: Witch-Hunting and Anti-Catholicism in 16th- and early-17th-century Scotland' (University of Glasgow MPhil thesis, 2004)

Margaret C. Kintscher, 'The Culpability of James VI of Scotland, Later James I of England, in the North Berwick Witchcraft Trials of 1590–91' (San Jose State University MA thesis, 1991)

Christina Larner (née Ross), 'Scottish Demonology in the Sixteenth and Seventeenth Centuries and its Theological Background' (University of Edinburgh PhD thesis, 1962)

Lauren Martin, 'The Devil and the Domestic: Witchcraft, Women's Work and Marriage in Early Modern Scotland' (New School for Social Research, New York, PhD thesis, 2003)

Joyce Miller, 'Cantrips and Carlins: Magic, Medicine and Society in the Presbyteries of Haddington and Stirling, 1600–1688' (University of Stirling PhD thesis, 1999)

Laura Paterson, 'The Witches' Sabbath in Scotland' (University of Edinburgh MSc by Research thesis, 2011)

Sarah Rhodes, 'King James VI of Scotland, His Treatise *Daemonologie*, and the Subsequent Influence on Witchcraft Prosecution in Scotland' (College of Charleston and the Citadel MA thesis, 2009)

Jane Ridder-Patrick, 'Astrology in Early Modern Scotland, ca. 1543–1726' (University of Edinburgh PhD thesis, 2012)

Elizabeth Robertson, 'Panic and Persecution: Witch-Hunting in East Lothian, 1628–1631' (University of Edinburgh MSc by Research thesis, 2009)

Liv Helene Willumsen, 'Seventeenth Century Witchcraft Trials in Scotland and Northern Norway' (University of Edinburgh PhD thesis, 2008)

Index

Note: Asterisks * denote persons accused of being witches.

Printed and bound by CPI Group (UK) Ltd, Croydon, CR0 4YY